WOMEN IN THE THIRD REICH

MATTHEW STIBBE

Department of History, Sheffield Hallam University, UK

A member of the Hodder Headline Group
LONDON
Co-published in the United States of America by
Oxford University Press Inc., New York

First published in Great Britain in 2003 by
Arnold, a member of the Hodder Headline Group,
338 Euston Road, London NW1 3BH

http://www.arnoldpublishers.com

Distributed in the United States of America by
Oxford University Press Inc.
198 Madison Avenue, New York, NY10016

The advice and information in this book are believed to be true and
accurate at the date of going to press, but neither the author nor the publisher
can accept any legal responsibility or liability for any errors or omissions.

British Library Cataloguing in Publication Data
A catalogue record for this book is available from the British Library

Library of Congress Cataloging-in-Publication Data
A catalog record for this book is available from the Library of Congress

ISBN 0 340 761059 (hb)
ISBN 0 340 761040 (pb)

1 2 3 4 5 6 7 8 9 10

Typeset in 10 on 12 pt Sabon by Phoenix Photosetting, Chatham, Kent
Printed and bound in Great Britain by Bath Press Ltd., Bath

What do you think about this book? Or any other Arnold title?
Please send your comments to feedback.arnold@hodder.co.uk

For Sam

Contents

List of Tables

Acknowledgements

Over the last few months a number of scholars have read through the draft version of this book and made many useful comments and suggestions, as well as saving me from some of the worst omissions and mistakes. In particular I would like to thank Jill Stephenson, Julie Gottlieb and Elizabeth Harvey. Richard Evans and Nik Wachsmann have also helped with their expert knowledge of capital punishment and the penal system in the Third Reich. All errors, it goes without saying, are my responsibility and mine alone.

Funds for research trips to Hanover, Bremen, Hamburg and Berlin were made available by the School of Humanities at Liverpool Hope University College. I am grateful to Janet Hollinshead and Terry Phillips for their promotion of my research activities in an ever tighter financial climate, and to David Giles for his efforts in tracking down obscure book orders for me via the inter-library loan system. My thanks are also due to Christopher Wheeler and Lesley Riddle at Arnold for their encouragement and interest in my project, and to the staff and directors of the various archives, libraries and museums I have used. In particular I would like to mention Angelika Eder, Angelika Voß and Linde Apel of the Forschungsstelle für Zeitgeschichte in Hamburg for their help in answering many of my questions and placing useful material at my disposal.

Finally thanks, as ever, to my family: Sam, Dad, Hazel, Emily, Alex, Simon, Katherine – you've been great, you are great.

Matthew Stibbe
Chorlton-cum-Hardy, Manchester
December 2002

List of Abbreviations

ANSt: *Arbeitsgemeinschaft Nationalsozialistischer Studentinnen* (Union of National Socialist Women Students)

BA Berlin: *Bundesarchiv* (German Federal Archives, Berlin section)

BDF: *Bund Deutscher Frauenvereine* (League of German Women's Organisations, umbrella organisation for the German Feminist Movement, 1894–1933)

BDM: *Bund Deutscher Mädel* (League of German Maidens – the female equivalent of the Hitler Youth)

CDU: *Christlich-Demokratische Union* (Christian Democratic Union, the main centre-right party in West Germany after 1945)

CSU: *Christlich-Soziale Union* (Christian Social Union, Bavarian wing of the CDU after 1945)

DAF: *Deutsche Arbeitsfront* (German Labour Front)

DDP: *Deutsche Demokratische Partei* (German Democratic Party)

DFO: *Deutscher Frauenorden* (German Women's Order)

DFW: *Deutsches Frauenwerk* (German Women's Bureau)

DNVP: *Deutschnationale Volkspartei* (German National People's Party)

DVP: *Deutsche Volkspartei* (German People's Party)

FDP: *Freie Demokratische Partei* (liberal party in West Germany after 1945)

FZH: *Forschungsstelle für Zeitgeschichte* (Research Centre for Contemporary History in Hamburg)

GDR: German Democratic Republic, 1949–90

Gestapo: *Geheime Staatspolizei* (Secret State Police)

HJ: *Hitlerjugend* (Hitler Youth)

JFB: *Jüdischer Frauenbund* (Jewish Women's League, founded 1904, dissolved 1938)

JM: *Jungmädel* (Young Maidens, the junior wing of the BDM for girls aged 10 to 14 years)

KdF: *Kraft durch Freude* (Strength Through Joy, the Nazis' main leisure organisation)

KLV: *Kinderlandverschickung* (Children's Wartime Evacuation Programme)

KPD: *Kommunistische Partei Deutschlands* (German Communist Party)

NHStA: *Niedersächsisches Hauptstaatsarchiv Hanover* (Main State Archives of Lower Saxony)

NSDAP: *Nationalsozialistische Deutsche Arbeiterpartei* (National Socialist German Workers' Party – the Nazi Party)

NSF: *Nationalsozialistische Frauenschaft* (National Socialist Women's League)

NSLB: *Nationalsozialistischer Lehrerbund* (National Socialist Teachers' League)

NSV: *Nationalsozialistische Volkswohlfahrt* (National Socialist Welfare Organisation)

RADwJ: *Reichsarbeitsdienst der weiblichen Jugend* (Women's Labour Service)

RLB-*Pressearchiv des Reichslandbundes* (Press archive of the Reichslandbund, held in the German Federal Archives, Berlin)

RMD: *Reichsmütterdienst* (Reich Mothers' Service)

SA: *Sturm-Abteilungen* (Stormtroopers or Brown Shirts)

SD: *Sicherheitsdienst* (Security Service of the Nazi Party)

SED: *Sozialistische Einheitspartei Deutschlands* (German Socialist Unity Party, the ruling party in East Germany after 1946)

Sopade: Organisation of the German Social Democratic Party in exile, 1933–45

SPD: *Sozialdemokratische Partei Deutschlands* (German Social Democratic Party, the main centre-left party in Germany, founded 1875)

SS: *Schutzstaffeln* (Nazi elite paramilitary formation)

StA Bremen: *Staatsarchiv Bremen* (State Archive of Bremen)

Vw/Hw: *Volkswirtschaft/Hauswirtschaft* (National Economy/Domestic Economy, a subsection of the DFW or German Women's Bureau)

Introduction

In September 1934, some 22 months after coming to power in Germany, Hitler gave an important address to the *NS-Frauenschaft*, the main political organisation for Nazi women, in Nuremberg. In it, he assured his listeners that 'the National Socialist movement has from the very beginnings of its existence not only seen but also found women to be its most loyal followers'. He continued: 'Our women's movement is for us not something that inscribes on its banner the fight against men, but something that has as its programme the common fight with men. For the new National Socialist people's community acquires a firm basis precisely because we have gained the trust of millions of women as fanatical fellow-combatants, women who have fought for the common task of preserving life ...'.[1] This, in other words, was the doctrine of the 'national community', the idea that women should not compete with men but work together with them for the achievement of common national goals and the welfare of the German people as a whole. What these common goals were, however, and how exactly they were going to benefit women, was less clear in Hitler's speech than how they were to be achieved: through a fanatical 'will to power' based on the re-assertion of male/female difference and a rejection of the 'Jewish doctrine' of equality between the sexes.[2]

Since the 1970s, writing on women in Nazi Germany has gone through a considerable expansion. Scholarly contributions from Jill Stephenson, Gisela Bock, Claudia Koonz, Ute Frevert, Dagmar Reese, Gabriele Czarnowski, Lisa Pine, Marion Kaplan and Elizabeth Heineman (to name but a few) have made a considerable addition to our knowledge both of the Third Reich and of women's experiences within it.[3] This book is not an attempt to compete with these previous works; rather, its aim is to offer a synthesis of the most recent research and to make some of the arguments and findings in German-language publications more accessible to readers of English. The emphasis will be on the distinct historical position of women in the Third Reich, whose position and status were sufficiently unique, especially in the realm of reproduction and the family, to justify assessing their experiences, opportunities and responses separately from those of men. Thus a sizeable portion of this book will focus on the Nazi pre-occupation with 'Aryan' motherhood as an ideal that was broadcast and propagated to women through a variety of state-controlled media and became a means of 'negating [female] sexuality and turning [women] into objects of procreation', as one recent study puts it.[4]

At the same time it is important to avoid making sweeping generalisations about women's experiences, such as the claim that women were all victims of the Nazi regime, or that they were all forced to identify positively with their new role as 'mothers of the *Volk*', producing lots of children for the Führer, which is patently untrue. In fact, as we shall see below, differences in age, class, religion, race, sexuality and marital status were as fundamental in determining the impact of Nazi policies on women's lives as gender itself. A subsidiary aim of the book, therefore, is to do justice to the variety and complexity of women's experiences during this period, and in particular to pay attention to that sizeable group of 'women standing alone': the never-married, the separated, the divorced, the abandoned, the imprisoned, the enslaved and the widowed, who between them numbered in the millions as a result of the dislocations, deportations and mass slaughter of the Second World War.[5]

Recent historiographical debate has pondered whether the Nazi regime was 'modern' or 'reactionary' (or both), whether it contributed, despite its own intentions, to the 'modernisation' of German society, with corresponding improvements in the social position and economic status of women, or whether it set back progress towards women's emancipation by several decades.[6] This discussion is highly relevant to some of the themes addressed in this study. For some historians, particularly those operating from older feminist assumptions, the language and imagery of the Third Reich offer an extreme example of how the nineteenth-century idea of 'separate spheres' of action for men and women has been used over time in order to maintain and reinforce inequalities based on gender.[7] Heroism and the warlike qualities of the German people, in Hitler's view, were situated in the male 'public' sphere, from which women were to be excluded for their own protection. The functions of the private sphere (motherhood and self-sacrifice in support of a husband) were to be kept strictly separate from, and subordinate to, those of the public. 'Equal rights for women', the Nazi leader once declared, 'means that they receive the respect they deserve in the sphere nature intended for them'.[8] Elsewhere he wrote: 'The "Aryan" hero must marry only his equal "Aryan" woman, but not one who goes out too much or likes theatres, entertainments, or sport, or who cares to be seen outside the house.'[9]

More recently, however, this rather one-dimensional view has been challenged by historians interested in exploring the complex relationship between image and reality in Hitler's Germany. In spite of surface appearances and popular perceptions, they argue, the gendered boundaries

between the 'male/public' and the 'female/private' sphere were never fixed,
even under the Third Reich, and were in fact considerably more flexible
than the 'separate spheres' model allows. To take one obvious example,
millions of German women worked outside the home for wages in Weimar
and Nazi Germany, in most cases for considerably less pay than men.[10] A
further 2.5 million non-German women worked as 'foreign' labourers in the
German war economy between 1939 and 1945, most of them deportees
from Poland and the occupied parts of the Soviet Union. Conditions for
such 'racially inferior' women amounted to little more than slavery, and
certainly they were not permitted to marry or enjoy a 'normal' heterosexual
family life in the way 'Aryan' women were. Strict laws prevented them from
socialising with the German population, and those who fell pregnant after
liaisons with French POWs and other male deportees from occupied Europe
were often subject to harsh punishments, including forced abortions and
sterilisations.[11]

At the other end of the scale, many politically active women from inside
the Nazi movement hoped to use the Nazi discourse on race and motherhood
to forge a radical new role for themselves within the National Socialist state
beyond the biological task of reproduction. This might involve helping to
train nurses and social workers in the fight against prostitution, alcoholism
and drug addiction, or providing assistance to charitable schemes such as the
Winter Relief Programme for poor Nazi families. During the war many
'eugenically valued' young single women were also encouraged to work
away from home, for instance in Nazi-controlled schemes like the Reich
Labour Service, or as auxiliaries with the armed forces or the SS.[12]
Furthermore, although after 1933 women were largely barred from holding
offices or positions of power within the upper echelons of the party and state,
they were nonetheless able, either as honorary or paid officials, to exert considerable influence over propaganda activities at grassroots level, for instance
through organisations such as the *NS-Frauenschaft* and *Deutsches
Frauenwerk*.[13] Those women involved in recruiting and motivating other
women for the Nazi cause often spoke of the pride they felt in the knowledge
that they were making a contribution, however small, to the great struggle
for national renewal, and also of their sense of solidarity with the fighting
men in the Wehrmacht or SS units. For them the most important thing about
National Socialism was its anti-communist and strongly nationalistic stance,
and not its conservative position on the 'women's question'.[14]

In terms of the broader debate, the argument presented in this book is
that the Third Reich was neither entirely reactionary nor entirely modern in
its policies and attitudes towards women. This is because its intentions lay
elsewhere, not in the repression of women per se or even in pushing women
back into the home and marriage, but in the reconstruction of society along
racial lines.[15] Of course, in a general sense women were discriminated
against in a variety of ways during the Nazi period, as indeed women in all
modern industrial societies have been and continue to be. Low wages,

hostility towards married women in work, and the stark under-representation of women in politics and in all senior administrative, managerial and professional posts were as much features of Hitler's Germany as they were of, say, inter-war Britain and France or of Fascist Italy.[16] Even after the defeat of fascism in 1945, men in all parts of Europe, through their predominance in governments, political parties, trades unions and religious bodies, retained the loudest voice in debates over national policies affecting women's reproductive rights and rights within the family.[17] In no country in western Europe until the 1960s were women afforded the legal right to an abortion, and access to information about birth control and family planning was (and continues to be) impeded by the hostility of the Christian churches and various other conservative and pro-natalist groups across Europe.[18]

Nonetheless, the Third Reich was unique because, as Gisela Bock astutely argues, racial hierarchies were given precedence over gender hierarchies, even if the basic underlying principles of patriarchy, male domination and female subordination remained in place.[19] The real female victims of the Nazi regime were those women who were considered 'racially inferior'. Alongside 'racially inferior' men they were subject to an appalling catalogue of cruelties and humiliations, ending in the ultimate horror of the death camps in occupied Poland. By and large, however, 'ordinary', 'Aryan' women did not have to face any of these experiences, unless they made a conscious decision to resist Nazism or to provide aid or shelter to its victims. Rather, they were often the beneficiaries of Nazi racial policies, receiving recognition and status as the mothers of the race while also exploiting pressures in the labour market to consolidate their position in employment outside the home, including – as Jill Stephenson has shown – some of the more highly paid professions.[20] In some contexts, especially in occupied Poland during the war, 'Aryan' women were even given opportunities to exercise power over 'racially inferior' women and men, helping to implement the policy directives of the all-male Nazi leadership. In such circumstances, women moved from being passive beneficiaries of the system to active participants in genocide and other Nazi war crimes.[21]

All this does not mean, of course, that gender is irrelevant to understanding Nazi racial ideology or the Holocaust. A large part of Nazi racial policy was built on the assumption that women were to be valued or not valued purely on the basis of their reproductive capacity – on whether, from a racial, biological and social point of view, they would make good mothers.[22] Racially 'inferior' and educationally disadvantaged women, for instance, were systematically excluded from the benefits offered to racially 'desirable' women, and instead were often forced into low-paid and monotonous 'gender-suitable' work that reinforced their status as 'undesirable' mothers.[23] During the war, as we have seen, thousands of eastern European women were also forced to work in appalling conditions, and in the event of pregnancy were denied access to proper pre- and post-natal care. Some even had their children taken away from them shortly after birth, while others were offered or coerced into accepting terminations, especially after an order of 1943 allowed eastern workers the right to abortion on demand.[24]

With Jewish women, Nazi policy went one stage further. The kind of work they were expected to perform in the death camps and forced labour camps of occupied Poland was often harder and more humiliating than that given to male prisoners, and resulted in a much shorter life expectancy within the camp system for women than men. In effect, they were being discriminated against twice, because of their race and because of their sex.[25] Some Nazi racial planners even held Jewish women responsible for alleged Jewish 'in-breeding', while blaming Jewish men for seducing or lusting after young 'Aryan' women – in their view a different, but no less reprehensible crime. This in itself demonstrates that traditional assumptions about gender continued to play an important role in Nazi racial discourse.[26]

However, it is important that this conceptual point should not blind historians to the possibility that one of the chief effects of Nazi racial policy and the Holocaust was to downgrade the importance of sexual differences in defining human experiences, to relegate gender to 'a kind of under-ground', as Bock puts it.[27] After all, women and men were killed in the same manner and in roughly the same numbers in the gas chambers of Auschwitz-Birkenau and other death camps. While men had a slightly higher chance of surviving the initial selections and the shock of forced labour, in the long run they too were doomed to perish at the hands of their tormentors, with only a handful of women and men living to tell the tale. What needs to be taken into account in any gender-based analysis of the years 1933 to 1945, in other words, are not just the differences, but also the similarities between the sexes, as well as the possible existence of degrees of difference and convergence, subtle and not so subtle forms of differences, and so forth.[28] Gender relations must be seen as dynamic, rather than created in a pre-determined historical vacuum; they may be subject to change and renegoti-ation even within relatively short periods of time – as evidenced by the frequent and sudden role-reversals that took place inside the typical German/Jewish family between 1933 and 1945.[29] As we shall see, this model is a crucial analytical tool for examining the position of women as a whole in the Third Reich. In essence it means that we need to explore women's experiences within the context of a dynamic interaction between everyday life and the changing nature (i.e. the growing radicalisation and destructiveness) of the Nazi regime itself.

Finally, the issues raised in this book also have an important bearing on recent developments in the social history of Germany during the Second World War, in particular with regard to popular attitudes towards issues like the persecution of the Jews and foreign workers, and also the vexed question of resistance and conformity to Nazism in general. As previous studies have found, the opposition of certain sections of the (female and male) population before the war was substantially weakened by develop-ments after 1939, when Gestapo and police terror increased massively while at the same time occupied territories were plundered for labour in order to shield German workers from the less palatable demands of the war economy.[30] Even as the military defeats mounted and the Allied bombing raids grew heavier from 1943, the general reaction was mostly one of passive acceptance of the need to fight, at least in order to defend Germany against the terrifying prospect of Soviet invasion and occupation. Against this background, the few women and men who did choose actively to resist the Nazi terror system appear even more remarkable and even more brave, precisely because they acted in conscious isolation from the majority of the population (in contrast to, say, Italian anti-fascists, who had a broad base of popular support in many parts of northern Italy during the final two years of the war). As Anthony Beevor writes in his recent study of the events leading up to the fall of Berlin in 1945, 'in a world of cruelty and horror, where any conception of humanity has been destroyed by ideology, just a few acts of human kindness and self-sacrifice lighten what would otherwise be an almost unbearable story'.[31] The evidence presented below would bear out this judgement in full.

Before going on to explore these issues in greater depth, however, it is first necessary to consider the position of women in Germany before the Second World War, including the question of women's support for, or opposition to, National Socialism in the period 1919–39. This will be the subject of the first two chapters of this book, which, for the purposes of simplicity, are separated by the turning point of 1933, the year in which Hitler came to power in Germany and set about establishing the Third Reich. Subsequent chapters will then look at important themes such as Nazi racial policy, Nazi policy towards women at work, youth movements and women's education, the role of women in the resistance, and the impact of the war on the home front. Finally, a short conclusion will examine some of the legacies of the Nazi regime and attempt to answer the question: What difference did the 12 years of National Socialist rule make to the attitudes and experiences of German women in the twentieth century, and to the struggle for equal rights and equal opportunities in particular? This, after all, seems to be one of the most pressing issues to emerge from a study of this kind.

Notes

1 'Rede des Führers auf dem Frauenkongreß in Nürnberg am 8. September 1934', in: *N.S. Frauenwarte* 3/7 (1934–35), p. 210.
2 On Nazi attitudes towards women a useful set of documents with commentary can be found in Jeremy Noakes and Geoffrey Pridham (eds), *Nazism, 1919–1945. A Documentary Reader. Vol. 2. State, Economy and Society, 1933–1939* (Exeter, 1984), pp. 448–70. On Nazi anti-feminism see also Chapter 1 below.
3 Jill Stephenson, *Women in Nazi Society* (London, 1975); Stephenson, *The Nazi Organisation of Women* (London, 1981); Stephenson, *Women in Nazi Germany* (London, 2001); Gisela Bock, *Zwangssterilisation im Nationalsozialismus*.

Studien zur Rassenpolitik und Frauenpolitik (Opladen, 1986); Claudia Koonz, *Mothers in the Fatherland. Women, the Family and Nazi Politics* (London, 1987); Ute Frevert, *Women in German History. From Bourgeois Emancipation to Sexual Liberation* (Oxford, 1989); Dagmar Reese, *'Straff aber nicht stramm – herb aber nicht derb'. Die Vergesellschaftung von Mädchen durch den Bund Deutscher Mädel im sozialkulturellen Vergleich zweier Milieus* (Weinheim and Basel, 1989); Gabriele Czarnowski, *Das kontrollierte Paar. Ehe- und Sexualpolitik im Nationalsozialismus* (Weinheim, 1991); Lisa Pine, *Nazi Family Policy, 1933–1945* (London, 1997); Marion Kaplan, *Between Dignity and Despair. Jewish Life in Nazi Germany* (Oxford, 1998); Elizabeth Heineman, *What Difference Does a Husband Make? Women and Marital Status in Nazi and Postwar Germany* (London, 1999).

4 Judith Tydor Baumel, *Double Jeopardy. Gender and the Holocaust* (London, 1998), p. 7.

5 Cf. Heineman, *What Difference Does a Husband Make?*, *passim*.

6 For a summary of the debate see Michael Burleigh and Wolfgang Wippermann, *The Racial State. Germany, 1933–1945* (Cambridge, 1991), pp. 7–22; and Ian Kershaw, *The Nazi Dictatorship. Problems and Perspectives of Interpretation*, 4th edn (London, 2000), pp. 161–82. Atina Grossmann's review essay 'Feminist Debates about Women and National Socialism', in: *Gender and History* 3 (1991), pp. 350–8, considers similar themes within the framework of women's history and feminist theory. See also Detlev J. K. Peukert, *Inside Nazi Germany. Conformity, Opposition and Racism in Everyday Life* (London, 1987), pp. 175–83; and Michael Prinz and Rainer Zitelmann (eds), *Nationalsozialismus und Modernisierung* (Darmstadt, 1991).

7 For two critical accounts of the historiography on this issue see L. K. Kerber, 'Separate Spheres, Female Worlds, Woman's Place. The Rhetoric of Women's History', in: *Journal of American History* 75 (1988), pp. 9–39; and A. Vickery, 'Golden Age to Separate Spheres? A Review of the Categories and Chronology of English Women's History', in: *Historical Journal* 36 (1993), pp. 383–414.

8 Quoted in Richard Grunberger, *A Social History of the Third Reich* (London, 1971), p. 313.

9 Quoted in Robert A. Brady, *The Spirit and Structure of German Fascism* (London, 1937), p. 187.

10 On women's employment in inter-war Germany see Renate Bridenthal 'Beyond Kinder, Kuche, Kirche: Weimar Women at Work', in: *Central European History* 6 (1973), pp. 148–66; and Tim Mason, 'Women in Germany, 1925–1940. Family, Welfare and Work', in: *History Workshop Journal* (1976), Part I, pp. 74–113, and Part II, pp. 5–32 (also reprinted in: Jane Caplan (ed.), *Nazism, Fascism and the Working Class. Essays by Tim Mason* (Cambridge, 1995), pp. 131–211; subsequent references to this work will refer to the later version). For a general overview of women's work see Eve Rosenhaft, 'Women in Modern Germany', in: Gordon Martel (ed.), *Modern Germany Reconsidered, 1870–1945* (London, 1992), pp. 140–58. On German women in the Second World War see Stephenson, *The Nazi Organisation of Women*, pp. 178–213; and Leila J. Rupp, *Mobilizing Women for War. German and American Propaganda* (Princeton, N.J., 1978).

11 The figure of 2.5 million for the total number of female foreign workers in Germany, including those from France and other parts of western Europe, is given in Gisela Bock, *Frauen in der europäischen Geschichte. Vom Mittelalter bis zur Gegenwart* (Munich, 2000), p. 301. On the wartime use of foreign labour in general see Ulrich Herbert, *Hitler's Foreign Workers. Enforced Foreign Labor in Germany under the Third Reich* (Cambridge, 1997).

12 Stephenson, *The Nazi Organisation of Women*, esp. pp. 178–213. On the Reich

Labour Service see also Stephenson, 'Women's Labor Service in Nazi Germany', in: *Central European History* 15 (1982), pp. 241–65, and Chapter 5 below.

13 Cf. Frevert, *Women in German History*, p. 217.

14 Stephenson, *The Nazi Organisation of Women*, pp. 35–6.

15 Cf. Burleigh and Wippermann, *The Racial State, passim*.

16 On inter-war Britain see Martin Pugh, *Women and the Women's Movement in Britain, 1914–1959* (London, 1992); and S.K. Kent, *Making Peace. The Reconstruction of Gender in Inter-War Britain* (Princeton, N.J., 1993). On Fascist Italy see Alexander de Grand, 'Women under Italian Fascism', in: *Historical Journal* 19 (1976), pp. 947–68; and Victoria de Grazia, *How Fascism Ruled Women. Italy, 1922–1945* (London, 1992).

17 See e.g. Robert G. Moeller, *Protecting Motherhood. Women and the Family in Postwar West Germany* (Berkeley, Calif., 1993); and Atina Grossmann, 'Pronatalism, Nationbuilding and Socialism. Population Policy in the SBZ/DDR, 1945 to 1960', in: David E. Barclay and Eric D. Weitz (eds), *Between Reform and Revolution. German Socialism and Communism from 1840 to 1990* (Oxford, 1998), pp. 443–65.

18 Cf. Stephenson, *Women in Nazi Society*, pp. 5–6.

19 Gisela Bock, 'Ordinary Women in Nazi Germany. Perpetrators, Victims, Followers and Bystanders', in: Dalia Ofer and Leonore J. Weitzman (eds), *Women in the Holocaust* (London, 1998), p. 94.

20 Jill McIntyre (i.e. Stephenson), 'Women and the Professions in Germany, 1930–1940', in: Anthony Nicholls and Erich Matthias (eds), *German Democracy and the Triumph of Hitler* (London, 1971), pp. 175–214.

21 The issue of whether and to what extent women acted as perpetrators in the Third Reich remains a highly controversial one. For a summary of the debate see Adelheid von Saldern, 'Victims or Perpetrators? Controversies about the Role of Women in the Nazi State', in: David F. Crew (ed.), *Nazism and German Society, 1933–1945* (London, 1994), pp. 141–65. Also Chapter 3 below.

22 Baumel, *Double Jeopardy*, p. 7. Cf. Burleigh and Wippermann, *The Racial State*, pp. 242–66.

23 See e.g. Annemarie Tröger, 'The Creation of a Female Assembly Line Proletariat', in: Renate Bridenthal, Atina Grossmann and Marion Kaplan (eds), *When Biology Became Destiny. Women in Weimar and Nazi Germany* (New York, 1984), pp. 237–70.

24 Herbert, *Hitler's Foreign Workers*, p. 270. See also Bock, *Zwangssterilisation*, esp. pp. 447–8, and Chapter 4 below.

25 Baumel, *Double Jeopardy*, p. 31. This point is also made by Primo Levi in his introduction to Liana Millu's memoir of the Holocaust, published in German as *Der Rauch über Birkenau* (Frankfurt/Main, 1999).

26 The idea of Jewish in-breeding can be traced back directly to a speech made by Hitler in Munich in August 1920, when he contrasted German racial purity, responsible for all that was good in the world, with Jewish in-breeding, responsible for all that was bad and corrupt in the world. For further details see Eberhard Jäckel, *Hitler's World View. A Blueprint for Power* (London, 1972), pp. 50–1.

27 Bock, 'Ordinary Women', p. 96.

28 Cf. Bock, 'Equality and Difference in National Socialist Racism', in: J. Wallach Scott (ed.), *Feminism and History* (Oxford, 1996), pp. 267–90; and Bock, *Frauen in der europäischen Geschichte*, pp. 281–96.

29 See Pine, *Nazi Family Policy*, pp. 147–78. Also Chapter 3 below.

30 See e.g. Herbert, *Hitler's Foreign Workers, passim*. Also Tim Mason, *Social Policy in the Third Reich* (Oxford, 1995).

31 Anthony Beevor, *Berlin. The Downfall 1945* (London, 2002), p. xxxv.

1

The Weimar Republic and the rise of the Nazis

In August 1919, on the day that the Weimar National Assembly finally approved a new constitution for Germany, the recently installed Social Democratic Minister of the Interior, Eduard David, declared before the elected delegates: 'The will of the people is now the supreme law. Our constitution provides the foundation for a social democracy. It guarantees not only political democracy, but also economic democracy'.[1] Over the past few decades, historians have often asked why it was that the first German republic, born of such rational, democratic and high-minded principles, should collapse so ignominiously after only 14 years in existence. Some accounts focus on the structural weaknesses of a western-style parliamentary system that succumbed to economic crisis and the rise of political extremism in the early 1930s. Others place more emphasis on a broader 'crisis of modernity', seen in such things as the loosening of class and family structures, the partial success and partial failure of pioneering welfare schemes, rising crime rates, and the pressures placed on traditional rural communities by the progressive modernisation of the economy and society. Fears for the future were exacerbated by the legacy of the First World War, which overthrew previously cherished assumptions about the political continuity of the German nation and led to the creation of what Detlev Peukert identifies as a 'popular mood oscillating between enthusiasm and anxiety, hopes of national reawakening and fears of national extinction'.[2]

One way of examining this 'crisis of modernity' in Germany in the 1920s is to place it in an international context, in order to see how developments in other European countries and even other continents influenced the attitudes of 'ordinary' Germans. One of the key events in international history in the twentieth century, for instance, was the Bolshevik revolution in Russia in 1917, which brought in its wake a radical change in the status of Russian women, even if this change was partially reversed under Stalin in the 1930s.[3] For a minority of German people in the 1920s, the Russian example was an inspiration and a hope, while for the majority – including the majority of the working class – it was something deeply alarming and abhorrent, conjuring up images of civil war, famine and the destruction of the family. Equally important for gender relations was the so-called 'American wave', which hit Germany in the inter-war period in the form of new fashions and new entertainments, modern advertising and department stores, nightclubs and jazz music, and above all the Hollywood blockbusters which pulled in millions of cinemagoers each week. In particular, the 'American wave' gave rise to the image of the 'new woman', the 'cigarette-smoking, motorbike riding, silk-stockinged or tennis-skirted young women out on the streets, in the bars or on the sports field', as Elizabeth Harvey puts it.[4] While for some, especially in the big cities like Berlin or Hamburg, the appearance of the 'new woman' was a welcome and acceptable sign of progress and rationality, for others it was a symbol of the collapse of the traditional patriarchal system and the 'decadence' of modern urban living, giving rise to a profound mood of cultural pessimism, particularly in conservative circles, and a belief that Germany was doomed unless it reasserted its own national identity and traditions.[5]

A second and related dimension to modernity, stressed by contemporaries of all political persuasions, was the steady drop in the number of young women opting for motherhood as a full-time career. For instance, the number of live births per 1,000 women of childbearing age fell from 128.0 in 1910–11 to 90.0 in 1922 and to an all-time low of 58.9 in 1933.[6] Concern about declining levels of fertility was of course common to nearly all European countries at this time, and affected France, Italy, Britain, Austria and Russia as much as it did Germany. It was in France, for instance, that the practice of giving state awards to prolific mothers was first introduced in 1920; and in Fascist Italy, too, large tax incentives were offered as a means of encouraging marriages and large families.[7] Nonetheless, in Germany the sense of 'demographic crisis' was particularly acute, and was made worse by the unusually large number of adult single women – war widows, divorcees, 'career girls' – within the population at this time, and the huge rise in the number of illegal abortions, especially during the periods of greatest economic dislocation (1919–23 and 1929–35). As Cornelie Usborne writes, population experts were especially worried by evidence that married couples were consciously and deliberating choosing to have smaller families (the 'two-child family', or sometimes one or no children at all) and were being aided in this by the increased availability of modern contraceptives and birth control methods. Furthermore:

The birth-rate was lowest and most conspicuously so in German cities, which encouraged the view that urban life was 'unnatural' and 'corrupting'. The capital featured regularly in the press as a warning example of what was in store for the nation. In 1924, newspapers announced with alarm that Berlin had the lowest birth-rate in the world (9.4 per 1,000).[8]

In order to gain a deeper understanding of the political choices that Germans faced in the 1920s, however, it is not sufficient to refer merely to broader international developments or demographic trends. What is also needed is a greater focus on the changing role and position of women in the economy of that time, coupled with an exploration of the continued importance of religion, habitat, employment status and class identity in determining political attitudes and voting patterns. First and foremost, this means examining in further detail the impact of the First World War and its immediate aftermath on German politics and society.

1. The position of women after the First World War

The First World War in Germany, as in other countries, brought about important changes in class and gender relations, which also had significant implications for the attempt by committed republicans to eradicate the most authoritarian and deferential features of imperial society in the aftermath of the 1918–19 revolution. True, an organised women's movement had already emerged before the war, and had won a number of important concessions, such as the entry of women into the universities. Nonetheless, the position of the women's movement was transformed by its official role in the mobilisation of women during the war and its promotion of the idea of female patriotic self-sacrifice for the good of the fatherland. Middle-class women certainly made a considerable contribution to nursing and social services during the war, and even larger numbers of working-class women entered the wartime labour force, for instance as munitions workers. The 'nation' and the women's movement, so it seemed, had come together after 1914, and even conservative and right-wing groups finally accepted – albeit reluctantly – that women would henceforth play a more prominent role in public and political life, not least in order to provide a counterweight to the growing power of organised labour.[9] Indeed, with ever greater numbers of women contributing directly to the war economy, it was not long before munitions factories were obliged to introduce an eight-hour day and to make other improvements to working conditions, such as the provision of daytime childcare and dormitories for single female workers. These concessions were wrested from employers in industry well before the November revolution of 1918, when the eight-hour rule was granted across the board.[10]

In fact, though, the war did not usher in a massive increase in female employment in Germany. What it did do was lead to significant changes in the types of work done by women. In particular 400,000 women now left domestic service and the agricultural sector, while a slightly higher number entered predominantly 'male' positions in war-related industries, for instance in metalworking, machine building and chemicals, or took on temporary administrative posts on behalf of the military or civilian authorities.[11] This was hardly enough to constitute a revolution in female employment patterns, but subjectively it may have increased the confidence of women by broadening the range of jobs open to them. More concretely, it offered some women the opportunity to escape from occupations that either paid less money for time given (e.g. textiles) or involved a greater degree of subordinate status (e.g. domestic service, agricultural work).[12] Indeed, while the total number of boys under 17 working in industry increased between 1913 and 1918, the number of girls under 17 decreased, suggesting that it was older women, married as well as single, who were the primary beneficiaries of the new employment opportunities created by the war.[13] Even so, in 1925 unpaid family assistants on small farms and in businesses still constituted the largest single group of 'economically active' women in the German Reich – some 4.63 million persons, compared to only 4.2 million women in all categories of regular employment (i.e. employment which involved paying contributions to the state sickness benefit scheme). There were also almost 1 million female agricultural workers and 1.3 million domestic servants. This might be compared to the 1.5 million women who were in white-collar jobs (three times as many as in 1907) and the 2.2 million in manual occupations of various kinds.[14]

The most important political gain for women from the war was of course the granting of female suffrage for national elections during the November revolution of 1918. It was expected, especially in view of the enthusiasm with which women initially responded, that this would lead to a further extension of women's rights in the future, as well as a strengthening of democratic values more generally. Nearly 80 per cent of all women who were eligible to vote did so in 1919, and nearly 10 per cent of the delegates to the new National Assembly were women.[15] Furthermore, feminist campaigners hoped that the presence of women in Reich and state parliaments would help to steer the language of politics away from a concern with war and other areas of male chauvinist culture towards a concern for the rights of the individual and the community. For those middle-class women who had enjoyed the benefits of a university education, new career opportunities seemed to beckon with the expansion of the welfare state and social services. The occupational census of 1925, for instance, revealed that just under 7,000 female graduates were employed in professional positions (mostly as teachers, social workers and doctors). By 1933 this figure had risen to 12,468.[16]

On the other hand, the November revolution and the years that followed it also saw great uncertainty for most German women. While capitalist employers saw working-class women as a reserve army of cheap labour, who could be paid less than adult men for doing the same work, the state and the trades unions often had a political interest in seeking to remove them from the workforce at times of high male unemployment. Indeed, many of those women who had taken on wartime positions in traditionally male-dominated industries and in the lower grades of the civil service were sacked after the war in order to make way for the returning soldiers.[17] There were also thousands of young war widows struggling to support themselves in a world dominated by chronic job insecurity and rampant inflation. Even those who were not widowed were often burdened by husbands who returned home crippled or psychologically disturbed by their wartime experiences. Others who wished to get married and start families were unable to do so because of the shortage of potential husbands (around 2 million men had been killed in the war, 85 per cent of whom were aged 18 to 34).[18] Poverty was a daily reality for many working-class women, whether single or married. Indeed, in 1925 over half of all female wage earners (2.2 million out of 4.2 million) were classified as manual workers in poorly paid unskilled or semi-skilled jobs. Furthermore, of the almost 2 million female manual workers in industry, over two-thirds were single and under 30, a fact used to justify lower rates of pay to the extent that skilled female workers were often paid less than unskilled men.[19]

Not surprisingly, the failure of successive republican governments to offer working women a better deal soon had its impact on politics and the trades union movement. Female membership of the General Federation of German Trade Unions, for instance, fell from an all-time high of 27.7 per cent of the total membership in 1920 to a mere 16 per cent by 1931.[20] Low wages and chronic job insecurity meant that many women saw work as a temporary state before marriage and therefore did not bother to join unions or engage in agitation for equal rights. Family and attracting a husband came first in the list of priorities, and work or a career a poor second. The commitment of the government and the political parties to the principle of female equality in the workplace also remained weak, a fact of some importance in the eventual triumph of Nazism in the early 1930s. Even the middle-class women's movement, the BDF, showed little concern for issues of women's rights, preferring to instruct its members on the importance of working in harmony with men for the renewal of the 'national community' and the 'spirit of 1914'. 'Organised motherliness' (*organisierte Mütterlichkeit*) and opposition to abortion and pornography were to be its main areas of concern during the 1920s, and the BDF also devoted much of its time to campaigning in favour of the new Reich Law for the Combating of Venereal Diseases, which came into force in 1927 and established a much harsher system of penalties for those convicted of running illegal brothels or of deliberately spreading sexually transmitted infections.[21]

Not all was lost, of course, of the emancipatory potential of 1918–19 or the radicalism of the pre-1914 era. In many of the bigger towns and cities, and some of the smaller ones too, women were actively engaged in politics at the local level, most notably for parties of the right such as the DNVP (German National People's Party) and the Catholic Centre Party, but also for parties of the left, including the SPD (social democrats) and the KPD (communists). In areas where the left-wing parties ran local government there were also some cautious moves towards addressing issues of birth control and female reproductive rights, usually in conjunction with broader programmes for the eradication of poverty and sexually transmitted diseases among the poorer sections of society. In Hamburg and Frankfurt-am-Main, for instance, special clinics were set up by volunteers from the *Bund für Mutterschutz* offering contraception and family planning advice to young women, and in Berlin the German-Jewish sexologist Max Hirschfeld opened his world-famous Institute for Sexology, which advocated (among other things) a more tolerant attitude towards homosexuality and female sexual liberation.[22] All of these institutions were shut down by the Nazis after 1933, but not before they had a chance to demonstrate that there was indeed a more enlightened and progressive side to Germany and German politics in the 1920s.

Where the left did fail, however, and fail spectacularly, was in its attempts to persuade more women to go out and vote for it at election times. Indeed, in each successive Reichstag election until 1930 the proportion of eligible women choosing to exercise their right to vote fell, from almost 80 per cent in 1919 to below 60 per cent in some towns and cities by 1928.[23] Those women who did bother to vote, moreover, showed a marked preference for parties that occupied a conservative position on the women's question, especially those connected to the established churches; namely the Catholic Centre Party and the Protestant DVP and DNVP parties. Certainly they did not seem attracted to the left-liberal DDP, the party most closely associated with the leadership of the bourgeois BDF feminist movement, which declined rapidly in support after 1918, nor to the SPD, the only party to have consistently upheld the demand for female suffrage in the Wilhelmine period. Indeed, women more than men seemed to look back on the 'good old days' of the empire with a feeling of nostalgia, a fact under-lined by the predominance of women among the supporters of the *Ersatzkaiser* Hindenburg in his successful campaigns for the presidency of the Republic in 1925 and 1932.[24]

Many experts explain German women's lack of commitment to republican and left-of-centre parties, and their apparent indifference to politics in general, by pointing to the limited benefits that emancipation brought women in the 1920s. Despite nominal recognition of equality of the sexes in the 1919 constitution, progress towards this goal was at best very slow. Few women won positions of independence, responsibility or professional status on a par with men; the majority of female workers (55 per cent) were still engaged in menial tasks in the least modernised sectors of the economy, either as unpaid workers in the family business or as hired domestic servants or agricultural labourers.[25] On the other hand, to many young, educated, middle-class women – who had been to university and took for granted the possibility of a career – the feminist movement, with its links to the political struggles of the pre-1914 era, seemed past its sell-by date, old-fashioned, prudish and unnecessarily antagonistic towards men. Certainly feminist criticisms of patriarchy seemed to have little relevance to their own lives and to the difficult choices they now faced between having a family or going out to work. As Emmy Beckmann, the chairperson of the German Women Teachers' Association, complained in a pamphlet published in 1932:

> ... a new generation of women has grown up, equipped with the education which a previous generation had fought for so hard, and with new rights and freedoms. These young women now see the tasks and lifestyles which await them as an unwanted burden and responsibility, a cold and empty substitute for the fulfilment to be gained from a peaceful home and the close family ties of husband, wife and child ... for [them] the ideal of liberation ... which the previous generation followed with such conviction, has faded away.[26]

The indifference of younger women towards the campaigns of their feminist forebears is hardly surprising, however, when one takes into account the failure of the established Weimar political parties to involve women in any meaningful way in policy formation or decision-making processes. In no party, for instance, did women ever fill more than 10 per cent of the leading positions, and at local level the proportion was between 1 and 2 per cent.[27] Even those parties with the highest proportion of female Reichstag deputies (DDP, SPD) tended to treat women as one 'interest group' among many to be represented. The SPD in particular developed all the hallmarks of a state-supporting mass bureaucratic organisation, with birth control and other 'family' issues unofficially reserved for the party's women's section, although women still had no real say when it came to defining broader policy areas. This enabled the party to pose as the chief advocate of women's rights even though, as a leading member of the government coalition between 1919 and 1923, and again between 1928 and 1930, it continued to obstruct or delay legislation that would establish the principle of equal pay for equal work.[28]

In fact, one of the chief paradoxes of Weimar politics is that it was the parties of the nationalist and conservative right – those that had originally opposed female suffrage – that proved to be more adept at mobilising women supporters at election time and holding their interest between elections. Campaigns against the post-1919 border with Poland or the use of African soldiers in the French occupation force on the Rhine, for instance, proved much more popular than those dealing with employment rights vis-à-vis men, and allowed some nationalist women to engage in politics at local and national level without compromising their middle-class respectability or femininity.[29] The gradual 'feminisation' of the nationalist and right-wing parties in Weimar Germany, especially at the provincial level, may help in part to explain why the left failed to capitalise on the initial electoral gains made in 1918. Another factor working against the left was the continued importance of religion and traditional patterns of deference, especially in rural areas where respect for the authority of the churches was still strong and where people of both sexes tended to vote either for the Catholic Centre Party or for the Protestant-dominated DNVP and DVP.[30] What still needs to be explained, however, is why so many women (as well as men) deserted the traditional conservative parties for the more radical Nazis in the early 1930s. We also need to know why many first-time voters, men and women, cast their ballots in favour of Nazi candidates at this time, instead of supporting the established parties of the left or right. Indeed, just as any examination of the Weimar Republic's failure to capture the hearts and minds of the German people must take women and their political attitudes into account, so too must an analysis of the reasons for the eventual triumph of Nazism in 1933.

2. Nazism and the 'woman question' in the 1920s

Between 1919 and 1933, 111 women served in the Reichstag as elected deputies. Most of them represented the parties of the left, the SPD and the KPD, although there were also a dozen or so from the DDP, the right-wing Protestant parties and the Catholic Centre Party.[31] Only one party could boast that it had no women MPs at all: the Nazi Party. This applied even after the huge electoral advances of the early 1930s, when at one point the NSDAP held 230 out of 608 Reichstag seats.[32] To put it quite simply, there was to be no room for women politicians in the coming Third Reich. Rather, as the *Nationalsozialistische Monatshefte*, one of the party's leading periodicals, declared in April 1930:

> The National Socialist movement is an emphatically male phenomenon as far as the political struggle is concerned. It regards women in parliament as a depressing sign of liberalism ... We believe that every genuine woman will, in her innermost being, pay homage to the masculine principle of National Socialism; for only then will she reemerge as a whole woman![33]

The Nazis' contempt for women politicians was of course well known to contemporaries and went hand in hand with their anti-communism and anti-Semitism, their glorification of violence and their demand for a one-party dictatorship in place of the democratic parliamentary system. However, it is also worth asking how far the Nazis' views on women in general differed from the attitudes of the average citizen in the post-1918 period. Like many other people in the 1920s, Hitler believed that men and women were essentially different, and that women had special qualities and responsibilities which made them unsuitable for work outside the home, except in compassionate or caring roles.[34] He was also obsessed, as were most other German politicians and church leaders, by the steep fall in the national birth rate and the apparent threat this represented to the revival of

Germany as a great power in the aftermath of the First World War.[35] Finally, Hitler's apparent concerns about rising crime rates and declining standards of sexual morality would have been familiar to conservative voters from all parts of the Reich. Indeed, in terms of his pro-family and anti-abortion rhetoric, Hitler was merely echoing the thoughts and feelings of millions of 'ordinary', provincial, middle-class Germans, many of whom voted for parties like the Catholic Centre, the DNVP, the DVP or even the DDP before turning to the National Socialists in the early 1930s.[36]

On the other hand, the Nazis stood out from most of the other right-wing parties in Weimar Germany when they called for the preservation of 'racial purity' as the answer to all of Germany's problems, and denounced feminism and the women's movement as part of a Jewish-led conspiracy designed to destroy Germany and weaken it from within. In this sense, hostility to women's emancipation was part and parcel of a broader anti-establishment rhetoric and was designed in particular to appeal to the lower middle class and anti-intellectual roots of the movement's early followers. One party spokesman, the Bavarian Landtag deputy Dr Buttmann, was clearly mindful of this constituency when he declared in a speech at Lahr on 10 October 1930:

> Women must support their men in the struggle, and they must do so from inside the home. There can never be healthy politics in the Reichstag, at the local level and in state parliaments, so long as gossipy old aunts and spinsters, with glasses on their noses, who belong to Christian women's societies and knitting clubs, are given representation.[37]

Another party slogan, associated in particular with the self-proclaimed Nazi 'philosopher' Alfred Rosenberg, was that German women should be 'emancipated from emancipation' – 'liberated' from the 'Marxist' dogma of sexual equality and returned to their 'natural' roles as mothers and house-wives. Feminism, in Rosenberg's view, was alien to the Germanic soul, a foreign import that came to central Europe through the insidious influence of the French enlightenment and its 'false' doctrine of the equality of all humans. Like liberalism, feminism would destroy all 'masculine' races, all the historical and cultural achievements of the German people, and lead directly to Bolshevism. Its ultimate aim was rule by the weak and the degenerate, the creation of a 'nation of Negroes and bastards'. Only if German women rejected once and for all the idea of sexual equality, and instead returned to their traditional roles as the reproducers of the race and the guardians of its biological inheritance, could there be any hope of national salvation. Politics could then be left once again in the hands of those who knew what was best for the state – men.[38]

Apart from these occasional outbursts of anti-feminist sentiment from people like Buttmann and Rosenberg, however, the NSDAP made few public statements about its policy towards women in the period before 1932, and instead concentrated on building up its support among men. The

SA in particular emerged after 1921 as the paramilitary wing of the movement and developed a fearsome reputation for violence and thuggery (matched by some of its rivals on the left). In spite of the violent, male chauvinist character of the early Nazi Party, though, it would be wrong to conclude that women played no part in its activities during the 1920s. True, women were formally banned from holding leading positions within the party hierarchy and from standing as Nazi candidates in elections. The number of women joining the party as fully paid-up members was very small, and actually fell from 8 to 5 per cent of the total between 1925 and 1933.[39] Only in a few places, such as the town of Barmen on the edge of the Ruhr industrial district in western Germany, did women make up more than 10 per cent of branch members after 1925.[40] Nonetheless, women could still be involved in Nazi Party affairs at local level, even if they did not officially join or pay membership fees. As Jill Stephenson notes, the wives and girlfriends of party members often 'sewed and cooked for male party activists, nursed the sick or injured among them, and made collections of clothes or other essentials for distribution to needy local people'. In so doing they were fulfilling Hitler's own conception of a gendered division of labour, with women permitted some activity outside the home, provided it was sufficiently 'womanly' and did not involve any competition with men.[41]

In some areas, too, small groups of women came together to form pro-Nazi associations of their own, which at first existed entirely separately of the male-dominated party organisation in Munich and were largely left to manage their own affairs.[42] The largest of these associations was Elsbeth Zander's *Deutscher Frauenorden* (DFO or German Women's Order). Founded in Berlin in 1923, it appealed to those women who rejected the conventional conservative parties and wished to engage in direct action against the communists and the 'red republic'. While Nazi men marched and fought in the streets, Zander mobilised her followers in public campaigns on behalf of the National Socialist cause, collecting cash donations and organising charity for poorer Nazi families, and even on occasion becoming involved in demonstrations and strikes. Through skilful manoeuvring, Zander also managed to gain Hitler's personal endorsement of the DFO as the party's official women's auxiliary group in July 1926.[43] According to its statutes, the order did not engage in political activity of any kind, but nonetheless stood at the service of the NSDAP and recognised Adolf Hitler as its leader. Its main purpose was the 'care of the fighting SA units' and their families as well as the training of nurses and social workers for work beneficial to the 'national community'. It also sought to educate its members in the importance of racial consciousness.[44] A police report in December 1930 concluded that the DFO already had 4,000 members in 160 branches by August 1930, rising to 5,100 by the end of the year. The largest branch was in Berlin, with 500 members, while other areas of strength were Bavaria, Thuringia, the Rhineland and Silesia.[45] Hamburg, on the other hand, had only 30 DFO members.[46]

With regard to the 'woman question', the views of the DFO were entirely at one with those of the male party leadership; in fact, if anything, Zander and her associates were even more violently anti-feminist and anti-Semitic than Hitler and Rosenberg. Emma Witte, a leading DFO member, for instance, made her mark in the 1924 Reichstag elections by launching a series of newspaper attacks on the nationalist DNVP, the NSDAP's main rival for the right-wing, conservative vote. The DNVP, she argued, had become too 'feminised' because it allowed one or two women to serve as Reichstag deputies and to sit on its policy committees. In her view, this was nothing less than an 'unmanly subservience ... towards the power-hungry claims of the party's leading women's libbers [*Rechtlerinnen*]'.[47] By contrast, the NSDAP was the only party that could lead Germany to recovery, through a decisive rejection of all forms of feminism and a return to a complete separation of male and female spheres of activity:

> The coming racial state must be masculine – or it will not be at all! Only men are in a position to overcome the state of female power-lessness which led us on towards the criminal act of revolution. Only a battle-hardened [and] ideologically armed people will conquer freedom for itself, will be able to assert itself as a nation! Only on its sword will Germany's future security rest.[48]

Not all Nazi women belonged to the DFO, however, and some preferred to lend their support through more indirect means, without having any formal links to the party. This applied, for instance, to those women who were members of front organisations like the *Kampfbund für deutsche Kultur* (Fighting League for German Culture), founded in Munich in 1928, or to those who belonged to other right-wing women's associations, like the Union for Women's Culture (*Verband Frauenkultur*) or the German-Colonial Women's League (*Deutsch-Kolonialer Frauenbund*), before moving on to join the NSDAP in the 1930s.[49] Meanwhile, within the party itself, chaos reigned as far as the organisation of women was concerned. In Lübeck in north Germany, for instance, a rival 'National Socialist German Women's Movement' had already been set up in 1924, while in Saxony Lotte Rühlemann established her own *Frauengruppe Leipzig* which (until 1933) refused to have anything to do with the other Nazi women's groups.[50] As if to add to the confusion, 1926 even saw the emergence of a new group of radical 'Nazi feminists', led by Emma Hadlich, who attacked the DFO's deferential attitude towards men and challenged the exclusion of women from leadership positions within the Nazi movement.[51] Another prominent national figure was Lydia Gottschewski, who joined the party in 1929 at the age of 23 and went on to become the first leader of the League of German Maidens (BDM or *Bund deutscher Mädel*) in 1930. In her view, Nazi women should not try to compete with men but instead should devote themselves to the task of motherhood and the nurturing of a community spirit among all Germans. This was to be their unique role within the National Socialist movement.[52]

Much less evidence is available on those ordinary women who were active in Nazism in a local context before 1933, since few have left behind written accounts. Some information is given, though, by the autobiographical data collected by the Polish-American sociologist Theodore Abel in his 1936 essay competition on the theme 'Why I Became a Nazi', which included 36 women out of 600 entries,[53] and by more recent discoveries such as the applications for party membership in the Hessian state archives used by Claudia Koonz in her study of Nazi women.[54] The impression given by this evidence is that female Nazi activists showed a strong tendency to identify with middle-class values and aspirations, were fiercely anti-communist and anti-socialist, and came overwhelmingly from Protestant backgrounds. On the whole they also represented a younger generation of women that had not experienced the feminist struggles of the pre-1914 era. Indeed, the average age for joining the party between 1925 and 1933 was 35, considerably lower than for any other party during this period.[55]

Julie Gottlieb's concept of a 'feminine fascism', developed in her recent study of the female members of the British Union of Fascists (BUF) and other extremist organisations in inter-war Britain, might also be used to categorise the outlook of some of the younger women involved in the various pro-Nazi women's groups of the pre-1933 era. According to Gottlieb, the ideology of 'feminine fascism' was characterised by the 'endowment of motherhood ... [and] of separate spheres' but within a context that also involved calls for the 'recognition of women's political grievances' and even 'the advocacy of some feminist goals'.[56] For instance, Nazi women, like women in the BUF, were partly attracted to the movement because of its promise to give women greater control over specific areas of public policy where successive democratic governments were seen to have failed, such as housing, consumption, welfare and the family. The chance to make new friends or to meet a potential husband at social events organised by the party may also have motivated some, especially those who had no particular interest in 'politics' but still wished to play a part in the newly emerging extreme nationalist subculture that stood against the 'Reds' and the 'traitors' republic'. Last, but by no means least, the members of the DFO and other Nazi women's groups often placed themselves at the forefront of Nazi anti-Semitic campaigns, helping to spread the message of racial hatred with at least as much enthusiasm as their male colleagues. A resolution passed by the Lübeck branch of the DFO in May 1930, for instance, condemned all forms of 'female sexual liberation' as 'Jewish' and 'unworthy of Germans', and continued:

> We German women refuse to allow our people to be swamped by the 'sexual reform' which the Jews have brought us. Never shall a Jew be allowed to dictate the sexual behaviour of the German people, since

the Jewish-blooded person has ... a different racial composition and follows a different, more licentious sex life than the German-blooded person.[57]

The Nazis' dependence on women like these for building up party organisation at grassroots level and developing new areas of support also forced a gradual, if grudging, recognition of their efforts from the (all-male) party leadership. This did not, of course, mean abandoning traditional patriarchal assumptions or gender inequalities, but it did mean an increased attention to women and the women's question as time went on. From 1926 onwards, for instance, the party's official newspaper, the *Völkischer Beobachter*, began publicising the activities of the DFO and other women's groups, and encouraged SA men to support these activities at all times.[58] Likewise, Goebbels, in his capacity as *Gauleiter* (district leader) of Berlin, started to mention women activists in his propaganda speeches in the mid- to late 1920s, for instance in his address to a meeting of DFO leaders in October 1927.[59] And even Alfred Rosenberg, the party's leading anti-feminist, found it necessary to make clear that his view that women were different to men was not meant to imply that they were in any way inferior.[60]

Much of this propaganda directed at women, however, was no more than a gesture by which the party leadership made concessions to those individuals and groups competing for Hitler's favour. Indeed, until 1932–33 the development of Nazi women's organisations lagged far behind the development of the NSDAP itself. Moreover, the DFO, despite winning official approval in 1926, was still expected to refrain from all political activities and to limit itself to traditional 'womanly' duties only. The fact that Zander received no financial support from the party until October 1931, when she agreed to merge the DFO into the new *NS-Frauenschaft* (NS-Womanhood), shows that even her version of ultra-loyal Führer worship was not enough to dispel the lingering doubts of the Munich leadership about the wisdom of involving women in the movement.[61] It was to take the economic crisis of 1929–33, and the political opportunities it presented, to bring about a change in the party's strategy.

3. The impact of the economic depression

Whatever the long-term causes of the rise of the Nazis, there can be little doubt that the most important short-term cause was the worldwide economic depression, which began with the Wall Street crash on 29 October 1929 and reached its peak in 1932, when over 6 million Germans were out of work. In the Reichstag elections of May 1928, before the Wall Street crash, the Nazis won only 2.7 per cent of the national vote. Their first major breakthrough came in September 1930, when they took 18.3 per cent of the vote and 107 Reichstag seats. In July 1932 the Nazis became the largest single party with 37.3 per cent of the vote and 230 Reichstag seats, and in November 1932 they still managed a respectable 33.1 per cent and 196 seats. Furthermore, we can assume that much of this extra Nazi vote came from first-time voters, who were either too young or too uninterested to exercise their right to vote before the early 1930s. Indeed, the statistics reveal that 2.3 million more Germans voted in the elections of July 1932 than had done so in the elections of June 1928.[62]

The economic depression aided Hitler's cause in a number of ways. Firstly, in electoral terms it was the extreme right rather than the democratic or revolutionary left that seemed to benefit most from the 'crisis of capitalism' and the ensuing violence on the streets. True, from 1930 both the SPD and the KPD positioned themselves as anti-fascist parties of the working class, albeit from radically different perspectives. But between them they were never able to attract more than about 50 per cent of the working-class vote, and their record among women was noticeably worse than among men.[63] The modest gains made by the KPD in the two Reichstag elections of 1932 were at any rate largely at the expense of the SPD, leaving the combined vote for the two bitterly divided anti-fascist parties at roughly 36 per cent. On top of this came the massive decline in the number of paid-up trades union members as unemployment grew and grew. By 1932–33 only a small percentage of Germans still believed in the possibility of a genuine workers' revolution – probably no more than the 10 per cent or so who voted for Ernst Thälmann, the KPD candidate, in the presidential elections of March and April 1932.[64] For the majority of the population the Soviet Union and its repressive domestic policy under Stalin, the collectivisation of agriculture and the beginning of the first Five Year Plan, served as an awful portent of what the extreme left might do should it come to power in Germany.

Secondly, the economic depression led to a huge backlash against feminism in Germany, with even moderate and pro-republican parties placing concern for women's rights on the back burner while seeking to increase their support among male voters. In 1931, for instance, the minority government of the Catholic Centre Party politician Heinrich Brüning introduced a new bill that demanded the dismissal of married women civil servants (including school teachers) if their financial circumstances 'seemed constantly secure', in order to create more jobs for men. Among the Reichstag parties, only the KPD opposed this blatantly anti-feminist piece of legislation when it came to a vote on 30 May 1932, while the SPD, to its discredit, agreed to support the bill provided that married women employed by the *Länder* or local authorities were exempted.[65] The Pope, too, in his encyclicals *Casti Connubii* of 30 December 1930 and *Quadragesimo Anno* of 15 May 1931, urged married Catholic women to stay at home rather than go out to work; and the Evangelical bishops also made known their opposition to the employment of housewives and mothers. All of this showed that a considerable body of opinion favoured some restrictions on women's rights, including Catholic and socialist politicians.

Thirdly, the economic depression caused a fatal split in the women's movement itself, especially when it came to differences of opinion regarding the need to defend the political and constitutional gains of 1918. Divisions came to a head in 1932 with the defection from the BDF of the Federation of German Housewives' Associations and the Federation of Rural Housewives' Associations, both of which had expressed dissatisfaction with the BDF's 'too liberal' leadership.[66] The BDF also had increasing problems in fending off criticism that it was academic, middle-class, unrepresentative of 'ordinary' women or simply outdated in its approach to contemporary issues. By contrast the NSDAP appeared to offer something new and fresh, a challenge to the staid old order. In particular it became associated with the idea of a 'national community' of all Germans cutting across the old boundaries of class and denomination, an idea partly borrowed from other right-wing parties like the DNVP and DVP. Whether such rhetoric helped to increase votes for the party overall is difficult to say, but certainly it served to strengthen anti-republican feeling in Germany and therefore paved the way for the acceptance of more authoritarian alternatives to the existing parliamentary system.[67]

Finally, the economic depression also helped to reinforce the views of conservative and pro-Nazi women's groups who argued that the best way to help women out of poverty was to protect and stabilise the family as the germ cell of the nation and the key to eventual economic recovery. The revolution of 1918, by contrast, was portrayed as a stab in the back, designed to cheat women out of their 'natural' roles as mothers and housewives and force them into work for slave wages in capitalist enterprises.[68] This was the view, for instance, of Guida Diehl, leader of the ultra-conservative Newland Movement (*Neulandbewegung*), an organisation founded in 1917 and dedicated to fighting communism and the perceived cultural decadence of the Weimar era.[69] In her many speeches and pamphlets Diehl argued that women had an important place in public life, but had been misled into thinking that their needs and aspirations could be met by demanding equality with men. In particular she blamed Jews and Marxists for alienating women from their true spiritual nature and leading them into rational thinking and an unhealthy preoccupation with issues of sexuality. Now the time had come to rid Germany of the menace of Judeo-Bolshevism once and for all, while also restoring honour and dignity to the uniquely female profession of motherhood. This could only be done, Diehl claimed, through a complete overhaul of the Weimar system and its replacement by more 'Germanic' forms of political organisation in which cooperation rather than conflict between the sexes could be promoted.[70]

The leaders of the NSDAP were undoubtedly aware of the potential advantages of using Diehl and other pro-Nazi women like Lydia Gottschewski for propaganda purposes, and women speakers did become an increasingly common sight at Nazi election rallies in the summer of 1932.[71] However, it is important not to overestimate the extent to which the Nazis changed the tenor of their policies in 1932–33 to attract more women voters. In fact, most of the party's policies on job creation and increased state support for those families living on the breadline were designed to appeal to men as much as to women. When women were specifically addressed, this was more often than not in response to the left's anti-fascist propaganda, which had done some harm to the Nazis' image, especially in the bigger cities. This was a particular concern after Hitler narrowly lost the presidential election to Hindenburg in April 1932; thenceforth the NSDAP deemed it expedient to devote at least some of its time to reassuring working women that it did not intend to take their jobs away.[72] Even so, when faced with criticism from other parties the Nazis' preferred line of defence was to stress their commitment to raising the status of the traditional house-wife and mother. This had the potential to appeal to all women, single or married, working or not. The largest constituency for the Nazis indeed remained the more conservative rural areas of northern and eastern Germany, where most women were either housewives or workers in the family business, and it was this group of people Hitler was most anxious not to alienate.[73]

Furthermore, evidence from party records suggests that by the middle of 1932 the NSDAP was also concerned with boosting its image among Christian voters of all kinds, and in particular to fend off accusations of being atheist or anti-religion. To this end it even began to emphasise its common ground with the Centre Party and the Catholic Church on a broad range of social issues, including its opposition to abortion and birth control. Instructions issued to party activists in Hanover during the Reichstag election campaign in November 1932, for instance, revealed that the main target of Nazi propaganda was to be the DNVP and the 'reactionary' Papen government, as well as the SPD and the communists. However:

> As far as the Centre Party is concerned, we are not expecting such a sharp struggle against us as last time. They are no longer portraying us as 'enemies of the church' ... in order to warn good Catholics away from us. We must constantly emphasise that we are absolutely pro-Church and Christian in outlook, but that we are otherwise concerned only with politics, and do not enter into denominational disputes. We also no longer regard the idea of a coalition with the Centre Party as a threat, since if the National Socialist movement is not in a position to survive a coalition with the Centre Party, then it also does not have the strength to create a German future.[74]

The political implications of this bid for the Catholic Church's approval were of course to become much more evident after the Nazi seizure of power in January 1933, and especially after the Concordat, signed between the new regime and the Vatican in July 1933.[75] Nonetheless, we can assume that the attempt to make the Nazis appear more *kirchenfreundlich* helped to reassure those women who would previously have been reluctant to vote for an extremist, radical party like the NSDAP.[76] The party's fierce anti-communism would also have been popular in the same religious circles. But above all it was the Nazis' strategic opportunism, their ability to appeal to a variety of conflicting interests, including those of women, that accounts for its success at the polls. Thus in November 1932 the party tailored specific approaches to farmers, artisans, the self-employed, students, white-collar workers, women workers, Social Democrat workers, housewives, war invalids, war widows, women from the middle class, educated women, and so forth.[77]

In the end, however, these efforts to win over the German electorate must be set alongside Hitler's attempts to gain the support of more powerful institutions – such as the army, the aristocratic *Junker* and big business – in his bid for the leadership of Germany. It was through these means, via the 'back door' rather than a convincing victory at the polls, that Hitler was eventually appointed by President Hindenburg to head a new right-wing coalition government on 30 January 1933.[78] This new government at first included only three Nazi ministers (including Hitler himself) in a total of 11. But it gave Hitler the chance he needed to transform Germany from a republic into a fascist-style dictatorship, one in which women were to have even fewer rights than men. Five weeks later, on 5 March 1933, elections of dubious validity gave the Nazis and their nationalist allies a narrow major-ity of 51 per cent, but even after the Reichstag fire and the forced exclusion of 81 KPD deputies from parliamentary proceedings they still needed the support of the Catholic Centre Party to obtain the two-thirds majority required to alter the constitution. This was given reluctantly, and after much intimidation of Catholic Reichstag deputies, on 23 March 1933.

4. The Nazi seizure of power

Given the constitutional nature of Hitler's appointment as Reich Chancellor in January 1933, and the apparent mandate he received from the electorate in March 1933, it may seem inappropriate to talk of a Nazi 'seizure of power'. However, the events of the next few months, when the National Socialists began to use the apparatus of the state to stamp out all opposition to one-party rule, lend a considerable degree of justification to historians' use of this phrase.[79] Socialist, communist and trades union organisations were almost immediately outlawed, and many of their leaders sent into exile or thrown into concentration camps. Other political parties chose to dissolve themselves before they too were banned. Organisations that were not overtly political were given a choice: either fall into line with the principles of National Socialism or face persecution and hostility from the

new regime. Falling into line (*Gleichschaltung*) usually meant agreeing to
expel Jewish or politically suspect members and adopting measures
designed to exclude non-Aryans. Meanwhile, a law passed in April 1933
allowed the state to fire Jewish and left-wing members of the civil service
and teaching profession.[80]

How did the middle-class German women's movement react to these
events? During the crisis years of the early 1930s, as we have seen, the BDF
failed to mount an active campaign against the Brüning government's plans
to move married women out of the civil service – a flagrant breach of article
218 of the constitution, which guaranteed equal access to public employment. Instead, in 1932 it demanded the replacement of the parliamentary
system with a corporate state along the lines of that in Fascist Italy, with a
separate corporation representing women, as the only genuine solution to the
'women's question'.[81] In May 1933 the BDF voted to dissolve itself rather
than submit to *Gleichschaltung*, but not – as Richard Evans has shown – as
an act of defiance towards the new regime. Rather, the BDF president Agnes
von Zahn-Harnack, declared: 'the new Germany will undoubtedly have
especial understanding for a whole series of tasks which the federation
believes to be urgent: in the first place a biological policy which supports the
German family through economic and eugenic measures'.[82]

Zahn-Harnack herself made speeches opposing Nazi anti-Semitism, but
this did not apply to many of the constituent organisations within the BDF,
most of which readily shed their Jewish members and agreed to be merged
into a new, Nazi-led organisation for all women's groups. Hence, far from
having to wage a war against the 'great fortress of German feminism' in
1933, the Nazis actually found in such organisations the most efficient
means of incorporating women into the new state (see also Chapter 2). Even
Hedwig Heyl, a leading figure in the women's movement in Berlin, who had
previously been close to the centre-left DDP, appeared to be won over to the
Nazi cause. In a speech delivered to a women's educational association soon
after January 1933 she glossed over the party's anti-Semitism and instead
declared:

> Our times place demands which are very simple when it comes to the
> content of Hitler's being and his laws ... The demand is that we only
> want the good, the noble ... The laws which Hitler has passed should
> only be understood in their entire whole, in their goodness, their love
> of the people, in their promotion of mutual goodwill and benevo-
> lence.[83]

The confused, contradictory and in part self-interested response of many
German women's leaders in 1933 has often been taken as a pretext for
pointing the finger at all German women and suggesting that they had a
special responsibility for the rise of National Socialism.[84] In fact, there is
little evidence for this. The Nazis were, it is true, increasingly reliant on

female voters as well as men in their quest to win power through the ballot box. Although the male vote for the NSDAP was still generally higher than the female, the difference did narrow and was even reversed in some Protestant areas. Even in Catholic Cologne, where men and women voted on differently coloured ballot papers, 19.2 per cent of women and 21.8 per cent of men voted Nazi in November 1932, compared to 15.5 per cent and 19.8 per cent in September 1930. By March 1933 this difference had narrowed to one percentage point, as Table 1 shows.

Table 1 Nazi share of the vote in Cologne, 1930–1933, by gender

Election	Men	Women	Difference
Reichstag, 14/9/1930	19.8%	15.5%	−4.3
Presidential, 13/3/1932	21.7%	16.7%	−5.0
Presidential, 10/4/1932	26.2%	19.7%	−6.5
Reichstag, 31/7/1932	26.4%	22.8%	−3.6
Reichstag, 6/11/1932	21.8%	19.2%	−2.6
Reichstag, 5/3/1933	33.9%	32.9%	−1.0

Source: Gabriele Bremme, *Die politische Rolle der Frau in Deutschland* (Göttingen, 1956), p. 74. Copyright © Vandenhoeck and Ruprecht, Göttingen.

Given the overall vote of 43 per cent that the Nazis received in March 1933 – an average of 10 points higher than in Cologne – we can conclude that at least 7 million women had supported the NSDAP in at least one election between 1930 and 1933. Allowing for tactical voting and some switching between parties, this figure was probably a lot higher.

These statistics, however, can be read in various ways and do not actually prove that German women were particularly susceptible to Nazism. In fact, as Jürgen Falter has recently pointed out, by 1933 women made up less than 6 per cent of NSDAP membership, accounting for less than 1 per cent of the entire female population.[85] Looked at from another point of view, women voters may actually have delayed Hitler's victory by nearly 12 months by voting predominantly for Hindenburg in the two-stage presidential elections of March and April 1932.[86] In some of the biggest cities, moreover, women outnumbered men among the supporters of the pro-Weimar SPD and were therefore a source of extra votes for the Republic as opposed to its enemies. This was the case in Berlin and Leipzig in 1928 and 1930, for instance, and in Frankfurt-am-Main in 1930.[87] In general, however, until 1930, and to some extent thereafter, female suffrage tended to work in favour of the Centre Party and the Protestant DNVP and DVP parties, and to the disadvantage of the Nazis as well as the SPD and KPD. This can be seen in Table 2, which analyses the impact of women's votes on the 1928 Reichstag election.

Furthermore, those millions of women who did vote for Hitler after 1928 were not necessarily expressing enthusiasm for his opposition to women's emancipation or female suffrage. Rather, as Helen Boak has shown in her study of working-class women, women's political choices and behaviour

Table 2 The impact of women's votes on the 1928 Reichstag election

Party	Total delegates elected	Estimated delegations based on male vote only	Loss or gain due to female vote
Catholic Centre Party (Zentrum)	62	50	+12
German Nationalists (DNVP)	73	64	+9
People's Party (DVP)	45	43	+2
Democrats (DDP)	25	26	−1
Social Democrats (SPD)	153	157	−4
Communists (KPD)	54	62	−8
National Socialists (NSDAP)	12	16	−4

Source: Renate Bridenthal and Claudia Koonz, 'Beyond *Kinder, Küche, Kirche.* Weimar Women in Politics and Work', in: Renate Bridenthal, Atina Grossmann and Marion Kaplan (eds), *When Biology Became Destiny. Women in Weimar and Nazi Germany* (New York, 1984), p. 37.
Copyright © Monthly Review Press, New York.

were as varied and as complex as men's, and had much more to do with the economic situation and fears about unemployment than anything any of the parties said about the 'women's question'.[88] Most women who voted Nazi were probably voting *against* other parties, especially the KPD or the SPD, or against the Weimar system as a whole, which seemed to have brought nothing but economic crisis and political instability. Others may have hoped that the Nazis would restore economic prosperity and save their husbands' jobs.[89] Anti-communism, as we have seen, was also a significant factor, and one Hitler played on with some success in the final years before 1933. Those women who were most resistant to the appeal of Nazism were either ultra-loyal Catholics (and there were many of these, especially in the rural areas of southern and western Germany) or committed socialists and trades unionists. On the other hand, it is impossible to say with any degree of accuracy exactly how many women (compared to men) voted for the Nazis in the early 1930s, or to prove that they were motivated by a specifically conservative or anti-feminist agenda.[90]

Finally, a vote for the Nazi Party (especially in the circumstances of depression-hit Germany) was not necessarily the same thing as a vote for fascist-style dictatorship or one-party rule. Nor was it always an expression of undying devotion to Hitler or the National Socialist cause. The ban on the KPD in February 1933 and the use of emergency legislation to imprison suspected communists was probably popular with most 'ordinary' Germans; the dissolution of other independent political organisations and the recourse to vulgar and violent forms of anti-Semitism less so. Catholic women often found it difficult to reconcile loyalty to their religion with the pressure to conform to the new regime, and some Nazi women even expressed their disappointment with the limited opportunities granted to them during the early years of the Third Reich.[91] As Tim Mason argues, 'in

January 1933 [Hitler] still had some leeway to make up in gaining the confidence of women'.[92] This also explains the increased attention the party devoted to family-oriented policies, and to the political and ideological organisation of women within its own ranks in the years after 1933.

Notes

1 Cited in Wolfgang Ruge, *Weimar – Republik auf Zeit* (East Berlin, 1969), p. 5.
2 Detlev J. K. Peukert, *The Weimar Republic. The Crisis of Classical Modernity* (London, 1991), p. 277.
3 On women in post-1917 Soviet Russia see Wendy Z. Goldman, *Women, the State and Revolution. Soviet Family Policy and Social Life, 1917–1936* (Cambridge, 1993).
4 Elizabeth Harvey, 'Culture and Society in Weimar Germany', in: Mary Fulbrook (ed.), *Twentieth Century Germany. Politics, Culture and Society, 1918–1990* (London, 2001), p. 61.
5 Cf. Cornelie Usborne, 'The New Woman and Generational Conflict. Perceptions of Young Women's Sexual Mores in the Weimar Republic', in: Mark Roseman (ed.), *Generations in Conflict. Youth Revolt and Generation Formation in Germany, 1770–1968* (Cambridge, 1995), pp. 137–63.
6 Figures cited in Stephenson, *Women in Nazi Germany*, p. 24.
7 Cf. Richard Vinen, *A History in Fragments. Europe in the Twentieth Century* (London, 2000), pp. 148–51.
8 Cornelie Usborne, *The Politics of the Body in Weimar Germany. Women's Reproductive Rights and Duties* (London, 1992), p. 32.
9 See Matthew Stibbe, 'Anti-Feminism, Nationalism and the German Right, 1914–1920. A Reappraisal', in: *German History* 20 (2002), pp. 185–210.
10 Frevert, *Women in German History*, p. 158. Cf. Ute Daniel, *The War from Within. German Working Class Women and the First World War* (Oxford, 1997).
11 Cf. Helen L. Boak, 'The State as an Employer of Women in the Weimar Republic', in: W.R. Lee and Eve Rosenhaft (eds), *State, Social Policy and Social Change in Germany, 1880–1994*, 2nd edn (Oxford, 1997), pp. 64–101.
12 Daniel, *The War From Within*, p. 278. See also Elizabeth Bright Jones, 'A New Stage of Life? Young Farm Women's Changing Expectations and Aspirations about Work in Weimar Saxony', in: *German History* 19 (2001), pp. 549–70.
13 Richard Bessel, *Germany after the First World War* (Oxford, 1993), p. 21.
14 Mason, 'Women in Germany', pp. 137–9.
15 Julia Sneeringer, *Propaganda and Politics in Weimar Germany. Winning Women's Votes* (Chapel Hill and London, 2002), p. 10.
16 Frevert, *Women in German History*, p. 197.
17 Daniel, *The War From Within*, p. 279.
18 Bessel, *Germany after the First World War*, pp. 6–10.
19 Helen L. Boak, 'Women in Weimar Germany. The "Frauenfrage" and the Female Vote', in: Richard Bessel and E. J. Feuchtwanger (eds), *Social Change and Political Development in Weimar Germany* (London, 1981), p. 162.
20 Frevert, *Women in German History*, p. 175.
21 Richard J. Evans, *The Feminist Movement in Germany, 1894–1933* (London, 1976), p. 237.
22 Usborne, *The Politics of the Body*, pp. 118–23. See also Atina Grossmann's extensive study, *Reforming Sex. The German Movement for Birth Control and Abortion Reform, 1920–1950* (Oxford, 1995).

23 Gabriele Bremme, *Die politische Rolle der Frau in Deutschland. Eine Untersuchung über den Einfluß der Frauen bei Wahlen und ihre Teilnahme in Partei und Parlament* (Göttingen, 1956), Table I, pp. 231–7, and Table II, pp. 238–9.

24 Ibid., Table IV, pp. 243–52.

25 For an excellent analysis of female employment patterns according to the 1925 census see Mason, 'Women in Germany', pp. 136–43.

26 Emmy Beckmann, *Um Stellung und Beruf der Frau* (Berlin, 1932), p. 2. Quoted in Elizabeth Harvey, 'The Failure of Feminism? Young Women and the Bourgeois Feminist Movement in Weimar Germany, 1918–1933', in: *Central European History* 28 (1995), p. 1.

27 Bremme, *Die politische Rolle der Frau*, pp. 121–5.

28 Werner Thönnessen, *The Emancipation of Women. The Rise and Decline of the Women's Movement in German Social Democracy, 1863–1933* (London, 1973).

29 This theme has been explored extensively by Raffael Scheck with respect to the DNVP (German National People's Party). See his essay 'German Conservatism and Female Political Activism in the Early Weimar Republic', in: *German History* 15 (1997), pp. 34–55; and a further essay, 'Women on the Weimar Right. The Role of Female Politicians in the Deutschnationale Volkspartei (DNVP)', in: *Journal of Contemporary History* 36 (2001), pp. 547–60. See also the study by Elizabeth Harvey, 'Pilgrims to the "Bleeding Border". Gender and the Rituals of Nationalist Protest in Germany, 1919–1939', in: *Women's History Review* 9 (2000), pp. 201–29.

30 On Catholic women see e.g. Doris Kaufmann, 'Vom Vaterland zum Mutterland. Frauen im katholischen Milieu der Weimarer Republik', in: Karin Hausen (ed.), *Frauen suchen ihre Geschichte. Historische Studien zum 19. und 20. Jahrhundert* (Munich, 1983), pp. 250–75; and Kaufmann, *Katholisches Milieu in Münster, 1928–1933. Politische Aktionsformen und geschlechtsspezifische Verhaltensräume* (Düsseldorf, 1984). On Protestant women see Nancy Reagin's study *A German Women's Movement. Class and Gender in Hanover, 1880–1933* (Chapel Hill and London, 1995).

31 Bremme, *Die politische Rolle der Frau*, Table 39, p. 124.

32 Koonz, *Mothers in the Fatherland*, p. 447, n. 6.

33 'Der Deutsche Frauenorden', in: *Nationalsozialistische Monatshefte* 1/1 (April 1930), p. 43. Copy in: StA Bremen, Nachrichtenstelle der Polizeidirektion 4, 65–175, Bl. 21.

34 Adolf Hitler, *Mein Kampf*, translated by Ralph Manheim (London, 1969), pp. 400–1.

35 Cf. Frevert, *Women in German History*, p. 188, for concern about falling birth rates.

36 On the pro-family rhetoric of all Weimar parties, including the SPD, see Sneeringer, *Winning Women's Votes, passim.*

37 Buttmann's speech at Lahr, as reported in: *Bayerische Kurier*, 28 November 1930. Copy in: Forschungsstelle für Zeitgeschichte, Hamburg (henceforth FZH), no. 951 – NS-Frauenschaft.

38 Alfred Rosenberg, 'Die Emanzipation der Frau von der Frauenemanzipation', extract from *Der Mythos des 20. Jahrhunderts* (Munich, 1930). Reproduced in: Annette Kuhn and Valentine Rothe (eds), *Frauen im deutschen Faschismus*, 2 vols (Düsseldorf, 1982), Vol. 1, pp. 58–60.

39 Michael H. Kater, 'Frauen in der NS-Bewegung', in: *Vierteljahrshefte für Zeitgeschichte* 31 (1983), p. 206.

40 Ibid., p. 204.

41 Stephenson, *Women in Nazi Germany*, p. 17.

42 For a detailed discussion of the phenomenon of pro-Nazi women's groups in

Weimar Germany see Stephenson, *The Nazi Organisation of Women*, pp. 24–37; Koonz, *Mothers in the Fatherland*, pp. 53–90; and Frevert, *Women in German History*, pp. 207–16.

43 In addition to the books noted above see also the extensive police records on the DFO in StA Bremen, Nachrichtenstelle der Polizeidirektion 4, 65–175.

44 'Aufgaben und Ziele des Deutschen Frauenordens', in: *Völkischer Beobachter*, 16/17 December 1928. Copy in: ibid., Bl. 4.

45 'Mitteilungen des Landeskriminalpolizeiamtes Berlin', 1 December 1930. Copy in: ibid., Bl. 22–4.

46 See Mädelgruppe des Deutschen Frauenordens an Herrn Standartenführer Conti, no date [1930]. Copy in: FZH, no. 951 – NS-Frauenschaft.

47 Emma Witte, 'Ein Mahnwort an die Leitung der NSDAP', in: *Deutsche Tageblatt*, no. 144, 27 June 1924. Copy in: Bundesarchiv, Abteilung Berlin-Lichterfelde, Pressearchiv des Reichslandbundes (henceforth BA Berlin, RLB-Pressearchiv), no. 7974, Bl. 109.

48 Witte, 'Völkische Frau und Staatsdanke', in: *Deutsche Zeitung*, 6 August 1924. Copy in: ibid., Bl. 111.

49 Alan E. Steinweis, 'Weimar Culture and the Rise of National Socialism: The *Kampfbund für deutsche Kultur*', in: *Central European History* 24 (1991), pp. 402–23. According to Steinweis, women made up 15.7 per cent of the *Kampfbund* members, with a total membership in January 1932 of around 2,100 (ibid., pp. 411–12). On the German-Colonial Women's Society see also Lora Wildenthal, 'Mass-Marketing Colonialism and Nationalism. The Career of Else Frobenius in the "Weimarer Republik" and Nazi Germany', in: Ute Planert (ed.), *Nation, Politik und Geschlecht. Frauenbewegungen und Nationalismus in der Moderne* (Frankfurt/Main, 2000), pp. 328–45.

50 Stephenson, *The Nazi Organisation of Women*, pp. 26–7.

51 See e.g. Hadlich's article, 'Aufgaben der Frauen in der Gegenwart', in: *Völkischer Beobachter*, 23 January 1926, and the response from other contributors.

52 Lydia Gottschweski, *Männerbund und Frauenfrage* (Munich, 1934). See also Koonz, *Mothers in the Fatherland*, pp. 114–15.

53 Theodore Abel, *Why Hitler Came to Power. An Answer Based on the Original Life Stories of Six Hundred of His Followers* (New York, 1938). See also Peter H. Merkl, *Political Violence under the Swastika. 581 Early Nazis* (Princeton, N.J., 1975), esp. pp. 119–37, which makes a further analysis of the data collected by Abel.

54 Koonz, *Mothers in the Fatherland*, pp. xii–xiii and 58.

55 Cf. Michael H. Kater, 'Generationskonflikt als Entwicklungsfaktor in der NS-Bewegung vor 1933', in: *Geschichte und Gesellschaft* 11 (1985), pp. 217–43.

56 Julie V. Gottlieb, '"Motherly Hate". Gendering Anti-Semitism in the British Union of Fascists', in: *Gender and History* 14 (2002), p. 296. See also Gottlieb's monograph on this subject, *Feminine Fascism. Women in Britain's Fascist Movement, 1923–1945* (London, 2000).

57 Cited in the second edition of the DFO's journal, *Opferdienst*, 5 May 1930. Copy in: FZH, no. 951.

58 Stephenson, *The Nazi Organisation of Women*, p. 29.

59 'Der Reichs-Vertretertag des Deutschen Frauenordens', in: *Völkischer Beobachter*, 25 October 1927.

60 See e.g. Alfred Rosenberg, 'Nachwort der Schriftleitung', in: *Völkischer Beobachter*, 23 January 1926, and 'Alfred Rosenberg und die deutsche Frau', in: *Völkischer Beobachter*, 27/28/29 March 1932.

61 See e.g. extract from a report of the Munich police office, 31 January 1929, explaining why, in spite of the efforts of local women, there was as yet no

support from party headquarters for the establishment of a local branch of the DFO. Copy in: StA Bremen, Nachrichtenstelle der Polizeidirektion 4, 65–175, Bl. 5.

62 Koonz, *Mothers in the Fatherland*, p. 447, n. 6. For a more critical interpretation see Jürgen Falter, 'The National Socialist Mobilization of New Voters, 1928–1933', in: Thomas Childers (ed.), *The Formation of the Nazi Constituency, 1919–1933* (London, 1986), pp. 202–31.

63 Cf. Mason, *Social Policy in the Third Reich*, pp. 51–3.

64 The results of the second round of voting on 11 April 1932 were as follows: Hindenburg 53 per cent, Hitler 37 per cent, Thälmann 10 per cent.

65 Boak, 'The State as Employer of Women', p. 88.

66 Evans, *The Feminist Movement*, pp. 244–53.

67 On the role of the myth of a German 'national community' in undermining the Weimar Republic and paving the way for Hitler see also Jeffrey Verhey's recent study, *The Spirit of 1914: Militarism, Myth and Mobilization in Germany* (Cambridge, 2000), esp. pp. 206–30.

68 See e.g. the article 'Nationalsozialismus und Frauenarbeit', in: *Bremer Volkszeitung*, 14 March 1932. Copy in: StA Bremen, Nachrichtenstelle der Polizeidirektion 4, 65–175.

69 On Diehl, see Koonz, *Mothers in the Fatherland*, pp. 80–5. Also the recent study by Silvia Lange, *Protestantische Frauen auf dem Weg in den Nationalsozialismus. Guida Diehls Neulandbewegung, 1916–1935* (Stuttgart, 1998).

70 See e.g. Diehl's pamphlet, *Die deutsche Frau und der Nationalsozialismus* (Eisenach, 1933).

71 See e.g. Propagandaleitung des Gau Südhannover-Braunschweig an die Gau-Frauenschaftsleiterin Frau Elisabeth Braun, 21 June 1932, in: NHStA Hanover, Hann. 310 I A, no. 1221, Bl. 122.

72 Frevert, *Women in German History*, p. 215.

73 Cf. Thomas Childers, *The Nazi Voter. The Social Foundations of Fascism in Germany* (London, 1983), esp. pp. 258–61.

74 'Kurzbericht über die Rednertagung in Hannover am 2. Oktober 1932', in: NHStA Hanover, Hann. 310 I B, No. 6, Bl. 124–5. Cf. 'Denkschrift zum Reichstagswahl am 6. November 1932', in: ibid., Bl. 131–44.

75 On the vexed issue of the relationship between the Catholic Church and the Nazi regime see Guenter Lewy, *The Catholic Church and Nazi Germany*, new edn (New York, 2000).

76 Cf. Mason, 'Women in Germany', p. 153.

77 'Personal letters' were sent out to each of these categories of voter as part of the election campaign in the Gau South Hanover-Braunschweig. See NSDAP Gau Südhannover-Braunschweig, Wahlrundschreiben an alle Ortsgruppen und Kreise, 25 October 1932. Copy in: NHStA Hanover, Hann. 310 I B, No. 6, Bl. 121–2.

78 On Hitler's appointment as Reich Chancellor in January 1933 see Henry Ashby Turner Jr, *Hitler's Thirty Days to Power* (London, 1999).

79 Cf. Peter D. Stachura (ed.), *The Nazi Machtergreifung* (London, 1983).

80 Gesetz zur Wiederherstellung des Berufsbeamtentums, 7 April 1933. Reproduced in: Noakes and Pridham (eds), *Nazism, 1919–1945*, Vol. 2, pp. 223–5.

81 Evans, *The Feminist Movement*, pp. 247–8.

82 Ibid., p. 258.

83 Wildenthal, 'Mass-Marketing Colonialism and Nationalism', p. 340.

84 Cf. Annemarie Tröger, 'Die Dolchstoßlegende der Linken. "Frauen haben Hitler an die Macht gebracht"', in: *Frauen und Wissenschaft. Beiträge zur Berliner Sommeruniversität für Frauen* (West Berlin, 1976).

85 Jürgen Falter, *Hitlers Wähler* (Munich, 1991), p. 143.
86 Mason, 'Women in Germany', p. 156.
87 Bremme, *Die politische Rolle der Frau*, Table 24, p. 76.
88 Helen L. Boak, 'National Socialism and Working-Class Women Before 1933', in: Conan Fischer (ed.), *The Rise of National Socialism and the Working Classes in Weimar Germany* (Oxford, 1996), pp. 163–88.
89 Ibid., p. 181. Cf. Frevert, *Women in German History*, pp. 214–15; Stephenson, *Women in Nazi Germany*, p. 15.
90 Boak, 'Women in Weimar Germany', pp. 167–8.
91 See e.g. the book of essays, *Deutsche Frauen an Adolf Hitler*, edited by Irmgard Reichenau (Leipzig, 1933). Also Clifford Kirkpatrick, *Woman in Nazi Germany* (London, 1939), pp. 60–1.
92 Mason, 'Women in Germany', p. 156.

2

The incorporation of women into the Nazi state

As mentioned in the previous chapter, the 1920s saw the formation of a number of ad hoc Nazi women's groups, which supported the idea of national revolution in the National Socialist sense, including (among others) Elsbeth Zander's *Deutscher Frauenorden* and Lotte Rühlemann's *Frauengruppe Leipzig*. At first such groups were granted considerable autonomy, reflecting both the party's preoccupation with recruiting and organising men, and the negative association of 'politicised' women with Marxism and the 'great betrayal' of 1918. Only gradually did the women's groups win recognition from the male leadership, and this in turn produced much rivalry and friction as the groups fought among themselves for favour. Eventually in October 1931 Gregor Strasser, the then head of the party bureaucracy, ordered the dissolution of all existing women's groups and created, in their stead, the *NS-Frauenschaft* (National Socialist Womanhood or NSF), the first official Nazi women's organisation under central party control. This reflected the importance the party attached to winning over the female vote in its bid for power by legal means, but also its determination to subordinate women's activities to the needs of the all-male party leadership.[1]

Although Elsbeth Zander was initially appointed head of the NSF, her rebellious nature and disrespect for authority soon isolated her from Hitler and other senior figures in the party, especially after the fall from grace of her main advocate, Gregor Strasser, who suddenly resigned from the NSDAP in December 1932 after a disagreement with Hitler over strategy.[2] Zander's eventual dismissal in April 1933 led to a fierce struggle between different factions of the party for control over women's activities, culminating in the appointment of Gertrud Scholtz-Klink as NSF leader in February 1934.[3] Scholtz-Klink was chosen deliberately by the male leaders of the party because she offered stability and absolute conformity to the demands of the new state. Unlike the earlier brand of rebellious Nazi women's leaders, she displayed little interest in ideology or political questions, but had distinguished herself as an able organiser, overseeing the 'coordination' of women's organisations in her home state of Baden. As a devoted mother of four children and an avid supporter of National Socialism, she agreed to run the NSF and its subordinate mass organisation, the *Deutsches Frauenwerk* (German Women's Bureau or DFW) with a profound sense that she would be able to resurrect the idea of the German family as the cornerstone of the Third Reich. But Scholtz-Klink ranked low in the Nazi hierarchy, and had very little say on matters of party and state policy, even in those areas directly affecting women and the family.[4]

By the time Scholtz-Klink took over as NSF leader, the Nazi women's organisation was no longer as powerful as it had been in 1931, nor its role so clear. Many of its former functions had been appropriated by rival agencies such as the National Socialist Welfare Organisation (*NS-Volkswohlfahrt* or NSV), which now took over the welfare activities of the party, and the Reich Food Estate (*Reichsnährstand*), which claimed a monopoly on the organisation of women from rural areas.[5] Much of Scholtz-Klink's time was spent fighting demarcation disputes with these groups, which she usually lost. Furthermore, the task Scholtz-Klink had set for herself – to educate the entire female population to think and act in a National Socialist way, so that they became loyal Nazis and brought up their children in accordance with National Socialist ideals – was a formidable one, far more demanding than persuading women to vote for the NSDAP at elections. As Jill Stephenson has argued, the majority of German women did not want to be organised, and full-time housewives in particular were resistant to the NSF's appeals for greater involvement in the 'women's work of the nation'.[6] As a result the NSF soon found itself cut off from its target audience. Likewise, the limited appeal of the DFW ensured that its ambition to become the mass organisation of German women under the NSF's leadership never materialised.

Nevertheless, the development of the Nazi women's organisations does tell us something important about the aims and goals of the regime and the way it sought to control and redefine women's activities in the interests of the (male-dominated) party and state. It also tells us something about the middle-class orientation of Nazi welfare schemes and the regime's lack of concern for the poor and the working class, unless they were deemed to be 'biologically worthy'. Indeed, as we shall see, despite their emphasis on a 'national community' of all Germans, the Nazis built their post-1933 organisations for women almost entirely on the foundations of older middle-class women's groups. Instead of being dissolved outright, they were persuaded to switch their allegiance from the now disbanded BDF to the newly created *Frauenwerk*, which came under the political control of the NSF. For radical Nazis, of course, this cooperation with traditional institutions was a betrayal of the revolutionary fervour of National Socialism and a violation of the party's stated aim of bringing Germans of all classes under one roof. For Scholtz-Klink, on the other hand, it was the only way of ensuring that the

National Socialist message reached the wider audience of non-Nazi, yet 'worthy' and 'respectable' German women of 'good racial stock' who, in her view, could still be won over to active support for the regime.

1. The DFW and the women's 'work of the nation'

In the early months of the Third Reich the Nazis gave absolute priority to destroying left-wing organisations such as the KPD and the SPD, as well as organisations deemed to be 'anti-national' or 'cosmopolitan' in inspiration. Only gradually were steps taken to bring other non-political agencies under the control of the party, including middle-class women's organisations, which gave instruction in household management and childcare or were intended to promote knowledge of German culture. Such domestic and cultural activities were now redefined in Nazi propaganda as the key areas in which women could contribute, through the structure of the *Frauenwerk* and under the ideological leadership of the NSF, to the rebirth of the German nation. Nazi women, in other words, were to learn proficiency in cooking and cleaning, develop an understanding of the regime's demographic and racial policies, and, as educators of the young, pass on their 'healthy' German views and standards to their children. In addition they were to be the first line of defence in the battle against the invasion of the German home by 'foreign' (i.e. Jewish or Marxist) cultural influences, and were also to participate in Nazi welfare schemes such as the Winter Relief programme (*Winterhilfe*) and the 'one-pot meal', under which on certain Sundays during the winter months well-off families ate a simple one-course dish only, instead of the traditional Sunday roast, and donated the savings to help pay for food and clothing for poorer 'Aryan' households.[7]

The idea of a specifically female contribution to the process of national rebirth had of course already been promoted by a wide variety of agencies in the 1920s, including some with pro-Nazi tendencies and others with more conservative or nationalist leanings. The demand that women be educated to accept marriage and motherhood as their national duty, for instance, or that they practise thrift in the kitchen and avoid consuming expensive foreign-grown foods, was not as original as the Nazis liked to proclaim. During the Weimar Republic, proposals of this kind had been put forward by the German Red Cross, the monarchist Queen Louisa League, the Federation of German Housewives' Associations, church groups of various kinds (for instance, the Catholic Women's League and the Evangelical Women's League) and even by organisations associated with the SPD.[8] Furthermore, in the early months of the Hitler dictatorship, a rather confused set of initiatives was used to promote training in motherhood and housewifery through state and party organisations. It was only with the appointment of Scholtz-Klink in 1934 that the first steps were taken to ensure uniformity of practice on the basis of the party's ideology and in line with Hitler's racial and population policies. All traces of individualism or class snobbery or confessional loyalty were now to be dissolved through the DFW and submerged into the collective whole, the 'women's work of the nation'. Or, as Joseph Goebbels put it:

> We must develop organisations in which every individual's entire life can take place. Then every activity and every need of every individual will be regulated by the *Volksgemeinschaft*, as represented by the Party. There is no longer arbitrary will. There are no longer any free realms in which the individual belongs to himself ... The time of personal happiness is over.[9]

One of Scholtz-Klink's first acts after her appointment in February 1934 was the establishment of the Reich Mothers' Service (*Reichsmütterdienst* or RMD), which was formally announced on Mother's Day in May 1934 and subsequently became one of the main departments (*Hauptabteilungen*) of the DFW.[10] The RMD was based largely on a number of older mothers' welfare organisations which had previously been run by church groups and were now coordinated under the leadership of the NSF. Its main task was to promote motherhood as a national cause of the highest significance, in which the interests of the state and the *Volk* came before the interests of the individual mother or child. To fulfil this role it set out to train women 'who are healthy in body and mind, convinced of the highest duties of mother-hood, experienced in nursing and educating their children, and who are capable of fulfilling their household duties'.[11] Specialist courses were given in cooking, sewing, book-keeping, pre- and post-natal childcare and the importance of 'racial hygiene' (of choosing, from a racial viewpoint, the 'right' husband). In towns and cities of over 50,000 inhabitants these courses were taught in permanent schools belonging to the DFW, of which there were a total of 80 by the end of 1935, while in rural areas they were provided by an ambulatory service.[12] The RMD funded its courses from the sale of badges on Mother's Day throughout Germany and by charging small enrolment fees to its students. By March 1939 over 1.7 million women had attended almost 100,000 RMD courses, despite the fact that they were voluntary and included a large element of ideological indoctrination as well as practical instruction.[13]

The other main working sections of the DFW were social assistance (*Hilfsdienst* – HD), national economy/domestic economy (*Volkswirtschaft/ Hauswirtschaft* – Vw/Hw), and border and foreign work (*Grenz- und Ausland* – GA). The last of these brought together a variety of women's groups that had long worked to uphold the national consciousness of ethnic Germans living abroad, especially in the disputed border areas of Poland and Czechoslovakia, as well as in South America and the former German colonies in Africa. Its officially stated aim was to 'keep women in touch with the women in foreign countries, and inform German women at home about foreign countries and their civilisation',[14] although its real purpose was to mobilise female support behind Hitler's policies of aggression abroad, including the dismantling of the Treaty of Versailles and the expansion of Germany's power on the continent at the expense of her European neighbours.

Meanwhile, the section for social assistance helped train women to become auxiliary nurses and social workers, partly so they could take part in the implementation of Nazi family and racial policies, and partly in order to overcome the expected shortage of professional nurses and home help staff as the economy geared itself up in preparedness for war, especially as the regime did not wish to become over-dependent on hospitals run by Catholic orders. In the late 1930s, when war seemed more imminent, the DFW also provided more general courses on civil defence and first aid for those who wished to volunteer for such 'patriotic' duties. In 1938, for instance, 580,000 women underwent training in air raid protection, almost twice as many as the year before. By contrast, the other courses run by the *Hilfsdienst* section could muster only 90,000 attendances between them, a clear indication of where priorities now lay.[15]

Finally, the national economy/domestic economy section had the dual objective of developing practical competence in household skills and ensuring ideological commitment to the economic and foreign policy aims of the Nazi state. This included, from 1936, the launching of an ambitious rearmament programme under the overall control of Hermann Goering and his 'Office for the Four Year Plan'. Even before 1936, however, the Vw/Hw was involved in propaganda campaigns designed to restrain consumer demand and alter the approach of urban housewives to household management and consumption, thus making important savings for the national economy and reducing the level of foreign imports needed to feed the population of the big cities. As Else Vorwerck, head of the Vw/Hw, put it in a newspaper article in 1934:

> No product of the German earth and of German toil should be allowed to go to waste or perish, and foreign imports can only be chosen as an option when nothing of equal value can be produced in Germany. This also makes it important to consider what kinds of German produce are available at particular times of the year. German cauliflower and tomatoes cannot be had in February, for instance, nor can German grapes be had in June. But this does not justify the purchase of foreign fruits and vegetables ...[16]

The Vw/Hw also worked closely with the women's division of the *Reichsnährstand*, which claimed responsibility for organising rural housewives and instructing them in the art of farm and household management.[17] After 1936, with the coming of the Four Year Plan, the work of these two agencies was coordinated, and their propaganda activities overseen by the

National Committee for Popular Economic Enlightenment (*Reichsausschuß für Volkswirtschaftliche Aufklärung*), a sub-division of the German Business Advertising Consultancy (*Werberat der deutschen Wirtschaft*), a private, state-sponsored agency charged with responsibility for Germany's national economic propaganda.[18]

Not all housewives were impressed by such efforts to reach them, however, and even DFW activists complained bitterly about the irony of persuading mothers to go on expensive and time-consuming cookery or nursing courses while neglecting their own children and housework. One Nazi woman wrote as early as 1934: 'The motherhood courses are wonderful, but what's the point of sponsoring them if the mothers are always away from their homes on party business?'[19] Another clearly resented the constant pressure to sell 'worthless badges' and other items of Nazi kitsch to poor and needy mothers in order to finance DFW activities:

> We have tried, and still continue to try to awaken in our women a feeling of responsibility for their families. But then we erode it by constant drives to sell something ... I love my work and my women, and I am ready to fight for them. But what is the point if it all looks great on the outside and does not nurture a true National Socialist human being [on the inside]?[20]

On a more general level, too, there was increasing discontent at the limited opportunities offered by the Nazi state to its 'loyal' female followers and a greater willingness to point out the gap between rhetoric and reality when it came to Nazi efforts to improve the position of women in society. In 1934, for instance, a group of 'loyal' Nazi women academics seized on a chance remark from Hitler that 'those who love Germany may criticise' to publish, under the title *German Women to Adolf Hitler*,[21] a set of proposals to rectify what they saw as glaring deficiencies in the position granted to women in the new organisations of party and state. One contributor complained: 'We see our daughters growing up in stupid aimlessness, living only in the vague hope of perhaps getting a man and having children. If they do not succeed, their lives will be thwarted.' Another spoke of the women being forced back into a 'shadow of loneliness' as the increasing demands of party activities took away their children and husbands.[22]

The criticisms and objections raised by some of the lesser figures within the Nazi women's organisations indeed go a long way to explaining why the DFW failed in its quest to bring the principles of National Socialism into the lives of ordinary German women and housewives. This failure is even more marked when we look at the membership figures for the NSF, which was intended to be the elite cadre organisation of Nazi women. By the end of 1938 it counted 2.3 million officials on its books, although 70 per cent of these were not card-carrying members of the NSDAP but merely organisers and educators of a non-political kind. The active (i.e. politicised) membership consisted of 3,500 full-time salaried staff at party head-quarters, 40,000 functionaries at the Gau, district and local branch level, and 280,000 cell and block leaders, most of whom were part-time and unpaid.[23] Like the DFW, the NSF experienced severe difficulties in recruiting working-class women, partly because most had no time for party activities and partly because the German Labour Front (see below) successfully asserted its claim to organise working-class women within the workplace. There were, of course, some working mothers as well as housewives among the officials of the NSF, but they were largely middle-class women and not from the manual working class. As one disappointed female party activist from before 1933 put it, the Nazis had 'offer[ed] us the same old song with new notes'.[24]

2. Nazi propaganda and the ideal Nazi woman

If the Nazi women's organisations themselves were something of a failure at driving home the message of National Socialist ideology, then there were other methods open to the Nazis in their effort to indoctrinate the population with National Socialist views and thereby create the 'ideal Nazi woman'. One such method was the increased use of the media, in particular the 'new media' of film and radio, which, like books, newspapers and theatre, came under the centralised control of Joseph Goebbels' Propaganda Ministry from March 1933 onwards.[25] Hitler himself was also known to be very keen on the revolutionary potential of propaganda to order the private lives of German citizens. 'My whole life was nothing but a constant effort to persuade others', he commented on one occasion during the Second World War, adding in another conversation shortly afterwards:

> For goodness' sake, let's not run to the police because of every peccadillo. Let us rather stick to educative measures. Don't forget, after all, that it was not by using fear inspired by police methods that we National Socialists won over the people, but rather by trying to show them the light and to educate them.[26]

Nazi propaganda typically sought to appeal to women by inducing them to celebrate their 'natural' domestic role as housewives and mothers, leaving the 'harsh' world of politics and work to men. In particular 'Aryan' women were to become the focus of the Nazis' drive to boost the birth rate. At least in the early years of the regime, they were systematically directed away from the idea of a full-time career towards starting or extending a family, and to this end a generous system of marriage loans was introduced in 1933. Under this scheme 'Aryan' couples could apply for an interest-free loan of 1,000 Reichsmarks (around a fifth of average yearly take-home pay) to be paid (to the husband) in the form of vouchers for furniture and other household goods, provided, of course, that the woman gave up work on marriage and devoted herself to motherhood. The amount to be paid back was reduced by a quarter for each child produced, so that after the fourth child no further repayments were necessary.[27] Mass weddings were also arranged as part of the propaganda drive to promote these marriage loans. In November 1933, for instance, the *Völkischer Beobachter* reported that 122 women workers from the Reemsta cigarette factory in Berlin had been married in a single mass ceremony before voluntarily resigning their jobs. The company replaced the women with unemployed German men, and thereby set a 'shining' example for other businesses to follow.[28]

The development of a 'cult of motherhood' was itself a key feature of Nazi propaganda, designed not to increase the number of births per se, but rather the number of 'racially desirable' births. The 'German mother', to be distinguished from the 'racially valueless' mother, was given an exalted place in Nazi imagery. Paintings, sculptures and posters frequently depicted the breast-feeding German mother surrounded by her healthy children in traditional rural settings, thus invoking the Nazi fantasy of ideal family life. 'We have given back to [the German mother] and [German] housewife the respect which they had lost under Marxist [i.e. republican] rule', wrote Gertrud Scholtz-Klink proudly in a pamphlet produced by the NSF in 1936.[29]

Mothers and housewives were indeed rewarded in various ways, not just financially through the marriage loans and other state benefits, but also in public celebrations of 'German womanhood'. In 1934, for instance, Mother's Day became an official holiday for the first time in Germany through a joint effort of the Ministry of Propaganda and Scholtz-Klink's *Frauenwerk*. This day of honour for mothers had first been established in the USA in 1907 and was observed on a small scale in Germany from 1923 onwards, largely at the behest of the florist industry and a few pro-family organisations. Under the Nazis, however, it acquired a new meaning and a new status. Thus, instructions issued by Reichsminister Goebbels in April 1934 demanded that this event be 'clearly distinguished from previous Mother's Days ... above all it should not be a coffee-and-cake event, but rather a day for the family, in which the mother is placed at the centre'.[30]

With this in mind, Goebbels ordered that all married men who normally worked in factories on Sundays be given a day off, and that all SA men, SS men, Hitler Youth and BDM members should also be released from duties so that they could attend to their families. Furthermore:

> In all the churches on this day the theme 'mother' and 'motherhood' must be addressed from the pulpit. The theatres can be put into service, both through the staging of appropriate and worthy plays and through the distribution of free tickets. These tickets must be for the whole family or single tickets for mothers whose children have already left home, especially for lonely old widows.[31]

As Irmgard Weyrather has written, Goebbels' attention to detail is indicative of the fact that Mother's Day was intended not just to be a means of manipulating women in order to persuade them to have more children, but also a fundamental part of the public celebration of National Socialism as a new national religion or *ersatz* political faith which would eventually replace Christianity in the hearts and minds of most Germans.[32] In this sense it ranks alongside other national holidays in the Nazi calendar, such as 30 January (*Tag der Machtergreifung* – anniversary of the seizure of power), 20 April (*Geburtstag des Führers* – the Führer's birthday), 1 May (*Tag der nationalen Arbeit* – National Labour Day) and 9 November (*Gedenktag für die Gefallenen der Bewegung* – day of mourning for the martyrs of the Nazi movement). Furthermore, during the war years Mother's Day was given even more emphasis than in peacetime. Thus in April 1942 Goebbels issued an order to all Gauleiter that they must 'organise celebrations for Mother's day on 17 May 1942 at all levels of the party (Ortsgruppen, Kreisen and Gauen) on a larger scale than ever before'.[33] Further instructions on 14 May 1942 from the Reich Minister for Labour Franz Seldte dealt with the issue of those mothers who were due to be awarded crosses but were supposed to be at work in war-related industries on the following Sunday:

> Those mothers who are due to be honoured on Mother's Day but who are also employed as workers or employees in public service and are expected to report to work on Sundays should be given the day off because of the great importance which the award of a Mother's Cross represents for German womanhood.[34]

The Mother's Honour Crosses were awarded for the first time on Mother's Day in May 1939, when 3 million women, mostly older women with four children or more, were solemnly granted the title of 'mother of the Reich' in special national ceremonies. The crosses came in three grades: bronze for four children, silver for six, and gold for eight or more. Recipients of the gold cross were honoured by Hitler himself. Meanwhile, Hitler Youth members were required to salute all holders of the Mother's Cross, and they were also granted other benefits and privileges, such as the right to jump queues in shops and to apply for extra ration cards during the war.[35]

In addition to propagating a 'cult of motherhood', Nazi propagandists were also keen to address women as consumers who had a special responsibility to safeguard the economic independence of the Third Reich in a world governed by intense competition for scarce resources and (in the Nazi view) by Jewish attempts to destroy and enslave the German nation. One Nazi pamphlet from 1934 declared:

> Every housewife needs to be aware of her responsibilities, needs to be clear that the manner of her housekeeping has a bearing not only on the welfare of her family, but also the welfare of the entire nation. It is

not insignificant how she decides to spend her housekeeping money, what she chooses to buy, in what proportions and in what order.[36]

In practice, this meant women were to be encouraged to use their power as consumers to contribute to the exclusion of Jews from the national economy and to the revival of a 'healthy' middle class that would form the backbone of German economic recovery.

> It is likewise important that there be a certain regularity in purchase and continuous reliance on dependable local merchants. This will bring about a steadiness in the market and certainty in keeping accounts; it makes it possible for the merchant to run his business according to plan, and thus better serve the wants of his customers. Between house-wife and merchant [there must be] honest cooperation ...[37]

In accordance with Nazi racial ideology, women were also discouraged from using cosmetics and wearing 'decadent' foreign modes of dress; sex appeal was considered to be 'Jewish cosmopolitanism', while excessive dieting was frowned upon on the grounds that it was counter to the birth drive. Efforts were made to establish a Germanic style of clothing and to this end a German Fashion Bureau was even set up in 1933 under the honorary presidency of Magda Goebbels.[38] Finally, Nazi propagandists also placed an increased emphasis on physical fitness for women, and smoking was strictly condemned, especially during and after pregnancy. The police commissioner of Erfurt, for instance, appealed to German citizens to 'remind women whom they meet smoking on the streets of their duties as wives and mothers'.[39] Meanwhile, the few birth control centres that had been set up in the Weimar years by female rights activists in the SPD and KPD were closed down, on the grounds that they were damaging to the health of the German nation. Access to contraceptives was made more difficult (although there was no formal ban on their manufacture or importation until 1941) and the sections of the Reich Penal Code dealing with abortion were toughened up, with harsh prison sentences meted out to those caught undergoing or assisting in the illegal termination of a pregnancy.[40]

The 'ideal Nazi woman', then, as she appeared in Nazi Party propaganda, was aware of her responsibilities to the race and the *Volk*, over and above her responsibilities to her family and herself. She was also well versed in the doctrine of National Socialism and willing to make sacrifices for the sake of the movement. Above all, as the American observer Clifford Kirkpatrick wrote in an important book published in the 1930s, the woman was seen in Nazi ideology as a 'giver rather than a taker of life'. This 'biological fact' made her unsuitable for military service and also for involvement in politics, since politics (in the Nazi view) was about one question only: war or peace. Indeed, the exclusion of women from the public sphere of politics and war was a crucial element in ensuring the survival of the Nazi regime and the success of its racist and expansionist policies, which could be realised only if women were given no real say in the decisions over life and death made by the leadership of the Third Reich.[41]

The extent to which National Socialism succeeded in getting its message across to women in the 1930s is an open and much debated question. On the surface, at least, it seems that certain aspects of the Nazi population policy aimed at women, such as the marriage loan scheme, and improvements in pre- and post-natal medical services, were highly successful. During 1934, for instance, the first full year of the marriage loan scheme, 224,619 loans were granted to newly wed couples. The figure fell to 156,788 in 1935 but rose again to 171,391 in 1936, so that by this time about one-third of all marriages were loan-assisted.[42] Furthermore, the scheme had a knock-on effect on certain types of economic enterprise, especially those involved in the production of furniture and other durable household items. The removal of the condition that women give up paid employment outside the home led to a sharp increase in the number of applications for marriage loans from 1937 onwards, also spurred on in part by the growth in the economy and the increase in consumer confidence. By 1939, indeed, 42 per cent of all marriages were supported by the scheme, and the percentage rose again in the early years of the war.[43]

Other parts of the National Socialist revolution, however, such as the anti-Semitic measures and the pressure to buy from 'Aryan' stores only, were far less popular and far less successful in propaganda terms. Indeed, as with the attempts to reorganise approaches to childrearing and housekeeping along National Socialist lines discussed above, most German women in the 1930s proved resistant to attempts by the party and state to tell them where they should shop and what they should wear. Thus, reports and eyewitness accounts from various sources on the 1 April 1933 boycott of Jewish shops indicate that the campaign was largely a failure. In bigger cities it was noted that many ordinary women and men had made a point of shopping at Jewish stores, and in some parts of the Gau Westfalen-Nord it was even necessary to admonish female party workers for ignoring the boycott.[44] As Richard Bessel has written, while the campaign of violence against the KPD was generally welcomed in Germany in 1933, early anti-Semitic measures, including the boycott, 'appear to have aroused widespread misgivings among the public and created difficulties for the Nazi leadership without offering compensating political dividends'.[45] The same can be said of the adulation of Hitler as the Führer, the God-like saviour of the German nation, which again aroused disquiet in some quarters. The Dresden philologist Victor Klemperer, for instance, noted a conversation with one of his Catholic students in June 1934, following her return from a youth camp:

> She said to me recently, 'A kind of catechism was read out to us. "I believe in the leader Adolf Hitler ... I believe in Germany's mission ..." Surely no Catholic can say that.'[46]

Women were also frequently resentful of the increasing demands placed on their husbands and children to devote time away from their families in 'voluntary' acts of service to the party or the state. Indeed, the rising divorce rate that followed the new Marriage Law of 1938, the encouragement given to children to denounce their politically unreliable parents to the Gestapo, and the introduction of compulsory military service for young men (1935) and of compulsory labour service for young women (1939), all exposed the contradictions in Nazi pro-family rhetoric. So too did the persistent rumours that teenage girls in the BDM (*Bund deutscher Mädel* – League of German Maidens) were returning home from weekend camps either pregnant or suffering from gonorrhoea or other sexually transmitted infections.[47] One very revealing joke about everyday life in the Third Reich ran: 'Where does the German family meet in the Third Reich? At the Reich party conference! The mother comes with the *Frauenschaft*, the daughter with the BDM, the son with the Hitler Youth, and the father with the SA'.[48]

In general, it is of course very difficult to say what kind of impact Nazi propaganda had on women. Despite the failure of initial anti-Semitic measures, for instance, recent studies by Robert Gellately and Eric Johnson suggest that the gradual exclusion of Jews from the 'national community' was made easier by the cooperation of large numbers of 'ordinary' German citizens with the state police, especially in the latter half of the 1930s.[49] Denunciations of those who committed the crime of *Rassenschande* – sexual relations with a member of an 'inferior' race – or who were simply known to be friendly with Jews or other 'undesirables', were not uncommon in Nazi Germany, and indeed formed the basis on which many routine police investigations began.[50] How many women were involved in denunciations is difficult to say, however, as is the question of motivation. In some circumstances, for instance, women might use the Gestapo in order to settle old scores with neighbours or escape from an unhappy marriage, and thus it is questionable whether the act of denunciation in itself was always necessarily a demonstration of loyalty to the regime. Rather, it could also have been a means of protecting oneself and one's family from the threat posed by a violent partner or ex-partner. It is not clear, either, whether female denouncers were typical of German women in general or much more the exception. Certainly Gestapo records indicate that on average men were more likely to make denunciations than women, although both Katrin Dördelmann, in her study of denunciations in the Cologne area, and Vandana Joshi, in her investigation of Gestapo files in Düsseldorf, also found many cases where women were the driving force behind the arrest and interrogation of suspects.[51] We will return to this theme in Chapter 7.

On a different note, Kate Lacey has explored the way in which the Nazis sought to reach women via the radio, then a relatively new medium and seen as an ideal means by which propaganda could penetrate the private female sphere of the German home.[52] Thus the speeches of top Nazi leaders could be beamed straight into women's homes as they went about their daily chores, as could regular programmed items that nurtured the idea of motherhood and the family or offered advice on childcare and managing household waste. Radio broadcasts were also a means of getting around the problem, identified in many reports from local and regional party organisers, that housewives were reluctant to attend courses or activities organised by the NSF or DFW because of the huge amount of time they took up. Indeed, in October 1933 the then head of the radio section within the Ministry of Propaganda, Horst Dreßler-Andreß, declared in a speech that no household should be without one of the newly launched *Volksempfänger* (people's radios), and by 1939 Germany had more radio sets per head of population – some 3.5 million had been sold – than any other country in continental Europe.[53]

Even here, though, there were problems and tensions. There was a necessary contradiction, for instance, between Nazi family ideology, which identified the man/father as head of household, and the penetration of a new non-familiar figure into the German home, the voice of the *Volksempfänger*, which could potentially challenge that authority over issues such as what to eat for Sunday lunch or how to manage the household budget. Women as mothers were also being exhorted to focus their lives around the wireless set and its daily broadcasts, even while other family members (including daughters) were being increasingly drawn into sports and other party-led activities outside the home. Indeed, the radio became yet another means by which married women's exclusion from the public sphere of politics and power was propagated, legitimised and reinforced. Life could be very lonely for those women whose world remained the smaller one of *Kinder* and *Küche*, except, of course, on certain occasions during the year, such as Mother's Day or the party congress in September, when they once again stepped briefly into the public limelight.

3. Strength through joy

While Scholtz-Klink and the NSF struggled to organise the education and training of millions of housewives and mothers in Germany, a significant number of female industrial workers – nearly 4 million in total by 1939[54] – were brought into the women's section of the German Labour Front (*Deutsche Arbeitsfront* or DAF), the organisation set up by Robert Ley in May 1933 to replace the now banned trades unions. Like the official Nazi organisations for women, the DAF was intended as a means of indoctrinating workers with the values of National Socialism and encouraging them to identify, at least outwardly, with the 'battle for births' and the rearmament programme of the late 1930s. Ley himself made no bones about what he saw as the totalitarian aims of the new regime:

> We start when a child is three years old. As soon as he even starts to think, he's given a little flag to wave. Then comes school, the Hitler

Youth, military service. But when all that is over, we don't let go of anyone. The Labour Front takes hold of them again, and keeps hold until they go to the grave, whether they like it or not.[55]

DAF efforts to improve the working conditions and thus the productivity of the workforce in the armaments factories will be discussed in Chapter 4. For the time being we will examine one of the DAF's other main functions: its attempt to supervise the leisure activities of female and male workers through its subsidiary organisation 'Strength Through Joy' (*Kraft durch Freude*, or KdF). Strength Through Joy was essentially a mass organisation for tourism, sport and popular entertainments. It sought to persuade German workers that, in spite of their low wages and longer shifts, they were much better off than they ever had been under the 'Marxist' Weimar Republic. It was also an instrument of Nazi racial policy, since Jews and other 'undesirables' were excluded altogether from the supposed 'joys' of KdF-sponsored activities. These included, among other things, state-subsidised holidays and theatre trips, cruises in the North Sea or Mediterranean, adult education classes, fitness clubs and hiking groups, and various sporting and outdoor events. Large open-air swimming pools and other leisure facilities were built for the use of workers and their families, and in 1938 plans were also laid for the mass production of the affordable 'KdF-car', otherwise known as the *Volkswagen* or people's car. The *Volkswagen* cars were never delivered, however, because of the outbreak of war and the subsequent retooling of car plants to manufacture tanks and other armoured vehicles for use by the Wehrmacht.[56]

As numerous accounts testify, the KdF organisation was probably the most popular of all the Nazi innovations in the sphere of social policy, even though much of its programme was borrowed from initiatives already undertaken in the 1920s. Surveys conducted at the time revealed that millions of ordinary workers and their families would take holidays away from home if they were provided at subsidised rates and with a reasonable amount of time off work. The Reichsbahn (state railway) and private bus companies, local guest houses and hotels, professional musicians and entertainers, and a host of other small businesses and self-employed people also benefited from the massive increase in tourism in the mid- to late 1930s. According to official statistics produced by the Strength Through Joy organisation itself, the number of people taking holidays away from home rose from 2.3 million in 1934 to 10.3 million in 1938.[57]

However, such figures must also be treated with some degree of caution. Only 180,000 people, the equivalent of one worker in every 200, actually went on one of the overseas cruises in 1938, while the majority took excursions of just a few days to resorts on the North Sea and Baltic coasts, or to previously hidden beauty spots such as the Harz Mountains, the Bavarian Alps or the area around Lake Constance.[58] Furthermore, as Ian Kershaw points out, in the most impoverished regions of Bavaria (and no doubt in other parts of Germany too) extremes of poverty prevented many working-class families from affording even the cheapest fares offered by the Strength Through Joy trips.[59] Conversely, many middle-class Germans were horrified by the expansion of mass tourism and gave KdF holiday resorts a wide berth. One report, penned by an SPD agent in Munich in April 1939, even spoke of a 'sharp social differentiation' in the way KdF activities were organised:

> The 'top people' only go on big trips where there will be a more select clientele. The big mass trips are for the proletariat. People now look for places where there are no KdF visitors ... A landlord in a mountain village in Upper Bavaria wrote in his prospectus: 'Not visited by KdF tourists'. The Labour Front, which was sent the prospectus by someone, took the landlord to court. He had to withdraw the prospectus and was not allowed to receive summer guests. Nevertheless, information about summer Pensions which are not used by KdF is becoming more and more widespread ...[60]

Apart from tourism, sport was the other major area of concern for the KdF organisation, and here it is possible to see a more concerted effort to break down class barriers. Sporting activities for women also fitted in well with the regime's priority of producing 'healthy' mothers with 'healthy' children in preparation for the racial tasks of the future. As early as 1935 it was claimed that the number of factory-based athletics courses offered by Strength Through Joy had risen from 8,500 to 48,500 over just one year. PE classes over the same period increased from 55,000 to 190,000, and the persons attending from 450,000 to 3,034,687.[61] By 1937–38 the number of women participating in basic fitness courses and especially in gymnastics had even begun to exceed the number of men, although, as Table 3 shows,

Table 3   Sports organised by Strength Through Joy

Type of course	Participants 1937	Participants 1938	of whom were female
Basic course	4,988,103	4,088,469	2,417,531
Special gymnastics	151,687	136,601	131,229
Light athletics	448,902	304,278	107,995
Swimming	1,809,873	1,582,427	710,416
Boxing, wrestling, etc.	208,762	203,252	8,415
Games	223,426	202,853	82,549
Water sports	19,393	9,641	5,399
Winter sports	53,839	92,631	55,656
Special sports	235,242	211,078	99,474
Youth in employment	1,262,267	3,004,071	140,720
Factory sports	–	12,297,026	2,048,200
Other (sailing, seaside resorts)	–	247,304	128,488
Total	9,401,494	22,379,631	5,936,072

Source: Jeremy Noakes and Geoffrey Pridham (eds), *Nazism, 1919–1945. A Documentary Reader, Vol. 2: State, Economy and Society, 1933–1939* (new edn) (Exeter, 2000), p. 155. Copyright © University of Exeter Press, Exeter.

women were clearly discouraged from participating in competitive ball games and factory sports, and instead were expected to stick to less strenuous forms of physical exercise in line with Nazi ideas about feminine 'beauty'.

Specialist evening and weekend courses were also laid on for women athletes, including bicycling, synchronised acrobatics, folk dancing and even pistol shooting.[62] Others worked towards winning a place in the 1936 Berlin Olympics or achieving the Reich Sport Medal, a less demanding honour which by 1944 had been awarded to some 5 million Germans of both sexes.[63]

As with the Nazi propaganda efforts described in the previous section, it is of course difficult to state the actual effects of Strength Through Joy in determining popular attitudes towards the regime, in particular the attitudes of women. Oral studies conducted after 1945 indicate a widespread tendency among the older generation of Germans to distinguish between the 'negative' and the 'positive' features of National Socialism. The 'positive' features relate mostly to the 1930s and include things like full employment and job security, the increasing availability of 'modern' consumer goods like radios and refrigerators, the potential for social mobility and higher wages, and the new leisure opportunities offered under the Strength Through Joy programme.[64] This impression is also confirmed in some of the reports commissioned by *Sopade*, the organisation of the German Social Democratic Party in exile, from its base in Prague in the 1930s. One report, written by a *Sopade* agent in Berlin in February 1938, read as follows:

> Strength through Joy is very popular. The events appeal to the yearning of the little man who wants an opportunity to get out and about himself and to take part in the pleasures of the 'top people'. It is a clever appeal to the petty bourgeois inclinations of the unpolitical workers. For such a man it really means something to have been on a trip to Scandinavia, or even if he only went to the Black Forest or the Harz mountains, he imagines that he has thereby climbed up a rung on the social ladder.[65]

On the other hand, the high point of popularity for KdF-sponsored activities in the late 1930s also coincided with a significant decline in levels of discipline at work and a corresponding increase in the number of complaints from employers about shoddy performance, absenteeism, illness, skiving off to smoke in the toilets and failure to meet targets. *Sopade* reports picked up on this, as did the security police and party spies who increasingly operated within the factories, workshops and industrial plants where 'ordinary' women and men worked.[66] Thus, ironically, the popularity of the KdF programme may have been more a symptom of growing worker disenchantment with the regime than a sign of support for its political and economic goals, although instances of open opposition, let alone resistance, were still extremely rare in the 1930s and only became apparent in the very different conditions of the Second World War. As Tim Mason has argued, Strength Through Joy was an instrument for the containment of working-class protest since it provided a necessary distraction from the 'pervasive fear, repression and alienation' which characterised industrial relations in the Third Reich.[67] In this regard women workers in the German Labour Front and its subsidiary organisations were probably no different from their male comrades.

4. The policing of female sexuality and the reproductive sphere

One final aspect of the Nazi organisation of women that should be mentioned here is the attempt to police the intimate sphere of male and female sexual relations in accordance with the overall aim of producing a new generation of 'hereditarily fit Aryans'.[68] As is to be expected, sex in Nazi Germany was officially defined as occurring solely within marriage, even though Nazi leaders themselves were known to be far from chaste in their personal lives. This petit-bourgeois attitude to sexuality was of course not specific to National Socialism, but rather built upon the conservative outlook of the majority of the German population, which was still heavily influenced by the traditional teachings of the churches and the anti-communist/anti-abortion temper of the Weimar period.[69] However, in the Nazi *Weltanschauung*, sex and marriage came to mean something else too – a means of fulfilling one's duty to the *Volksgemeinschaft* and the National Socialist state.[70] Women who failed to marry or who remained in childless marriages were not just pitied or chastised in private but were also publicly stigmatised for helping to undermine the nation's health and were accused (among other things) of 'racial desertion'. True, as Jill Stephenson points out, it would be wrong to give the impression that women were actually coerced into motherhood or forced to have children against their will.[71] Nonetheless, many couples were undoubtedly subject to social pressures of a kind that led them to have children soon after marriage simply to avoid drawing attention to themselves.

Furthermore, unmarried men, and from 1938 childless couples, were also forced to pay additional taxes to the sum of 10 per cent of their income as a punishment for their 'refusal to multiply' (*Fortpflanzungsverweigerung*).[72] And finally, the 1938 Marriage Law allowed the courts to approve the dissolution of marriages in the interests of the 'national community' if one partner turned out to be infertile or refused to have children (or, regardless of the above, if the marriage was between a German and a Jew). In some cases, divorces were granted even to those couples who had children if the husband could demonstrate that his plans to marry a second partner would result in him fathering more children than if he stayed in his original marriage. Here we can safely assume that the wishes of the first wife and her children were not taken into account by the courts or were set aside in favour of the higher interests of the *Volk*. Indeed, the man might even be relieved of his obligation to pay maintenance if the condition of the labour market allowed his first wife to take up paid employment outside the home.[73]

The propaganda and divorce legislation that targeted single and childless women was also bound to affect lesbians and gay men living in Germany, whether married or not. Male homosexuality was already a criminal offence under Section 175 of the Reich Penal Code of 1871, but in practice during the 1920s Germany had developed a reputation as one of the most sexually tolerant countries in Europe. Indeed, one of the most urgent tasks for Nazi policy on sexual matters, in addition to cracking down on abortion and contraception, was the destruction of homosexual institutions and cultural life in Berlin and other major cities. This involved, among other things, the closing down or close surveillance of known gay bars and clubs, and the dissolution of organisations that promoted homosexual rights, such as Max Hirschfeld's Institute for Sexology.[74] However, as Claudia Schoppmann has argued, Nazi persecution of homosexuals differed fundamentally from the racial war of destruction waged against the Jewish population and against Sinti and Roma.[75] For one thing, the aim was not the extermination of all homosexuals – although many did die as a result of appalling brutality and ill-treatment in concentration camps – but rather 'deterrence through punishment' and in some cases 're-education'.

For another thing, the main targets of the anti-homosexual police hunts that followed the violent purge of the SA in 1934 were gay men and rent boys rather than lesbians. Indeed, no criminal prosecutions of lesbians took place in the Third Reich, whereas some 50,000 men were convicted of 'indecency' under a revamped version of Section 175. Of these, between 10,000 and 15,000 were sent to concentration camps, where over two-thirds of them died.[76] National Socialist policies on female homosexuality proceeded on the basis that lesbianism was not something to be punished as an individual misdemeanour and therefore did not require the intervention of the Gestapo or the courts. According to Otto Thierack, later the Minister of Justice, lesbians were at worst 'pseudo-homosexuals' because 'a woman – in contrast to a man – is always capable of intercourse'. Female homo-sexuality might well be 'racially damaging' since it ran counter to the birth drive, but most Nazi legal and population experts took the view that it was less of a danger to the state than male gay relations, since 'a woman seduced in this way is not permanently withdrawn from normal sexual intercourse, but retains her utility for population policies'.[77]

Accordingly, Nazi agencies involved in the policing of sexuality took the view that lesbianism could best be eradicated through propaganda and public enlightenment. Only one or two legal experts called for the extension of

Section 175 to women; the rest accepted that criminalising female homosexuality or prosecuting offenders would not be as effective as the use of social
and political pressure to secure conformity to heterosexual norms. In addition
to the pro-natalist and pro-marriage campaigns directed at all 'Aryan'
women, two approaches in particular were taken to prevent the spread of
lesbianism. Firstly, the NSF was asked to develop a campaign against the
supposed 'masculinisation' of women through 'modern' clothing and hairstyles, which was seen as a particularly insidious feature of 1920s 'decadent'
(or 'Jewish') fashions. Thus one NSF pamphlet from 1934 warned:

> Where one finds in women's clothing a tendency to blur the differences
> between the sexes, for instance an emphasis on narrow hips and broad
> shoulders in imitation of the male figure, these are signs of degenera-
> tion emanating from an alien race: they are inimical to reproduction
> and for this reason damaging to the *Volk*. Healthy races do not
> artificially blur sexual differences.[78]

A second method was the emphasis that leading Nazi figures like Hitler and
Goebbels, as well as Hitler Youth leader Baldur von Schirach, placed on the
qualities of 'feminine grace' and 'female charm', not just in clothing and
hairstyles (although this was important) but also in codes of deportment,
manner of speech, and choice of sporting and other activities. Schirach, for
instance, once told one of his subordinates, the BDM organiser Jutta
Rüdiger:

> When I sometimes watch women getting off a bus – old puffed-up
> women – then I think: 'you should be prettier women'. Every girl
> should be pretty. She doesn't have to be a false, cosmetic and made-up
> beauty. But we want the beauty of graceful movement.[79]

Gay women who still refused to conform outwardly to Nazi ideas about
'German womanhood' exposed themselves to varying degrees of stigmatisa-
tion and prejudice but were not at risk of prosecution under Section 175, as
we have seen. However, an unknown number may have been caught up in
the persecution of so-called 'asocials': petty thieves, prostitutes, drug users
and drunks who had committed no identifiable crime but were nonetheless
taken into 'protective custody' by the police or the SS, which usually meant
a spell inside a concentration camp.[80] Accounts of life in Ravensbrück and
other women's concentration camps indicate that there were some gay
women among the prisoners. Unlike gay men they were not forced to wear
a pink triangle, but rather the black triangle of the 'asocial' or the red
triangle of the 'political'.[81] It is also rumoured that some lesbians were
forced by the SS to work in the brothels set up for gay men inside the
concentration camps for purposes of 're-education'. However, Claudia
Schoppmann has found no supporting evidence for this.[82]

In the meantime, many gay women as well as gay men in Nazi Germany undoubtedly chose to get married in order to avoid raising suspicions, and in some cases, in order to save their jobs or careers as well. This fact alone must put a serious question mark over the claims made by Nazi propagandists that the party's population policies were responsible for the sudden increase in marriages and births after 1933. The relevant figures are given in Table 4, and are worth considering in more detail. At first sight they do show a significant increase in the total number of live births during the first six years of Nazi rule, from under 1.1 million in 1931 to just over 1.4 million in 1939, an increase of 27.2 per cent. During the same period, however, the number of marriages grew almost as quickly, from 516,793 in 1932 to 645,062 in 1938, an increase of 24.8 per cent.[83] In other words, those couples who did get married were choosing to have smaller families: on average only 1.8 children per family in 1940 compared to 2.3 per family in 1920, in spite of the state subsidies and other rewards given to prolific mothers.[84]

Table 4 Population statistics in Germany, 1929–1939

Year	Marriages	Live births	Births per 1,000 inhabitants
1929	589,600	–	–
1931	–	1,047,775	16.0
1932	516,793	993,126	15.1
1933	638,573	971,174	14.7
1934	740,165	1,198,350	18.0
1935	651,435	1,263,976	18.9
1936	609,631	1,277,052	19.0
1937	620,265	1,277,046	18.8
1938	645,062	1,348,534	19.6
1939	772,106	1,407,490	20.3

Source: Jeremy Noakes and Geoffrey Pridham (eds), *Nazism, 1919–1945. A Documentary Reader, Vol. 2: 1933–1939* (new edn) (Exeter, 2000), p. 259.
Copyright © University of Exeter Press, Exeter.

Furthermore, even if we accept that the Nazis were able to increase the underlying birth rate in the period before the Second World War, then it is still debatable how far this can be attributed directly to the popularity of Nazi pro-natalist policies. Gisela Bock, for instance, in her study of reproductive issues in the Third Reich, argues that other factors were far more important in determining the relatively favourable birth rate of the mid- to late 1930s, in particular the 'economic miracle' that saw the German economy switch from mass unemployment to virtually full employment (for men) in the space of three or four years. Of all the births between 1934 and 1939, she argues, two-thirds would have occurred anyway, judging by population trends that had already emerged in the 1920s. Of the remaining third, '60% can be put down to subjective motives which led men and women to spend their moderate increase in income on a child'. The other 40 per cent occurred for a variety of reasons, some to do with support for the regime, but others including the Third Reich's clampdown on abortions and the desire of some women to escape from the world of repetitive and poorly paid work into the relative comfort of the family.[85]

The increase in births cannot therefore be taken as evidence of growing support for the Nazi regime among German women in the late 1930s. At best women were prepared to tolerate a regime that provided them with improved welfare and maternity benefits on the one hand, but forced them to be more thrifty and economical with housekeeping on the other. Furthermore, in spite of all the pro-natalist propaganda directed at 'Aryan' women, illegal abortions continued (according to Gestapo estimates) at a rate of between half a million and a million a year during the late 1930s, partly, it seems, because of the greater difficulty in obtaining contraceptives.[86] Certainly there was no attempt at a 'birth strike' in Nazi Germany (as had once been mooted by radical feminists in Wilhelmine Germany),[87] but hundreds of thousands of married and unmarried women, nonetheless, continued to opt out of motherhood altogether, either from individual choice, or because poverty, unemployment, low wages or failure to secure a marriage loan made it preferable to remain childless. Indeed, as Elizabeth Heineman has shown, applying for a marriage loan sometimes meant having one's medical records and 'racial value' closely scrutinised, which might have acted as a deterrent for some potential couples.[88]

In the meantime, the increased use of the Gestapo to persecute gay men and lesbians, and clamp down on illegal abortions,[89] as well as the employment of police and Nazi Party spies in factories and workshops,[90] demonstrates the growing reliance of the regime on intimidation and terror as a means of realising its racist and totalitarian agenda. Personal decisions about who to choose as a sexual partner, or how many children to have, were no longer seen as a matter of individual choice (as they had been, in some quarters, in the 1920s), but were regarded as matters in which the Nazi state could intervene in order to protect the interests of the 'Aryan' race and the 'national community'. This can also be seen when we examine the impact of Nazi racial policies on the lives of ordinary women, men and children.

Notes

1 The background to the formation of the NSF is dealt with in detail in Stephenson, *The Nazi Organisation of Women*, pp. 50–8.
2 On Strasser see the study by Peter D. Stachura, *Gregor Strasser and the Rise of Nazism* (London, 1983).
3 For a detailed account of the background to Scholtz-Klink's emergence as NSF leader see Stephenson, *The Nazi Organisation of Women*, pp. 97–129.
4 Ibid., p. 121. Scholtz-Klink's own account of her role in the Third Reich,

published under the title *Die Frau im Dritten Reich* (Tübingen, 1978), should be read with caution because of its tendency to gloss over the less pleasant sides of the National Socialist regime, especially the persecution and murder of the Jews.

5 On the NSV see Herwart Vorländer, *Die NSV. Darstellung und Dokumentation einer nationalsozialistischen Organisation* (Boppard am Rhein, 1988). On the *Reichsnährstand* see Daniela Münkel, *Nationalsozialistische Agrarpolitik und Bauernalltag* (Frankfurt/Main, 1996).

6 Stephenson, *The Nazi Organisation of Women*, pp. 156–72. Cf. Stephenson, 'The Nazi Organisation of Women, 1933–1939', in: Peter D. Stachura (ed.), *The Shaping of the Nazi State* (London, 1978), pp. 186–209.

7 On the 'one-pot meal' see Grunberger, *Social History of the Third Reich*, pp. 109–10.

8 See e.g. Nancy R. Reagin, 'Comparing Apples and Oranges. Housewives and the Politics of Consumption in Interwar Germany', in: Susan Strasser, Charles McGovern and Matthias Judt (eds), *Getting and Spending. European and American Consumer Societies in the Twentieth Century* (Washington D.C., 1998).

9 Koonz, *Mothers in the Fatherland*, p. 179.

10 Stephenson, *The Nazi Organisation of Women*, p. 137.

11 NSF pamphlet of 1934 quoted in Brady, *The Spirit and Structure of German Fascism*, p. 202.

12 See the article 'Die Arbeit des Reichsmütterdienstes', in: *Völkischer Beobachter*, no. 349, 15 December 1935. Copy in: BA Berlin, RLB–Pressearchiv, no. 7977, Bl. 93.

13 Figures in Noakes and Pridham (eds), *Nazism, 1919–1945*, Vol. 2, pp. 459–60.

14 Brady, *The Spirit and Structure of German Fascism*, p. 205.

15 Stephenson, 'The Nazi Organisation of Women', p. 196.

16 Else Vorwerck, 'Wirtschaftliche Alltagspflichten der deutschen Frau beim Einkauf und Verbrauch', in: *Berliner Börsen-Zeitung*, 18 November 1934. Copy in: BA-Berlin, RLB-Pressearchiv, no. 7976, Bl. 160.

17 Details of a new cooperation agreement between the *Reichsnährstand* and the NSF can be found in: *Zeitungsdienst des Reichsnährstandes*, no. 244, 8 November 1934. Copy in: BA-Berlin, RLB-Pressearchiv, no. 7977, Bl. 156.

18 Cf. Nancy Reagin, '*Marktordnung* and Autarkic Housekeeping. Housewives and Private Consumption under the Four Year Plan, 1936–1939', in: *German History*, 19 (2001), pp. 162–84.

19 Koonz, *Mothers in the Fatherland*, p. 210.

20 Ibid., p. 211.

21 *Deutsche Frauen an Adolf Hitler*, edited by Irmgard Reichenau (Leipzig, 1933).

22 Ibid., p. 57. Cf. Grunberger, *Social History of the Third Reich*, p. 330.

23 Membership figures in Noakes and Pridham (eds), *Nazism, 1919–1945*, Vol. 2, p. 460.

24 Koonz, *Mothers in the Fatherland*, p. 211.

25 On Nazi propaganda in general and the structure of the Reich Ministry of Propaganda and Popular Enlightenment in particular see the excellent study by David Welch, *The Third Reich. Politics and Propaganda* (London, 1993), esp. pp. 23–49.

26 Hitler's *Tischgespräche*, 18 January and 23 June 1942. Quoted in Mason, *Social Policy in the Third Reich*, p. 26.

27 On the marriage loans see Heineman, *What Difference Does a Husband Make?*, pp. 21–6.

28 'Die Frau in den Haushalt, der Mann an die Arbeitsstätte', in: *Völkischer Beobachter*, 1 November 1933. Cf. Stephenson, *Women in Nazi Society*, pp. 87–8.

29 Gertrud Scholtz–Klink, *Verpflichtung und Aufgabe der Frau im nationalsozialistischen Staat* (Berlin, 1936), p. 13.
30 Der Reichsminister für Volksaufklärung und Propaganda an die Reichspropagandastelle Weser–Ems, 30 April 1934. Copy in: StA Bremen, Senatsregistratur 3-V.2, no. 2112.
31 Ibid.
32 Weyrather, *Muttertag und Mutterkreuz*, p. 7.
33 Ibid., p. 200.
34 Der Reichsarbeitsminister an die nachgeordneten Dienststellen, 14 May 1942. Copy in: StA Bremen, Senatsregistratur 3-V.2, no. 2112.
35 Stephenson, *Women in Nazi Society*, p. 50.
36 Anna Zühlke, *Frauenaufgabe, Frauenarbeit im Dritten Reich* (Leipzig, 1934), pp. 48–9. Reproduced in: Kuhn and Rothe (eds), *Frauen im deutschen Faschismus*, Vol. 1, p. 27.
37 Brady, *The Spirit and Structure of German Fascism*, p. 204, quoting from speech given by Scholtz–Klink in London in July 1935.
38 Haste, *Nazi Women*, p. 97.
39 Ibid., p. 96.
40 On the destruction of sex reform organisations and the crackdown on abortion see Grossmann, *Reforming Sex*, pp. 136–53.
41 Kirkpatrick, *Woman in Nazi Germany*, pp. 112–13.
42 Ibid., p. 121.
43 Noakes and Pridham (eds), *Nazism, 1919–1945*, Vol. 2, p. 451.
44 Reagin, '*Marktordnung* and Autarkic Housekeeping', p. 171, n. 23. Cf. Marion Kaplan, *Between Dignity and Despair. Jewish Life in Nazi Germany* (Oxford, 1998), p. 22.
45 Richard Bessel, *Political Violence and the Rise of Nazism. The Storm Troopers in Eastern Germany, 1925–1933* (London, 1984), p. 108.
46 Victor Klemperer, *I Shall Bear Witness. The Diaries of Victor Klemperer, 1933–1941* (London, 1998), p. 64 (diary entry for 13 June 1934).
47 See e.g. ibid., p. 131 (diary entry for 19 October 1935).
48 Weyrather, *Muttertag und Mutterkreuz*, p. 53.
49 Robert Gellately, *The Gestapo and German Society. Enforcing Racial Policy, 1933–1945* (Oxford, 1990); Eric A. Johnson, *Nazi Terror. The Gestapo, Jews and Ordinary Germans* (New York, 1999). On the process of isolating Jews from the *Volksgemeinschaft* more generally see also the comments made by Kaplan, *Between Dignity and Despair*, p. 44, and Chapter 3 below.
50 See e.g. the figures for Würzburg cited in Gellately, *The Gestapo and German Society*, p. 162.
51 Katrin Dördelmann, '"Aus einer gewissen Empörung habe ich nun Anzeige erstattet". Verhalten und Motive von Denunziantinnen', in: Kirsten Heinsohn, Barbara Vogel and Ulrike Weckel (eds), *Zwischen Karriere und Verfolgung. Handlungsräume von Frauen im nationalsozialistischen Deutschland* (Frankfurt/Main and New York, 1997), pp. 189–205; and Vandana Joshi, 'The "Private" became "Public". Wives as Denouncers in the Third Reich', in: *Journal of Contemporary History* 37 (2002), pp. 419–35.
52 Kate Lacey, 'Driving the Message Home. Nazi Propaganda in the Private Sphere', in: Abrams and Harvey (eds), *Gender Relations in German History*, pp. 189–210.
53 Ibid., pp. 192–3. Nonetheless, according to Angus Calder, *The People's War. Britain, 1939–1945* (London, 1969), p. 358, nearly 9 million radio sets had been sold in Britain by 1939, giving it almost three times as many radios per head of population as the German Reich. I would like to thank Jill Stephenson for pointing this out to me.

54 Scholtz-Klink, in her account, gives the number of women in the DAF as 3,572,897 in June 1937, rising to 3,833,903 by June 1938. See Scholtz-Klink, *Die Frau im Dritten Reich*, p. 321.
55 Frevert, *Women in German History*, p. 243.
56 On the Strength Through Joy organisation see Brady, *The Spirit and Structure of National Socialism*, pp. 143–50; Grunberger, *Social History of the Third Reich*, pp. 254–6; Schoenbaum, *Hitler's Social Revolution*, pp. 104–7; and Mason, *Social Policy in the Third Reich*, pp. 158–61.
57 Mason, *Social Policy in the Third Reich*, p. 160.
58 Grunberger, *Social History of the Third Reich*, p. 255.
59 Ian Kershaw, *Popular Opinion and Political Dissent in the Third Reich. Bavaria, 1933–1945* (Oxford, 1983), p. 81.
60 Noakes and Pridham (eds), *Nazism, 1919–1945*, Vol. 2, p. 353.
61 Figures in Brady, *The Spirit and Structure of National Socialism*, p. 147.
62 See e.g. the illustrations for the section 'Kraft durch Freude', in: Maruta Schmidt and Gabi Dietz (eds), *Frauen unterm Hakenkreuz* (West Berlin, 1983), pp. 58–62.
63 Grunberger, *Social History of the Third Reich*, p. 286.
64 See e.g. the many oral studies conducted by Lutz Niethammer and colleagues into working people's experiences and memories of everyday life in the Ruhr area, which are briefly summarised for English-language readers in Ulrich Herbert, 'Good Times, Bad Times. Memories of the Third Reich', in: Richard Bessel (ed.), *Life in the Third Reich* (Oxford, 1987), pp. 97–110.
65 Noakes and Pridham (eds), *Nazism, 1919–1945*, Vol. 2, p. 353.
66 See the examples in ibid., pp. 370–4. Also Kershaw, *Popular Opinion and Political Dissent*, pp. 95–110.
67 Mason, *Social Policy in the Third Reich*, p. 161. Cf. Mason, 'The Containment of the Working Class in Nazi Germany', in: Mason, *Nazism, Fascism and the Working Class*, pp. 231–73.
68 For a useful introduction see Stefan Maiwald and Gerd Mischler, *Sexualität unter dem Hakenkreuz. Manipulation und Vernichtung der Intimsphäre im NS-Staat* (Hamburg and Vienna, 1999). Also Czarnowski, *Das kontrollierte Paar*, *passim*.
69 For a broader look at German and European attitudes towards sexuality in the nineteenth and twentieth centuries see also George L. Mosse, *Nationalism and Sexuality. Respectable and Abnormal Sexuality in Modern Europe* (London, 1985). On the 1920s in particular see Cornelie Usborne, *The Politics of the Body*, *passim*.
70 Cf. Gabriele Czarnowski, '"Der Wert der Ehe für die Volksgemeinschaft". Frauen und Männer in der nationalsozialistischen Ehepolitik', in: Heinsohn, *et al.* (eds), *Zwischen Karriere und Verfolgung*, pp. 78–95.
71 Stephenson, *Women in Nazi Germany*, p. 30.
72 Maiwald and Mischler, *Sexualität unter dem Hakenkreuz*, p. 107.
73 Stephenson, *Women in Nazi Society*, pp. 43–4; Czarnowski, '"Der Wert der Ehe"', p. 89.
74 Among the various English-language works on the Nazi persecution of homo-sexuals the most important are Heinz Heger, *The Men with the Pink Triangle* (London, 1980); and Richard Plant, *The Pink Triangle. The Nazi War Against Homosexuals* (New York, 1986). See also the short essay by Hans-Georg Stümke, 'The Persecution of Homosexuals in Nazi Germany', in: Michael Burleigh (ed.), *Confronting the Nazi Past. New Debates on Modern German History* (London, 1996), pp. 154–66.
75 Claudia Schoppmann, 'National Socialist Policies Towards Female Homosexuality', in: Abrams and Harvey (eds), *Gender Relations in German*

History, pp. 177–87. See also Schoppmann's larger German-language work, *Nationalsozialistische   Sexualpolitik   und   weibliche   Homosexualität* (Pfaffenweiler, 1991).

76 Schoppmann, 'National Socialist Policies', p. 179. Cf. Stümke, 'The Persecution of Homosexuals', p. 160; and Plant, *The Pink Triangle*, p. 235.

77 Schoppmann, 'National Socialist Policies', p. 182.

78 Ibid., p. 183.

79 Haste, *Nazi Women*, p. 137.

80 On the Nazi persecution of 'asocials' see Jeremy Noakes, 'Social Outcasts in the Third Reich', in: Bessel (ed.), *Life in the Third Reich*, pp. 83–96. Also Chapter 3 below.

81 Plant, *The Pink Triangle*, pp. 114–16.

82 Schoppmann, 'National Socialist Policies', *passim*.

83 The much bigger increase between 1938 and 1939 can be put down to the growing fear of war, which led many young couples to get married as quickly as possible in order to provide some form of stability in the uncertain times that lay ahead.

84 Stephenson, *Women in Nazi Germany*, p. 32, citing Wolfgang Wippermann, *Umstrittene Vergangenheit. Fakten und Kontroversen zum Nationalsozialismus* (Berlin, 1998), p. 182.

85 Bock, *Zwangssterilisation*, pp. 166–7.

86 Stephenson, 'Women, Motherhood and the Family', in: Burleigh (ed.), *Confronting the Nazi Past*, p. 173. Cf. Koonz, *Mothers in the Fatherland*, p. 187.

87 On the 'birth strike' episode of 1913 see Usborne, *The Politics of the Body*, pp. 8–10.

88 Heineman, *What Difference Does a Husband Make?*, pp. 24–5.

89 Through a new 'Reich Central Office for the Combating of Homosexuality and Abortion', established by Gestapo headquarters in Berlin in 1936. Cf. Stümke, 'The Persecution of Homosexuals', p. 159.

90 Kershaw, *Popular Opinion and Political Dissent*, pp. 71 and 110, n. 31.

3

The impact of Nazi racial policies

The idea and goal of a 'racially pure' Germany was, without doubt, the *raison d'être* of the Nazi regime, and the ultimate motivation for its genocidal policies in the Second World War. Indeed, as one recent study puts it, in the Third Reich 'race was meant to supplant class as the primary organising principle in society', with no place afforded for 'lesser races' or those deemed biologically 'unfit'.[1] The Jews in particular were singled out as the 'anti-race', the alleged polluters of the German biological stock who would never give up in their attempts to destroy Germany from within. As a result they were systematically excluded from the 'national community', were faced with ever more restrictions on their personal freedom, and were eventually expelled to the east, becoming the main victims of the purpose-built extermination camps set up in occupied Poland between 1941 and 1945. Alongside the 6 million Jews, up to 500,000 'Gypsies' and an unknown number of Slavs were also murdered.[2]

The Nazi emphasis on racial purity also provided an additional justification for attempts to police and circumscribe women's choices in the sexual and reproductive sphere, and to establish control over women's bodies. Thus, while 'racially valuable' German women were encouraged to reproduce, 'lesser breeds' were systematically prevented from doing so through the techniques of 'modern' medicine. Gisela Bock even claims, on the basis of her study of the Nazi sterilisation laws, that the ultimate intention of Nazi population policy was anti-natalist rather than pro-natalist.[3] Between 1934 and 1939 about 320,000 women and men were compulsorily sterilised against their will under the new Law for the Prevention of Hereditarily Diseased Offspring. Some of the victims were alcoholics or prostitutes; some had a history of mental illness or schizophrenia; others were young women deemed to be 'at risk' of unwanted pregnancy or 'mentally defective' to the point where they were considered incapable of making decisions for themselves. Women were the primary victims, not only because they accounted for 80 per cent of the fatalities that resulted from botched abortions and sterilisations, but also because of what sterilisation meant to them: the destruction of their bodies and their female identities. The Nazi regime, argues Bock, was first and foremost anti-women rather than pro-family in its policies; it 'by no means broke with birth control (Malthusianism) but institutionalised it'.[4]

Racism and sexism were indeed two sides of the same coin in the Nazi treatment of those women considered to be 'undesirable' as breeders. Thus racism sharpened the hostility that Nazi population 'experts' felt towards 'asocial' women and prostitutes, while sexism meant that Jewish and 'Gypsy' women were often treated with even less respect for their human rights and dignity than Jewish and 'Gypsy' men. This can be demonstrated by examining the various 'selection' procedures that took place in the Nazi death camps of occupied Poland. As Atina Grossmann writes, 'the stark fact remains that on the ramp [where selections were made], men and women were separated, and women with small children or visibly pregnant [women] were marked out for immediate extinction'.[5] In other words, gender, as well as age, could make the crucial difference between instant death or a chance of survival through being assigned to a work camp. Jewish women were also targeted by the SS because of their reproductive capacity; pregnancy was the surest guarantee of selection for the gas chamber.[6] Another expert, Gabriele Pfingsten, agrees: 'Jewish women were persecuted and murdered all the more aggressively because, as women, they were potential bearers of the next Jewish generation'.[7]

Jewish men were more likely to survive for other reasons too, although there were some, more limited, circumstances in which it was better to be a woman than a man. Of the 163,000 Jews remaining in Germany in October 1941 – those who had not been able to secure exit visas or who had chosen to stay – two-thirds were over 45 years of age, with 20 per cent more women than men.[8] Immigration quotas and visa restrictions imposed by potential host countries like Britain and the United States were not gender-neutral but clearly favoured men over women, and the young over the old. Finally, emigration may have been delayed because husband or wife were reluctant to abandon relatives, homes and friends. In many cases husbands left first, because they were considered to be most at risk of arrest or harassment by the Gestapo and the SS, with the hope that their families would follow soon afterwards. Then, after 1939, it became much more difficult to leave, until there came a point in late 1941 when it was all but impossible to do so. Women, in other words, did not have the same status or authority within the traditional German-Jewish family as men, which left them with fewer choices and less say when it came to decisions about whether to emigrate. It did not leave them entirely bereft of influence and power, however, as we shall see.

1. Nazi policies towards the Jews

In 1933, according to the census records for that year, about 525,000 people, or less than 1 per cent of the German population, were Jewish.[9] Some (just under one in five) were first-generation immigrants from Russia and eastern Europe, but the vast majority had been born and raised in Germany and considered themselves loyal German citizens. They were involved in all areas of economic life and all occupations, but were particularly prominent in business and commerce, and in certain professions such as medicine and law, and were also significantly under-represented in the agricultural sector and in almost all branches of the rural economy. In terms of religious views, only a small minority were of the ultra-orthodox persuasion; most observed Jewish customs and rituals in a formal sense only, while some had abandoned their faith altogether, either converting to Christianity or becoming agnostics or atheists. Above all, Germany's Jews were prosperous, educated and well integrated into society. In 1933 almost 70 per cent of them lived in cities of over 100,000 inhabitants and 32 per cent lived in Berlin alone, where they made up close to 4 per cent of the population. By contrast, over half of non-Jews in Germany lived in towns and villages of fewer than 100,000 inhabitants.[10]

Generalisations about the position and status of Jewish women in Germany before 1933 are as difficult to make as about the Jewish population as a whole. Most lived in 'respectable' bourgeois households, although some rebelled against middle-class values and became, in the language of the 1920s, 'new women', determined to enjoy the sexual freedoms of big city life. Others turned to radical politics and became active in the SPD or the KPD or (more rarely) in Zionist organisations. The proportion of Jewish women in paid employment outside the home increased steadily from 18 per cent in 1907 to 27 per cent in 1933, although this was slightly lower than the percentage for non-Jewish women (34 per cent). Married Jewish women were expected to stay at home and look after their children, but parents often encouraged their unmarried daughters to study for a career. In 1932, 7 per cent of all women students in Germany were Jewish, as were 10 per cent of women lawyers and – most striking of all – 33 per cent of women doctors. The adult female Jewish population itself, according to 1933 figures, consisted of 45 per cent married women, 41 per cent single women and 14 per cent widows.[11]

In spite of the huge diversity within the Jewish community in Germany, Nazi propaganda insisted on treating all Jews – men and women, the pious and the non-observant, housewives and professionals – as a homogenous group of 'aliens', to be expelled as soon as possible from the 'national community'. The first official anti-Semitic measure undertaken by the Nazis, the national boycott of Jewish shops and businesses, took place on 1 April 1933, and this was followed on 7 April by the 'Law for the Restoration of the Professional Civil Service', which called for the compulsory 'retirement' of all Jews in public employment. As a consequence numerous Jews were sacked from their jobs as teachers, judges, mayors, state prosecutors, and so forth, although for the time being Jewish frontline war veterans were exempted, and Jewish doctors and lawyers could continue in private practice.[12] Others were forced to 'resign' from professional bodies and business associations that adopted 'Aryan-only' clauses in order to fall in line with the requirements of the new regime. As Marion Kaplan has shown, this process applied as much to women's professional groups as to men's. Thus a few weeks after the German Doctors' League (*Verband der Ärzte Deutschlands*) voted to exclude Jews, the League of German Women Doctors (*Deutscher Ärztinnenbund*) decided to follow suit. Herta Nathorff, a former member and a Jew, recorded in her diary:

> April 16, 1933: Meeting of the League of German Women Doctors. As usual I went today, after all, this is where the most respected and the best known women colleagues in Berlin gather. 'Strange atmosphere today, I thought, and so many strange faces'. A colleague whom I did not know said to me, 'You must be one of us?' and showed me the swastika on the lapel of her coat. Before I could answer, she stood up and fetched a gentlemen into our meeting, who said that he had to demand the *Gleichschaltung* of the League in the name of the government ... Silently we 'Jewish and half-Jewish' doctors stood up and with us some 'German' doctors – silently we left the room – pale, outraged to our innermost selves. We then went ... to discuss what we should do now. 'We should quit the League as a united group' said some. I was opposed. I will gladly allow them the honour of throwing us out, but I will at least not voluntarily abandon my claim to membership ... I am so agitated, so sad, so confused, and I am ashamed for my 'German' colleagues.[13]

Many other Jewish professionals – teachers, lawyers, judges and civil servants as well as doctors – faced similar humiliating experiences in the early years of the Nazi regime. Worse was to follow after the passing of the Nuremberg Laws of 15 September 1935. Of these, the most important were the 'Reich Citizenship Law', which denied Jews basic civil rights such as the right to vote or to claim state benefits, and the 'Law for the Protection of German Blood and Honour', which prohibited marriage and extramarital sexual relations between Jews and 'Aryans'. Previous exemptions for Jewish war veterans and their families were now also removed and they too lost their civil rights. Members of the Jewish community were now in effect outcasts within their own country, and as a final insult they were no longer permitted to hoist the German national flag above their houses.[14]

From a reading of memoir literature, it is clear that Jewish women were more sensitive to the low-level discrimination they now faced in everyday life, the snubs they encountered from neighbours and acquaintances, the discomfort they felt when going out shopping or travelling on public transport, and the harassment of their children at school by teachers and fellow pupils, whereas Jewish men tended to dwell more on their loss of professional status and, especially if they had served in the war or as Prussian state officials, on their feelings of having been betrayed by the fatherland. Claire Dratch (née Bachrach) recalled how her own life was affected by the passing of the Nuremberg Laws:

> My childhood was happy and carefree. I grew up secure in the love and warmth of my family and my friends ... When did things in my life begin to change? Not at the beginning of the 1930s. At that time the predominantly Catholic population of Seligenstadt valued and respected its Jewish friends and fellow citizens as before. But at the end of 1935, after the announcement of the Nuremberg Laws, the influence of the Nazis began to affect me and my family more strongly ... Friends no longer wanted to walk down the street with me. They no longer wished to sit next to me on the train, eventually they did not wish to be seen with me at all ... I had became a non-person.[15]

Likewise, Rahel Beer, who was brought up in the small town of Harburg in northern Germany, remembered a particular incident that caused her a great deal of pain and upset:

> I once had a boyfriend who I often went dancing with. Then one night we walked back home, and we were standing out on the street, and he began to sing the anti-Semitic song 'Blut vom Messer fließt, dann geht's noch mal so gut'. You cannot imagine what that does to a person. Of course I said good-bye there and then, and that was that.[16]

The growing atmosphere of persecution and social exclusion also affected the relationship between Jewish men and women. While husbands and fathers lost their careers and businesses, and therewith their traditional role as the family breadwinner, women were obliged to take on new, degrading and sometimes dangerous roles, for instance agreeing to work as domestic servants and maids in wealthier Jewish households in order to make up for their husbands' loss of income, or interceding with state and party officials on behalf of their husbands and fathers. Lisa Pine even talks of an 'enforced equality between men and women' brought about by the progressive impoverishment of the Jewish community. As she writes:

> Broken men were seen differently in the eyes of both their wives and their children. Furthermore, frustration, fear and indecision often led to friction in the home between parents and children.[17]

Within the family, women often proved better equipped to sustain morale and deal with the psychological strains of daily life under the Third Reich. While continuing to work for the family business and/or to do domestic chores, they were expected to perform the additional task of providing emotional support for angst-ridden husbands and children. One woman wrote of her husband:

> He stopped eating, as he said no one had the right to eat when he did not work and became ... despondent ... He feared we would all starve ... and all his self-assurance was gone ... These were terrible days for me, added to all the other troubles, and forever trying to keep my chin up for the children's sake.[18]

Women, because of their greater social skills, were also often better at organising self-help groups within their own neighbourhoods and communities. When the Nuremberg Laws of 1935 excluded Jews from the Winter Relief programme, for instance, members of the League of Jewish Women (JFB or *Jüdischer Frauenbund* – an organisation founded in 1904 and continuing to exist, under close Gestapo surveillance, until 1938) came together to collect money, clothing and fuel for poorer Jewish families. The League also set up communal kitchens, playgroups for children of working mothers, and discussion sessions at which women could talk about their problems and receive practical and moral support. The League's newsletter, the *Blätter des jüdischen Frauenbundes*, contained advice on a variety of pressing concerns and urged Jewish women to do their utmost to preserve a mood of optimism and cheerfulness within the home environment in order to raise the spirits of other family members. By 1936 Jewish women were also running practical training sessions for would-be emigrants, including instruction in agriculture, domestic service and handicrafts – skills that, it was presumed, would help them to find employment abroad.[19]

At first, men were much more reluctant than women to consider emigration as an option. They were more status-conscious, less willing to take lower-paid jobs abroad, and more integrated into the German community. Often they saw themselves as indispensable to their business partners, patients or congregations, and could not contemplate leaving them in the lurch. Marta Appel, for instance, who was married to a rabbi in Dortmund and was herself active in Jewish communal organisations, later remembered a discussion among friends about a doctor who had left Germany in 1935.

> 'It takes more courage to leave,' the ladies protested. 'What good is it to stay and wait for ... ruin? Is it not far better to ... build up a new existence somewhere else in the world, before our strength is crippled by the everlasting strain on our nerves ...? Is not our children's future more important than a fruitless holding out against Nazi cruelties and prejudices?' Unanimously we women felt that way, and took the

doctor's side, while the men ... [spoke] against him. On our way home I still argued with my husband. He, like most other men, could not imagine how it was possible to leave our beloved homeland, to leave all the duties which constitute a man's life. 'Could you really leave behind all this to enter nothingness?' ... 'I could,' I said ... and there was not a moment of hesitation on my part.[20]

Sometimes, though, attitudes towards emigration were as much about generational differences as they were about gender. Marta Appel came to recognise this through her work with the Dortmund branch of the Zionist organisation *Youth Aliya*. As she also wrote:

The rising new enthusiasm of the Jewish youth for Palestine caused ill-feeling in a great many homes. Often we had to smooth the friction between parents and children. The youth did not want to wait any longer, while the parents' hearts and hopes still belonged to the German fatherland.[21]

Indeed, in addition to being more sceptical towards Zionism, women over 30 years of age often shared the view of their husbands that it was better to stay in Germany and defend Jewish honour than to flee overseas in disgrace. Occasional acts of kindness from non-Jewish colleagues or acquaintances also led many Jewish families to misread the situation and believe that they would be safe as long as they kept their heads down. As a result, the number of Jews leaving Germany failed to rise above 40,000 per year before 1938 and dipped to as low as 21,000 in 1935 (see Table 5).

Table 5   Jewish emigration from Germany, 1933–1938

Year	No. of emigrants
1933	37,000
1934	23,000
1935	21,000
1936	25,000
1937	23,000
1938	40,000

Source: adapted from Marion Kaplan, *Between Dignity and Despair. Jewish Life in Nazi Germany* (Oxford, 1998), pp. 72–3.

On 9–10 November 1938, however, came *Kristallnacht*, or the 'night of broken glass', which saw a nationwide orgy of violence against the Jewish community in supposed retaliation for the murder of Ernst vom Rath, a German official in the Paris embassy, by a young Polish Jew called Hershel Grynszpan.[22] Some 91 people were killed or committed suicide on *Kristallnacht*, most of them men, and in the aftermath a further 30,000

Jewish men were arrested in their homes, beaten up and taken to concentration camps for no other reason than that they were Jewish. In the absence of their husbands – and because they were told that their husbands would be released only if they agreed to leave Germany immediately – some women now broke with traditional gender stereotypes and took over the decision-making role within their families. Else Gerstel, for instance, who had 'fought desperately' with her husband, a judge, over the question of whether to emigrate, decided to ignore his continued objections and sent a telegram to her brother Hans in New York: 'Please send affidavit.'[23] Likewise Hertha Merlan, from Hamburg, remembered how her mother was galvanised into action by the arrest of her father on 10 November and his imprisonment in Dachau:

> My mother did everything possible to get out, she went to all the consulates [in Hamburg] and tried to find somewhere we could emigrate to ... Eventually she got to the Uruguayan consulate, and they gave her a visa ... but then a few days before we were due to leave we heard that Uruguay had closed its borders and were letting no more refugees in ... even those who had a visa ... So then my mother went to the Brazilian consulate and got a visa from them ... My mother knew that Brazil was much bigger than Uruguay and that the opportunities to get ahead were also much better. And she was right. At that time it was still relatively easy to make money.[24]

Between November 1938 and September 1939 a total of 112,000 Jews left the Third Reich, but thousands more were turned down for exit visas. On top of the financial and bureaucratic obstacles imposed by the Nazis and by potential host countries, many were simply too poor to emigrate or lacked contacts abroad who could vouch for them. Women in particular were under pressure to stay behind in order to look after elderly or sick relatives, and even Jewish women's organisations encouraged wives to let their husbands emigrate alone if there were no viable alternatives.[25] Some parents made the heartbreaking decision to send their children alone on the so-called *Kindertransporte* to England, while they remained in Germany hoping to follow on in due course. By such means just under 10,000 children were brought to safety in the last few months of peace, while smaller numbers of 'unaccompanied' children went to Palestine, the USA or other European countries.[26] In the meantime, the longer people delayed their decision to apply for exit visas, the harder it became to leave, not least because of the outbreak of war in September 1939. Elderly housewives or widows were especially vulnerable to being left behind, while even those with the advantages of youth and contacts abroad faced continued setbacks in their emigration plans. Elisabeth Freund, for instance, whose three children had already left Germany before *Kristallnacht*, suffered one disappointment after another:

In the spring of 1939 ... we obtained an entry permit for Mexico for 3,000 marks. But we never received the visa, because the Mexican consulate asked us to present passports that would entitle us to return to Germany, and the German authorities did not issue such passports to Jews. Then, in August 1939, we did actually get the permit for England. But it came too late, only ten days before the outbreak of war, and in this short time we were not able to take care of all the formalities with the German authorities. In the spring of 1940 we received the entry permit for Portugal. We immediately got everything ready and applied for our passports. Then came the invasion of Holland, Belgium and France by the German troops. A stream of refugees poured into Portugal, and the Portuguese government recalled by wire all of the issue permits. As it happened, we were lucky that we had not given up our apartment and not yet sold our furniture.[27]

Eventually, Elisabeth and her husband succeeded in leaving Berlin for Cuba in October 1941, just days before the German authorities banned all further Jewish emigration from occupied Europe. Few of the approximately 163,000 Jews remaining in Germany at this time were able to escape the deportations to the death camps in Poland, which began in several waves from 18 October 1941 onwards. In May 1945 around 12,500 Jews were still living in Germany, some in hiding, although most protected by marriage to 'Aryans'.[28] A further 5,000 or so German Jews managed, against all the odds, to survive the death camps themselves.[29]

2. 'Mixed' marriages and 'mixed' partnerships

Throughout the period of the Third Reich, and especially in the years before the war, the Nazi persecution of Jews was augmented by their persecution of 'mixed' families, i.e. those in which one partner was Jewish (even if non-practising) and the other 'Aryan'. Indeed, the statistics suggest that large numbers of people fell into the category of 'mixed' marriage, 'mixed' parentage, or both. In 1933 approximately 35,000 'mixed' marriages existed, a majority being between Jewish men and 'Aryan' women. Due to emigration, divorce or death, this figure fell to 20,000 by May 1939, 16,760 by December 1942 and 12,487 by September 1944. By the end of the Third Reich, 98 per cent of the 'full' Jews who were still living as free persons in Germany had avoided deportation and extermination only because they were married to non-Jews.[30]

As we saw above, the Nazis abhorred 'racial mixing' of any kind, and prohibited both marriage and extramarital relations between Jews and 'Aryans' under the 1935 Nuremberg Laws. Even before this, couples of different races who were intending to marry or who were engaged in extramarital sexual relations faced harassment and persecution. As early as

1933, for instance, 'Aryan' women with real or alleged Jewish lovers were forced to parade through the streets of their home towns with signs around their necks declaring: 'I have committed racial treason' or: 'I fornicate with Jews'. And in the autumn of 1935, a special edition of the anti-Semitic magazine *Der Stürmer* published the names and addresses of 'recent mixed marriages' in order that local party officials in charge of housing and employment might be aware of their existence and take 'appropriate action' against them.[31]

After the Nuremberg Laws, the punishments for the new crime of *Rassenschande* (racial defilement) became much more harsh. Men accused of racial defilement, whether 'Aryan' or Jewish, were invariably treated by the Nazi authorities with greater harshness than women, and Jewish men often ended up in a concentration camp, which from 1939 effectively meant a death sentence.[32] 'Aryan' women were more likely to suffer public humiliation rather than imprisonment, although, as Eric Johnson has shown, there were instances when Jewish women were taken into custody by the Gestapo and forced to go through humiliating interrogations merely to satisfy the voyeuristic pleasures of the Gestapo officials present. Often such women were sent for short periods to a concentration camp for 're-education', while their 'Aryan' lovers typically served a prison sentence of between one and two years. This, as we have seen, was far more lenient than the treatment given to Jewish men accused of defiling 'Aryan' women.[33]

Those 'mixed' couples who had married before 1935 and whose marriages could not therefore be legally dissolved were subject to different kinds of pressure and harassment. From April 1939 some lived in so-called 'privileged marriages', and were shielded from the effects of anti-Jewish legislation, although this seems to have applied mainly to Jewish women with 'Aryan' husbands and not the other way around.[34] The Nuremberg Laws also created two legal categories of *Mischlinge*, or mixed-race, Jews (*Mischlinge* first degree and *Mischlinge* second degree), who were given more rights than 'full Jews'. First-degree *Mischlinge* – those who were not practising Jews but had two Jewish grandparents – could not marry 'Aryans' but could marry full Jews or second-degree *Mischlinge*. If they married a full Jew, they were in effect 'marrying down' and any offspring would be counted as 'full Jews' as well. If they married a second degree *Mischlinge*, they were 'marrying up' and their children too would be classified only as second-degree *Mischlinge*. Second-degree *Mischlinge*, those with one Jewish grandparent, found similar dilemmas: they were able to marry 'Aryans' and first-degree *Mischlinge* but not full Jews. Both categories of *Mischlinge* were usually spared the full horrors of the Holocaust, although they did face a variety of petty restrictions and humiliations which made life unpleasant for them. Some estimates suggest that as many as 300,000 Germans fell into one of the categories of *Mischlinge* and were thus affected by the racial laws of the Nazi state.[35]

Finally, in the aftermath of the new Marriage Law of 1938, the Gestapo and other agencies placed increasing pressure on 'Aryans', especially 'Aryan' women, to divorce their Jewish spouses, occasionally even offering this as a means of saving their children from deportation or their spouses from torture and death. One woman, for instance, whose father had been arrested in 1943, remembered the Gestapo's frequent attempts to blackmail her mother into agreeing to terminate her marriage:

> My mother was repeatedly told by Gestapo officers, by representatives from the Jewish community and by others who were facing similar persecution that holding onto her marriage would do my father a great deal of harm. If the current situation – then known as 'blood-defilement' – should continue, then my father would be sent to a concentration camp where he would probably die. If the marriage were dissolved, on the other hand, my father could count on better treatment. From families of 'evacuees' we had heard that 'evacuation' merely meant 'relocation' and that a postal service had been in existence for months so that the 'evacuated' could receive parcels.[36]

In most books on the Third Reich, it is assumed that 'Aryan' men were more likely to divorce Jewish wives than vice versa, mainly because the Gestapo could threaten their careers and livelihoods, or even have them imprisoned in a concentration camp if they refused to cooperate.[37] Yet Beate Meyer found a very different picture in her recent study of 130 'mixed-race' divorce cases that went to court in Hamburg during the Nazi period. Of these, 103 involved 'Aryan' women divorcing Jewish men, and only 27 'Aryan' men divorcing Jewish women. According to Meyer:

> Those who wanted a divorce were mostly German-blooded women ... Divorce seemed to them to be the only means of ensuring their own survival while at the same time ... also giving their husbands a fighting chance. The judges were enthusiastic participants in this process of racial segregation. However: the actual decision to divorce a partner was made in the majority of cases by non-Jewish women, who thereby became if not perpetrators, then nonetheless participants in the expulsion and persecution of the Jews, and thus played a role which they preferred to forget after the war was over.[38]

The chances of survival for a divorced Jewish man were also a lot lower than for a divorced Jewish woman. After 1942 the former were usually sent to the 'old people's' ghetto at Theresienstadt, and then on to Auschwitz where they faced forced labour or immediate 'selection' for death. The latter, on the other hand, could usually avoid deportation if they had children under 14 who were being raised outside the Jewish faith. They also remained 'privileged' in the sense that they did not have to wear the yellow star in public, which had been made compulsory for all 'non-privileged'

Jews from September 1941 onwards. Thus, on the specific issue of 'mixed marriages', Nazi policy was neither race-neutral nor gender-neutral but rather favoured the 'Aryan' over the Jew, the wife over the husband and the mother over the childless woman.[39]

However, in spite of the evidence presented by Meyer, it remains the case that surprisingly few 'Aryan' partners of either sex were willing to file for divorce against Jewish partners. Precise figures are hard to come by, but estimates indicate that only 7 per cent of mixed marriages were legally dissolved in Baden and Württemberg, and only 20 per cent in Hamburg.[40] Anecdotal evidence also suggests that many 'Aryan' women and men who may have wished for a divorce in 'normal' times, stayed in broken marriages in order to protect their Jewish spouses from deportation (or until both had succeeded in emigrating). Verena Groth, for instance, who was born in Stuttgart in 1922 to a part-Jewish father and an 'Aryan' mother, later recalled:

> My mother would never have divorced [my father], even in what was an unhappy marriage, and especially not after she knew it would be his downfall. Especially not then. I mean, many men sent their wives to England. I know of several who said, we'll divorce pro forma, and later I'll come and get you. And many, along with their wives, broke down. They went with their Jewish part, they could not bear the strains, and they [thereby] killed themselves.[41]

Meanwhile, in some desperately sad situations, where the pressure on mixed marriages became too much to bear, Jewish spouses saw suicide as the only option to safeguard the future of their families and especially their children. In other cases, couples went through the motions of getting divorced, while in fact the 'Aryan' partner continued to support his or her Jewish spouse in secret. This was the case, for instance, with a Hamburg couple where the Jewish wife suggested divorce to her 'Aryan' husband in 1939 in order to save the business they had built up together; in the end she survived the war, mainly because she had a son by her husband in 1935 who was being raised as a Catholic. Other divorces were complicated by the existence of third parties or stepchildren or both, not to mention Gestapo intimidation and the threat of imminent deportation. Nonetheless, Marion Kaplan, in her study, still found that a 'remarkable number of mixed marriages remained firm', a testament to the bravery of both partners in the marriage and to their refusal to bow before Nazi terror and intimidation.[42]

3. The 'hereditary ill', 'asocials' and others 'unworthy of life'

While anti-Semitism was one aspect of the Nazi racial programme, the persecution of women and men deemed to be biologically 'unfit', 'asocial' or

carriers of supposedly hereditary illnesses like manic depression or schizophrenia was another. Indeed, many of those targeted for eventual deportation
and extermination were people who had suffered from discrimination and
social exclusion long before Hitler came to power in 1933: the physically dis-
abled, the mentally ill, the homeless, 'habitual criminals', carriers of sexually
transmitted diseases, and so forth. As early as 1926, for instance, the Bavarian
Landtag had passed a 'Law for Combating Gypsies, Travellers and the Work-
Shy', and similar legislation was enacted by the state governments in Prussia
and Hesse in 1927 and 1929 respectively.[43] What set the Nazis apart,
however, was their emphasis on biological solutions to social problems like
poverty, alcohol addiction, underachievement at school, and criminality.
Thus, as the philologist Victor Klemperer noted in his book *The Language of
the Third Reich* (1946), the ideology of National Socialism was based on a
'scientific, or rather pseudo-scientific theory of race' which was used to justify
'every excess and every claim to national superiority, every tyranny, every
atrocity and every act of mass murder'.[44] Jews were without doubt the main
victims of this system, but they were by no means the only victims.

Alongside the expulsion of Jewish women and men from the 'national
community', compulsory sterilisation of the 'weak' and 'degenerate' was
one of the main instruments of Nazi racial policy between 1933 and 1939.
Sterilisations without the individuals' or guardians' consent were legalised
under the Law for the Prevention of Hereditarily Diseased Offspring of 14
July 1933, which set up nine diagnostic causes under which a person could
be sentenced by a genetic health court to sterilisation.[45] Five of the
categories related to mental and cognitive disorders ('congenital feeble-
mindedness', 'schizophrenia', 'manic depressive illness', 'hereditary
epilepsy', and 'Huntingdon's Chorea'); three to physical disabilities
('hereditary blindness', 'hereditary deafness', 'serious physical deforma-
tion'); and the final one to alcoholism. All nine 'invalidities' were considered
to be inherited from the parents, although alcoholism was not treated as an
hereditary illness but rather as 'evidence of mental and moral inferiority'.
While the law was the work of the new Nazi regime, it also had the support
of a variety of non-political medical experts who had long advocated sterilisation and other eugenic measures as a means of improving the health of
the 'national body' and preventing the birth of 'degenerate individuals'.[46]
Men with criminal records or chronic personality disorders were the
intended targets as much as women. Nonetheless, women who failed to
conform to the expected norms of middle-class society, especially prostitutes or so-called 'asocial' women who 'burdened' the welfare state by
having large numbers of children by different sexual partners, were a
particular cause for concern for Nazi and non-Nazi health 'experts' alike.[47]

The sterilisation law itself came into effect on 1 January 1934 and was
supplemented by various additional measures against those with alleged
'hereditary illnesses' or those in danger of propagating 'life unworthy of
life'. In 1935, for instance, a supplementary law allowed for abortions to be

carried out in the first six months of pregnancy on women who had been categorised as 'hereditarily ill' by one of the genetic health courts, and in 1938 it was announced that Jewish women could apply for abortion on demand.[48] In 1937 the small number of black Germans (the so-called 'Rhineland bastards', most of them born in the 1920s) had been summarily sterilised on racial grounds even though they suffered from no manifest 'hereditary' illnesses.[49] Thousands of 'asocials', petty criminals, drunks and prostitutes, whose 'asociality character' was defined as being the result of 'congenital feeble-mindedness', were also sterilised, as were a number of 'Gypsies' (Roma and Sinti), the latter being targeted on both racial and social-biological grounds.[50] The most vulnerable group, however, accounting for some 30 to 40 per cent of all sterilisations in the period 1934 to 1936, were the inmates and former inmates of psychiatric institutions and asylums. Often they were discharged from hospital only after agreeing to undergo the operation that would prevent them having children.[51]

In total, as we saw above, some 320,000 people were sterilised between 1934 and 1939, representing 0.5 per cent of the population. The figure also includes 5,000 'eugenic' abortions with subsequent sterilisations.[52] In the same period compulsory sterilisation was also practised in 30 states in the USA following a supreme court ruling in favour of the state of Virginia in 1927, and in Sweden, which was ruled by a supposedly progressive centre-left government for much of the 1930s and 1940s. However, the numbers involved here were much smaller; for instance, a total of 60,000 operations were carried out in the USA between 1927 and the end of the 1970s in a population about six times that of Germany.[53] In Nazi Germany the two most common reasons given for sterilisation were 'hereditary feeble-mindedness' and 'schizophrenia', with a tendency for female victims to fall under the former and male victims under the latter diagnosis. Between 1934 and 1937 about 80 men and 400 women died during the course of the operation. Most victims of the sterilisation programme came from the poorer sections of society, although a few were middle-class women who had in some way contravened the norms and expectations of their class. The 'good housewife' and the mother of 'valuable' children, on the other hand, could be sure to evade sterilisation.[54]

Gisela Bock, in her study of the sterilisation programme, came across a number of examples of women prepared to resist their forced sterilisation at the hands of the state and the medical profession. In May 1934, for instance, Emma F., a 29-year-old unmarried and childless women from Freiburg who had once spent some time in a psychiatric hospital, where she was diagnosed as 'schizophrenic', was informed that she would be sterilised against her will. In response she wrote a long letter of protest to the genetic health court:

> I am working regularly in the cigar factory since I left the clinic. I am
> able to earn the highest wage and my employer is satisfied with my

work ... I have recovered and am now as normal as anyone else ... All human beings differ from one another ... I do not understand why I should be sterilised. I have not done any moral or sexual wrong. A nervous mental disease can happen to every human being and is just like any other illness ... I do not have sexual intercourse with men and I do not intend to marry.

In spite of Emma's claim that she had merely suffered a nervous breakdown and was not ill with 'hereditary schizophrenia', a higher court rejected her appeal and she was forcibly sterilised in 1935.[55]

In another case, the husband of Olga G., a factory worker from Lörrach, told a court hearing in 1934 that he did not believe his wife was 'congenitally feeble-minded', even if she had experienced difficulties at school:

My wife and I will not consent to sterilisation. I also cannot understand why my wife would even be considered for sterilisation, since in my opinion she is not feeble-minded.

Olga's boss, the foreman from the factory where she worked, also told the court that he found her to be of 'normal' intelligence. A subsequent appeal failed, however, when a local priest testified that not only Olga, but also her father and brother were 'abnormal'; the entire family, he argued, was 'tainted' [*schwerbelastet*] and Olga herself displayed 'strong psychopathic traits' [*starke psychopathische Züge*], being easily distracted, bad-tempered and obdurate. She had also had to stay down a year at school and had once, 'hung herself, half-naked and with her hair untied, out of the top window and stared as if catatonic up to the skies'. This, apparently, was enough to prove that she was suffering from a 'hereditary' disorder which could be passed on to future generations if it were not checked now. Indeed, the appeal court itself found that 'even a small degree of congenital feeble-mindedness can be passed on and therefore can do harm to the next generation'. Olga was finally sterilised against her own wishes and those of her family in June 1936.[56]

While sterilisation represented an unwarranted and dangerous interference in the bodies of both women and men, an even worse fate awaited the long-term inmates of psychiatric institutions who were considered ineligible for release at any point in the future and who were therefore not offered sterilisation as a means of securing their re-entry into society. Between 1939 and 1941, under the 'euthanasia' project known by the code name 'Aktion T-4', some 70,273 mentally and physically handicapped adults were murdered as so-called 'useless eaters' or 'life unworthy of life', in part, as Michael Burleigh has argued, in order to save money and create more bed space for military casualties at a time of war.[57] The killings were organised under the greatest secrecy by Dr Karl Brandt, Hitler's chief physician, and Philipp Bouhler, the head of the Chancellery of the Führer, in accordance with Hitler's own written instructions dating from 1 September 1939. Six asylums were selected as killing centres, and specially trained SS personnel were sent in to carry out technical 'modifications', namely the installation of gas chambers disguised as showers. Patients 'selected' for 'euthanasia' from other asylums were then sent to the special asylums where, on arrival, they were photographed and then gassed. Their corpses were burned in specially designed crematoria. The relatives of those killed received notification of the patients' transfer to the new asylum and information that 'she/he had arrived safely', followed one week later by a letter of condolence announcing the person's death from an unsuspected illness, for instance appendicitis or epilepsy. Alongside the 70,273 adults murdered in this way, some 5,200 'deformed' children were also killed in a separate programme launched by Brandt and Bouhler at the end of 1938.[58]

Although 'Aktion T-4' and the 'children's euthanasia programme' were meant to be kept secret, news spread rapidly, especially as the families of the victims were not always satisfied with the official explanations of cause of death. Partly in response to complaints from relatives, which were backed by the Catholic Bishop of Münster, Clemens von Galen, Hitler called an official halt to the 'euthanasia' programme on 24 August 1941.[59] Nonetheless, many of the 'T-4' personnel were transferred to occupied Poland, where they worked as 'experts' in the newly established death camps at places such as Belzec, Sobibor and Treblinka. The killing of asylum patients inside Germany also continued unofficially until the end of the war, using lethal injections and by deliberate starvation. It is not known how many people died in this manner, but the figure is likely to run into tens of thousands.[60]

In the meantime, alongside the operation of the 'euthanasia' programme and the extermination camps in Poland, mass sterilisations and forced abortions continued to function as an instrument of Nazi racial policy. In September 1940, for instance, plans began for the drafting of a special Protection Law, never implemented, that would allow for the sterilisation of those not covered by the original Law for the Prevention of Hereditarily Diseased Offspring. The intended targets included prostitutes, women of 'inferior character' and anyone categorised as being 'asocial' (*gemeinschaftsfremd*).[61] Within the borders of the old Reich the forced sterilisation of more than 2,000 German 'Gypsies' (Sinti and Roma) took place between 1943 and 1945 under the watchful eye of the SS, while several thousand others were deported to the east and later gassed at the Auschwitz 'Gypsy' camp.[62] The mass sterilisation of the 107,000 part-Jews (*Mischlinge*) still living in Germany in 1942 was discussed and agreed as an alternative to their deportation, but not carried out in practice. In this way the second-degree *Mischlinge* and most of the first-degree *Mischlinge* were saved from the death camps, although their fate might well have been different had the Nazis won the war.[63]

Thousands of Polish and Soviet women workers deported to Germany from the east as forced labourers (the *Ostarbeiterinnen*) were also made to undergo abortions and sterilisations, partly for racial reasons and partly in order to maintain the women as productive workers for the German war economy (see also Chapter 4).[64] By this time some Nazi racial 'experts' were calling for the compulsory sterilisation of up to 20 per cent or even 30 per cent of the indigenous German population itself. Significantly, however, in March 1942 it was declared that 'no more applications for the sterilisation of [full] Jews need be made'.[65] The reason for this is clear: by this time it had already been decided that all full Jews were to be deported to Poland and exterminated *en masse* under the programme known euphemistically as the 'final solution to the Jewish question in Europe'.[66] In this way the Jews were singled out for 'special treatment' within the overall framework of the Nazi drive for a new racial order on the European continent.

4. Women as agents of Nazi racial policy

Though many women were victims of Nazi racial policy, others were to be found among its agents, actively participating in the enforcement of racist laws and measures drawn up by men. Thus, as we have seen, the League of German Women Doctors was among the first women's organisations to exclude Jewish members, eager to conform to the requirements of Nazi *Gleichschaltung*. Likewise, many 'ordinary' German women helped to isolate their Jewish neighbours and acquaintances from the 'national community', thus contributing to their 'social death' even before the organised violence of *Kristallnacht* in 1938.[67] And finally, the leaders of the Nazi women's organisations, in particular the NSF under Gertrud Scholtz-Klink, openly supported Nazi policies that targeted the 'unfit' and the 'asocial' for sterilisation while providing extra material and financial support for 'racially valuable' families.[68]

The drawing up and enforcement of the sterilisation laws was first and foremost, of course, the responsibility of the male-dominated medical profession, which worked hand in hand with so-called 'experts' from the Race-Political Office of the Nazi Party and the SS Race and Resettlement Office. Nonetheless, many female nurses and social workers reported possible sterilisation candidates to their superiors, who then investigated such cases before deciding whether to proceed with an application to the genetic health courts.[69] From August 1939 midwives were also required to report 'deformed' births to their nearest Health Office, and from November 1939 psychiatric nurses working in asylums were required to assist in the transportation of 'euthanasia' candidates to the 'T-4' killing centres. The evidence suggests that most nurses performed these duties willingly and without protest, although degrees of complicity and knowledge of the 'euthanasia' programme itself varied from individual to individual.[70]

Women doctors and nurses were also among the perpetrators of the so-called 'wild' or unofficial 'euthanasia' that took place in German asylums between 1941 and 1945. Nurses now assisted directly in the killing process, holding patients down while they were given lethal injections, or sometimes administering the injection themselves, as well as being party to the policy of systematic starvation. According to Michael Burleigh, 'literally hundreds' of nurses and nursing orderlies, as well as a handful of female doctors, became, in effect, murderers or accomplices to murder during the war.[71] At no point were they forced into this; no nurses were sacked or disciplined for refusing to participate in acts of 'euthanasia', and those who objected could not merely apply for, but actually insist on, a transfer to another post. Some nurse-killers undoubtedly felt uncomfortable with doing what they were asked to do, but continued to follow orders out of a sense of duty or deference to their superiors, a phenomenon doubtless reinforced by the gendered hierarchy within the medical profession. Others became so hardened that they no longer considered killing patients to be a crime, adopting instead the view that it was a form of 'deliverance' for those whose life was deemed not to be worth living. Sometimes parents or family members also made it clear to nursing staff that they would rather their relatives were dead so they did not have to continue to visit them any more. This, undoubtedly, made the task of killing easier.[72] A small minority of female asylum workers went further than this, however, and seem to have derived a perverse form of pleasure from tormenting their patients. In her recent study Bronwyn McFarland-Icke gives the example of a former patient at the Eichberg asylum in the Rheingau who witnessed a deliberate murder in 1942:

> A nurse pulled the hair of an old woman when she did not direct her gaze properly. When the woman defended herself, the nurse pulled her down and repeatedly struck her head against the floor until the woman was dead.[73]

Elsewhere, women school teachers and social workers often collaborated with the Nazi regime's harassment of Jews and other 'racial inferiors', helping to make life difficult, if not intolerable, for them. Often this was simply a routine part of their jobs, but, as numerous accounts suggest, it could be done with varying degrees of enthusiasm or reluctance. For instance, Marta Appel, the rabbi's wife from Dortmund, remembered with great bitterness the behaviour of one of the music teachers at the local school, who deliberately chose to humiliate her two daughters on the occasion of Mother's Day:

> 'You have to be present for the festival,' the teacher told them, 'but since you are Jewish, you are not allowed to join in the songs'. 'Why can't we sing?' my children protested with tears in their eyes. 'We have a mother too, and we wish to sing for her'. But it seemed that the teacher did not want to understand the children's feelings. Curtly she

rebuked their protest. 'I know you have a mother,' she said haughtily, 'but she is only a Jewish mother'. At that the girls had no reply; there was no use to speak any longer to the teacher, but seldom had they been so disturbed as when they came home from school that day ...[74]

Fewer women than men were involved in the Holocaust itself, i.e. in the systematic deportation and mass murder of Jews in the extermination camps of occupied Poland between 1941 and 1945, or in the mass shootings of Soviet Jews undertaken by the *Einsatzgruppen* following the Nazi invasion of the USSR in 1941. There were no women among the personnel of the death camps at Belzec, Sobibor and Treblinka.[75] Nonetheless, within the Nazi concentration camp system as a whole, women made up an estimated 10 per cent of the guards, including at Auschwitz-Birkenau in Upper Silesia, which was a slave labour camp as well as an extermination camp. Most members of the SS female guard units came from 'normal' lower middle- and working-class backgrounds, and were recruited from other Nazi organisations such as the BDM or the NSF. Not all had previous connections with the party, however, and some were drafted into working for the SS as *Dienstverpflichtete*, or conscripts, especially towards the end of the war.[76] In May 1945 there were roughly 3,000 fully trained women SS guards (*Oberaufseherinnen*), together with 3,000 auxiliaries of the security police (*Helferinnen der Ordnungspolizei*) and a further 4,000 wartime auxiliaries of the SS (*Kriegshelferinnen*).[77] The usual age range was between 17 and 30, and only those who passed rigorous racial and aptitude tests achieved the distinction of becoming fully fledged members of the *SS-Frauenkorps*. Among the more lowly ranks of the camp guards, however, it seems that almost anyone could join, regardless of previous employment history, marital status or class background. Germaine Tillion, for instance, a French resistance fighter who was deported to the women's concentration camp at Ravensbrück in 1942 and had privileged access to camp records, found that the women guards included 'tram conductors, factory workers, opera singers, qualified nursery teachers, hairdressers, farmers, young girls from middle class homes who had never worked before, retired school teachers, circus-riders, former prison warders, officers' widows and so on'.[78]

Eyewitness accounts and testimonies offered at post-war trials also indicate that some of the female SS guards could be as brutal and sadistic as their male colleagues. Olga Lengyel, for instance, a Romanian doctor who survived the women's forced labour camp at Auschwitz, was able to observe at first hand the many crimes of Irme Griese, one of the most notorious SS guards who was known by the camp inmates as the 'blonde angel of death' because of her role in the 'selections' and her frequent use of the whip:

> She [Griese] was of medium height, elegantly attired, with her hair faultlessly dressed. The mortal terror which her mere presence inspired visibly pleased her ... With her sure hand she chose her victims, not

only from the well but from the sick, the feeble and the incapacitated. Those who, despite hunger and torture, still evidenced a glimmer of their former physical beauty were the first to be taken. They were Irme Griese's special targets.[79]

Besides concentration camp guards and SS auxiliaries, various other women were directly or indirectly involved in Nazi war crimes. The wives of SS men, for instance, saw themselves as part of an elite who were helping to realise the dream of a racial revolution and a racially structured new order in the heart of Europe. Those married to the commandants of concentration and death camps often chose to live with their husbands within the camp compounds, or at least visited these places, and were thus able to observe their husbands' work at close hand.[80] Sometimes they turned up to act as voyeurs in the torture and murder of inmates or helped to 'select' victims for the camp gallows, and less frequently they took part in such acts themselves. More importantly, they often sought to enrich themselves through the SS terror system, either by the forced labouring of prisoners as maids and servants in the family home or through their involvement in corruption, the black market and the theft of confiscated Jewish property. One former inmate of the Hrubieszow ghetto in Poland, for instance, wrote after the war:

> At that time it was widely known that the wives of Gestapo officers and other German officials helped themselves to the property of Jews, especially suitcases, clothing and other personal items, and took these things back to Germany.[81]

Between 1940 and 1944 several thousand young and single women from the 'old Reich' were also recruited for education and welfare work among indigenous and 'resettled' ethnic Germans in occupied Poland, and thereby took part in or witnessed acts of brutality against the non-German population, including the forcible expulsion of Polish and Jewish families from their homes and the removal of Polish children from their parents.[82] From the mid-1930s female students and university graduates often took jobs in genealogical record offices or in racial science institutes, which involved compiling data on potential victims of the Third Reich's racial polices. An example would be the women who worked for the criminal-biological department of the Reich Health Office, based in Berlin-Dahlem, which collected information about 'Gypsies' and other 'asocials'.[83] And finally, during the war, the Gestapo and the SS employed thousands of women as typists, stenographers and telephonists, helping to oil the wheels of the Nazi killing machine and ensuring its smooth functioning.[84]

Various explanations and theories have been put forward to explain why so many women as well as men were willing to act as agents of or accessories to Nazi racial crimes. Some historians have argued that female perpetrators were, like all women, victims of patriarchy and male oppression, that they 'compensated for their own enslavement by picking on those who were more severely oppressed'.[85] Others suggest that they used their traditional roles as mothers and housewives to encourage their husbands' greater crimes, thereby helping to make genocide possible.[86] Still others maintain that the highly qualified female scientists who worked for Nazi racial institutes and thereby helped to formulate the genocidal objectives of the regime were rare examples of 'emancipated women' because they transcended traditional gender boundaries and competed with men for men's work. This implies that they were not 'normal' women but exceptions, which proved a general rule about the passive, supportive, home-making role of women in the Third Reich.[87]

In a recent essay, however, Gisela Bock has argued convincingly that none of these explanations is satisfactory because they all assume an 'idealised' version of 'normal' female behaviour which does not reflect the social reality of the Third Reich or the real intentions of the Nazi regime.[88] The female perpetrators of Nazi crimes against humanity were in fact qualitatively no different from their male colleagues in terms of motivation and degree of culpability, even if they were fewer in number. For most, upward mobility and career enhancement were the key aims, followed closely by opportunities for self-enrichment through involvement in corruption.[89] A few were psychopaths or 'natural born killers', but the vast majority were not. Some were married, some even had children, but this did not in itself determine their participation in Nazi crimes, which was more often a function of their extra-domestic activities – their leadership in one of the Nazi women's organisations, their employment as teachers, scientists or nurses, and their desire to leave low-paid jobs or domestic drudgery for something better. Or, to put it another way, the female perpetrators were 'ordinary' women, just as ordinary as the women who did not participate in crimes against humanity, and just as ordinary as the men who did.

True, on some occasions in occupied Poland an old-fashioned taboo seemed to operate, dictating that women be spared the sight, sound and smell of direct contact with violence. For instance, women social workers and auxiliaries working with ethnic German settlers in the east would be brought to an area of resettlement only after the original Polish or Jewish inhabitants had already been 'evacuated' and any evidence of atrocities cleared away. However, there are so many examples where this taboo did not come into play and where it was deliberately broken by SS men who wanted women (wives and girlfriends, colleagues, even German Red Cross nurses) to witness forced expulsions, that it can hardly be said to have existed in practice.[90] Indeed, as Bock concludes, the real novelty of the Nazi regime was the use it made of 'ordinary' people – women as well as men, non-Germans as well as Germans – to carry out its programme of racially motivated mass murder. Those who became killers or accessories to genocide and acts of 'ethnic cleansing' under the Third Reich were not usually sadists or psychopaths but *ganz normale Leute* – normal people.[91] And in the final analysis, they should be judged for what they did and not for who they were in terms of gender, class or nationality.

Notes

1 Burleigh and Wippermann, *The Racial State*, p. 4.
2 Figures in ibid., p. 364. The word 'Gypsies' is placed in inverted commas here because it is considered a term of abuse by the Sinti and Roma communities who have lived in several parts of Europe since the medieval period. The term is derived from the word 'Egyptian', although there is no evidence that any of the 'Gypsies' ever came from Egypt – in fact they originated from the Punjab region of northern India. For further details see ibid., p. 113.
3 Bock, *Zwangssterilisation*, *passim*.
4 Ibid., p. 10.
5 Grossmann, 'Feminist Debates about Women and National Socialism', p. 356.
6 Cf. Baumel, *Double Jeopardy*, p. 22.
7 Gabriele Pfingsten in *Holocaust and Genocide Studies* 14 (2000), p. 460 (review of Andreas Baumgartner, *Die vergessenen Frauen von Mauthausen. Die weiblichen Häftlinge des Konzentrationslagers Mauthausen und ihre Geschichte* (Vienna, 1997)).
8 See the figures on emigration in Monika Richarz (ed.), *Jewish Life in Germany. Memoirs from Three Centuries* (Bloomington and Indianapolis, 1991), p. 37.
9 Kaplan, *Between Dignity and Despair*, p. 10.
10 Ibid., p. 11.
11 Ibid., p. 240.
12 Burleigh and Wippermann, *The Racial State*, p. 78.
13 Kaplan, *Between Dignity and Despair*, pp. 26–7.
14 *Gesetz zum Schutze des deutschen Blutes und der deutschen Ehre*, 15 September 1935, and *Reichsbürgergesetz*, 15 September 1935. For an English translation of these texts see Noakes and Pridham (eds), *Nazism, 1919–1945*, Vol. 2, pp. 535–7.
15 Lisa Pine, *Nazi Family Policy, 1933–1945* (Oxford, 1997), p. 153.
16 FZH/Werkstatt der Erinnerung (henceforth WdE), no. 565 T.
17 Lisa Pine, 'German Jews and Nazi Family Policy', *Holocaust Educational Trust Research Papers*, Vol. 1, no. 6 (London, 2000), p. 9.
18 Kaplan, *Between Dignity and Despair*, p. 61.
19 Ibid., p. 49.
20 Marta Appel, unpublished memoirs written in the USA in 1940–41, reproduced in: Richarz (ed.), *Jewish Life in Germany*, pp. 351–61.
21 Ibid., p. 359.
22 On *Kristallnacht* see Wolfgang Benz, 'Der Novemberpogrom 1938', in: Benz (ed.), *Die Juden in Deutschland, 1933–1945. Leben unter nationalsozialistischer Herrschaft* (Munich, 1989), pp. 499–544.
23 Kaplan, *Between Dignity and Despair*, p. 69. See also Kaplan, 'Keeping Calm and Weathering the Storm. Jewish Women's Responses to Daily Life in Nazi Germany, 1933–1939', in: Ofer and Weitzman (eds), *Women in the Holocaust*, p. 44.
24 FZH/WdE, no. 434 T.
25 Kaplan, 'Keeping Calm and Weathering the Storm', p. 49.
26 See the figures cited in Baumer, *Double Jeopardy*, p. 8.

27 Elisabeth Freund, undated manuscript written in Havana (Cuba), December 1941, reproduced in: Richarz (ed.), *Jewish Life in Germany*, pp. 412–24.

28 Figure cited in Sybil Milton, 'Women and the Holocaust. The Case of German and German-Jewish Women', in: Bridenthal *et al.* (eds), *When Biology Became Destiny*, p. 321.

29 Cf. Koonz, *Mothers in the Fatherland*, p. 379.

30 On mixed marriages see Nathan Stoltzfus, *Resistance of the Heart. The Rosenstrasse Protest and Intermarriage in Nazi Germany* (New York, 1996); and Stoltzfus, 'Protest and Silence. Resistance Histories in post-war Germany. The Missing Case of Intermarried Germans', in: Ruby Rohrlich (ed.), *Resisting the Holocaust* (Oxford, 1998), pp. 151–78. On the offspring of mixed marriages see Kaplan, *Between Dignity and Despair*, pp. 74–93. Also the recent study by Beate Meyer, *'Jüdische Mischlinge'. Rassenpolitik und Verfolgungserfahrungen, 1933–1945* (Hamburg, 1999).

31 Kaplan, *Between Dignity and Despair*, p. 79.

32 Burleigh and Wippermann, *The Racial State*, p. 84.

33 Johnson, *Nazi Terror*, pp. 111–16.

34 'Privileged' mixed marriages comprised those where the children had been baptised, and those between 'Aryan' men and Jewish women, regardless of whether there were children or not. 'Non-privileged' marriages were marriages between 'Aryan' women and Jewish men that remained childless, and also all marriages where children had been enrolled in the Jewish religious community as of September 1935. For further details see Kaplan, *Between Dignity and Despair*, pp. 148–9.

35 Ibid., p. 75.

36 Meyer, *'Jüdische Mischlinge'*, p. 89.

37 See e.g. Kaplan, *Between Dignity and Despair*, p. 91.

38 Meyer, *'Jüdische Mischlinge'*, pp. 91–2.

39 Ibid., p. 92.

40 Kaplan, *Between Dignity and Despair*, p. 250, n. 4.

41 Quoted in Alison Owings, *Frauen. German Women Recall the Third Reich* (London, 1993), p. 105.

42 Kaplan, *Between Dignity and Despair*, pp. 92–3. Cf. FZH/WdE, no. 339 T.

43 Guenter Lewy, *The Nazi Persecution of the Gypsies* (London, 2000), pp. 7–9.

44 Victor Klemperer, *LTI (Lingua Tertii Imperii). Notizbuch eines Philologen* (Leipzig, 1975), p. 171.

45 On the sterilisation law see also Gisela Bock, 'Racism and Sexism in Nazi Germany. Motherhood, Compulsory Sterilization and the State', in: Bridenthal *et al.* (eds), *When Biology Became Destiny*, pp. 271–96.

46 See e.g. Usborne, *The Politics of the Body*, pp. 148–55. Also Paul Weindling, *Health, Race and German Politics between National Unification and Nazism, 1870–1945* (Cambridge, 1989), esp. pp. 383–93 and 450–7.

47 On the persecution of 'asocial families' see Pine, *Nazi Family Policy*, pp. 117–46; and Pine, 'Hashude. The Imprisonment of "Asocial" Families in the Third Reich', in: *German History* 13 (1995), pp. 182–97.

48 Bock, 'Racism and Sexism in Nazi Germany', p. 283.

49 Burleigh and Wippermann, *The Racial State*, pp. 128–30.

50 Pine, *Nazi Family Policy*, p. 128. On 'asocials' see also the recent volume of essays edited by Robert Gellately and Nathan Stoltzfus, *Social Outsiders in the Third Reich* (Princeton, N.J., 2001).

51 Michael Burleigh, *Death and Deliverance. 'Euthanasia' in Germany, 1900–1945* (Cambridge, 1994), p. 61.

52 Bock, 'Racism and Sexism in Nazi Germany', p. 279.

53 See e.g. the report by Matthew Engel in the *Guardian*, 4 May 2002, p. 21 on the

unveiling of a memorial to the 7,000 victims of the compulsory sterilisation programme in Virginia between 1927 and 1979.

54 Bock, 'Racism and Sexism in Nazi Germany', p. 287.
55 Bock, 'Ordinary Women', pp. 86–7. Cf. Burleigh and Wippermann, *The Racial State*, pp. 254–6.
56 Bock, *Zwangssterilisation*, pp. 228–9.
57 Michael Burleigh, 'Saving Money, Spending Lives. Psychiatry, Society and the "Euthanasia" Programme', in: Burleigh (ed.), *Confronting the Nazi Past*, p. 106. On the 'euthanasia' programme see also Burleigh, *Death and Deliverance*, esp. pp. 93–129.
58 On the 'children's euthanasia programme' see also Jeremy Noakes and Geoffrey Pridham (eds), *Nazism, 1919–1945. A Documentary Reader. Vol. 3: Foreign Policy, War and Racial Extermination* (Exeter, 1988), pp. 1005–9.
59 Ibid., p. 1040.
60 On the involvement of 'T-4' personnel in the murder of Jews and on the so-called 'wild euthanasia' between 1941 and 1945 see Burleigh, *Death and Deliverance*, pp. 220–66.
61 Pine, *Nazi Family Policy*, p. 119. Cf. Bock, 'Racism and Sexism in Nazi Germany', pp. 286–7.
62 Michael Zimmermann, 'The National Socialist "Solution of the Gypsy Question". Central Decisions, Local Initiatives and their Interrelation', in: *Holocaust and Genocide Studies* 15 (Winter 2001), pp. 412–27.
63 On the SS's plans to sterilise *Mischlinge* see Heinz Höhne, *The Order of the Death's Head. The Story of Hitler's SS* (London, 1969), p. 367. Also Isabel Heinemann's recent article, '"Another Type of Perpetrator". The SS Racial Experts and Forced Population Movements in the Occupied Regions', in: *Holocaust and Genocide Studies* 15 (Winter 2001), pp. 387–411, esp. pp. 397–9.
64 Burleigh, *Death and Deliverance*, p. 255. See also Herbert, *Hitler's Foreign Workers*, pp. 268–73.
65 Bock, 'Racism and Sexism in Nazi Germany', p. 283.
66 When exactly the decision to murder the Jews was made is still a matter of debate, although most historians agree that it took place at some point in the second half of 1941, and certainly before the infamous Wannsee conference of 20 January 1942. For a useful summary of the different points of view see Mark Roseman, *The Villa, the Lake, the Meeting. Wannsee and the Final Solution* (London, 2002), esp. pp. 36–64.
67 Cf. Kaplan, *Between Dignity and Despair*, p. 5.
68 See e.g. the article 'Zur bevölkerungspolitischen Lage', in: *NS-Frauenwarte*, 6/1 (1937–38), p. 1. Also Else Frobenius, *Die Frau im Dritten Reich* (Berlin, 1933), pp. 47–8.
69 Cf. the evidence presented in Stephenson, *Women in Nazi Germany*, p. 147.
70 Noakes and Pridham (ed.), *Nazism, 1919–1945*, Vol. 3, pp. 1006 and 1022–4. On the involvement of women in the 'euthanasia' programme see also Ernst Klee, *'Euthanasie' im NS-Staat. Die Vernichtung 'lebensunwerten Lebens'* (Frankfurt/Main, 1983), esp. pp. 80ff.; and the recent study by Bronwyn Rebekah McFarland-Icke, *Nurses in Nazi Germany. Moral Choice in History* (Princeton, N.J., 1999).
71 Burleigh, *Death and Deliverance*, p. 250.
72 Ibid., p. 251.
73 McFarland-Icke, *Nurses in Nazi Germany*, p. 216.
74 Marta Appel, unpublished memoirs (1940–41), in: Reicharz (ed.), *Jewish Life in Germany*, p. 354.
75 Bock, 'Ordinary Women in Nazi Germany', p. 89.

76 Milton, 'Women in the Holocaust', p. 308.
77 Figures cited in Gudrun Schwarz, 'Frauen in der SS. Sippenverband und Frauenkorps', in: Heinsohn *et al.* (eds), *Zwischen Karriere und Verfolgung*, p. 238.
78 Germaine Tillion, *Frauenkonzentrationslager Ravensbrück* (Frankfurt/Main, 2001), p. 153.
79 Olga Lengyel, *Five Chimneys* (St Albans, 1972), pp. 100–1.
80 On SS wives in general see Gudrun Schwarz's study, *Eine Frau an seiner Seite. Ehefrauen in der 'SS-Sippengemeinschaft'* (Hamburg, 1997). On the particular example of Ilse Koch, wife of Karl Koch, the commandant of Buchenwald concentration camp, see also Alexandra Przyrembel, 'Transfixed by an Image. Ilse Koch, the "Kommandeuse of Buchenwald"', in: *German History* 19 (2001), pp. 369–99.
81 Schwarz, 'Frauen in der SS', p. 229.
82 On this theme see Elizabeth Harvey, '"We forgot all Jews and Poles". German Women and the "Ethnic Struggle" in Nazi-Occupied Poland', in: *Contemporary European History*, 10 (2001), pp. 447–61. Also Harvey, '"Die Deutsche Frau im Osten". "Rasse", Geschlecht und öffentlicher Raum im besetzten Polen, 1940–1944', in: *Archiv für Sozialgeschichte* 38 (1998), pp. 191–214.
83 Burleigh and Wippermann, *The Racial State*, p. 119.
84 Cf. Gudrun Schwarz, 'Verdrängte Täterinnen. Frauen im Apparat der SS (1939–1945)', in: Theresa Wobbe (ed.), *Nach Osten. Verdeckte Spuren nationalsozialistischer Verbrechen* (Frankfurt/Main, 1992), pp. 197–227.
85 Rita Thälmann, *Frausein im Dritten Reich* (Munich, 1984), p. 270.
86 Koonz, *Mothers in the Fatherland*, p. 5.
87 See e.g. Götz Aly and Susanne Heim, *Vordenker der Vernichtung. Auschwitz und die deutschen Pläne für eine neue europäische Ordnung* (Frankfurt/Main, 1993), pp. 198–202. Here Aly and Heim discuss the careers of the Austrian scientists Dr Elfriede ('Fritzi') Fliethmann and Dr Dora Maria Kahlich, colleagues at the *Anthropologisches Institut* attached to the University of Vienna. During the war Fliethmann was appointed to a senior position at the *Institut für Deutsche Ostarbeit* in Cracow.
88 Bock, 'Ordinary Women', *passim.*
89 Cf. Schwarz, 'Frauen in der SS', pp. 235–6. Holocaust survivors Ota Kraus and Erich Kulka also noted in their post-war investigation of the Nazi concentration camp system that 'all the SS guards and wardresses had but one aim: to get rich as quickly as possible, to acquire luxury goods which could not be acquired elsewhere' – see Kraus and Kulka, *The Death Factory. Documents on Auschwitz* (London, 1966 [1946]), p. 162.
90 For further evidence see Harvey, '"We forgot all about Jews and Poles"', esp. pp. 452–8; and Daniel Goldhagen, *Hitler's Willing Executioners. Ordinary Germans and the Holocaust* (London, 1996), pp. 241–4. One SS commandant, Captain Wohlauf, even invited his visibly pregnant wife to watch a massacre of Jews that took place on the market square in Miedzyrzec, Poland, on 25 August 1942, although some of the men he was commanding later expressed their astonishment and anger at this breach of decorum, especially 'since [Wohlauf] knew full well before an "action" what was going to happen' (cited in Goldhagen, p. 242).
91 Cf. Tillion, *Frauenkonzentrationslager Ravensbrück*, pp. 154–8.

|4|

Women and work

Increasingly, when discussing Nazi racial policy, historians are struck by the wide range of competing agencies and rival power centres feeding into the decision-making process, so that the genocidal priorities of the regime emerged only gradually and in piecemeal fashion between September 1939 and the end of 1941.[1] Another area where there were a great many twists and turns was the party's attempt to regulate and influence the domestic labour market in order to meet its racial, ideological and economic objectives. Thus, as we have already seen, during the economic slump of the early 1930s the NSDAP had been among the fiercest critics of so-called 'double-earners', and had promised to remove married women from waged work as part of its proposed solution to the unemployment crisis facing Germany. The *ABC of National Socialism*, published in 1933, declared:

> National Socialism aims to allow the German woman the opportunity to fulfil the calling which nature has given to her, namely to be a wife and mother! She has no desire to work in the factory and no desire to enter parliament. A comfortable home, a loving husband and a multitude of happy children are much more to her taste. National Socialism will ensure that the men get jobs again so that they can establish and feed a family and so that they can rescue women from the current need to work [outside the home].[2]

Such views were of course typical of Nazi propaganda in the earlier years of the Third Reich. As we have seen, they also struck a chord with large sections of the German population, including women as well as men. However, it is important to distinguish clearly between image and reality when discussing Nazi labour policy. True, in the early 1930s some women, especially married women professionals and civil servants, were encouraged or forced to leave their jobs in order to prevent a man from having to do so or in order to save costs. Carrot followed stick here with the introduction of the Marriage Loan Scheme in 1933, which offered women the opportunity to exchange dead-end factory jobs for the supposed benefits of enforced domesticity (see also Chapter 2). In practice, however, millions of middle-class and working-class women continued to work in the wage economy in the mid-1930s, and many more were brought into the workforce after the rearmament programme got fully under way from 1936. Richard Overy even argues that in international terms Germany had 'an exceptionally high level of female employment in the late 1930s', especially when one takes into account those types of unwaged work, such as helping out on the family farm or small business, that did not appear in the official health insurance statistics but were nonetheless vital to the German economy.[3] This made the task of mobilising additional women for war work after 1939 even more difficult, particularly as women, both married and single, were 'already employed in great numbers, often for long hours, and for consider-ably less pay than men'.[4]

On the other hand, most historians agree that the efforts to coax more married women and housewives into the labour market during the Second World War were contradictory, half-hearted and largely unsuccessful.[5] Instead of removing the allowances paid out to soldiers' wives who refused to work, the regime preferred to exploit the labour of young single women who were drafted into a variety of more or less compulsory service schemes in German agriculture and industry or into auxiliary work with the Wehrmacht.[6] In addition, and on a much larger scale, the Nazis also relied on the forced labour of millions of foreign deportees, prisoners of war and concentration camp inmates in order to keep the economy going, especially in the final years of the war. The reasons for this are complex, and will be discussed below in greater detail. Before moving on to the war years, however, it is first necessary to consider the state of the German labour market in the 1930s.

1. Women and the labour market in the 1930s

When the Nazis came to power in Germany in 1933 unemployment stood at over 6 million and many working-class families were facing a future of dire poverty and even destitution. In fact, the Great Depression, which began with the Wall Street crash in October 1929, had affected mainly the traditional producer-led, male-dominated industries, such as the building, engineering and iron and steel trades, where few women were employed. Subsequently, many families were forced to rely on the mother or daughters as the sole breadwinners, at least during the worst period of the depression between 1930 and 1932 (see also Table 6).

Before coming to power, Hitler had promised to resolve this economic crisis firstly by removing married women from the workforce and secondly by introducing an ambitious programme of public works such as the

Table 6 Employment status of the insured German workforce in 1932

	Men	Women
Unemployed	45.6%	32.7%
On short time	20.8%	32.8%
In full employment	33.6%	34.5%

Source: Dörte Winkler, *Frauenarbeit im 'Dritten Reich'* (Hamburg, 1977), p. 193.
Copyright © Hoffmann und Campe Verlag, Hamburg.

construction of motorways (*Autobahnen*), which would provide more work for men.[7] In the early years of the regime, however, reducing the adult male unemployment rate was easier said than done. For one thing, employers were often reluctant to replace cheap female labour with more expensive adult male labour, especially in industries such as textiles where women traditionally made up the majority of the workforce and were often hired on short-time contracts. For another, single women, of whom there were several million in 1933, still had a right, and in many cases, an economic need to earn a wage of their own. This applied in particular to women aged 18 to 25 whose families could not afford to support them and who had yet to find a husband.[8] Finally, although married women accounted for only 29.9 per cent of all 'economically active women' in 1933, and were mostly employed in agriculture and the rural economy, the Nazis knew that they could not afford to rely on single women alone as the only 'suitable' female workforce, especially as most financial experts agreed that the key to economic recovery lay not in agriculture but in the regeneration of the industrial sector.[9] Or, as the *Berliner Tageblatt*, a formerly left-liberal newspaper, pointed out in an article in August 1933, economic logic dictated 'that in the future too a considerable portion of those taking jobs in industry – perhaps up to 20 per cent of the total – will have to be made up by women':

> In textiles, for instance, over 50% of production is currently carried out by women, and the same applies in the clothing industry. In the paper industry women account for 35% of the workforce, in the food industry for 30% and in the electro-technical and chemical industries for over 20%.[10]

Instead of campaigning for their dismissal upon marriage, the article continued, it was better to ensure that working women were educated as to their duties and responsibilities through the women's section of the DAF, so that they too could become 'active members of the (National Socialist) Volksgemeinschaft'.[11]

As the recession passed, the question of female employment returned in a different guise as more and more women workers were needed to fulfil the demands of the Four Year Plan and at the same time to meet the requirements of an increasingly buoyant consumer-led economic recovery. Indeed, as Tim Mason argues, it was the shortages of labour, especially skilled labour, as the economy geared itself up for war that really exposed the contradictions in Nazi attitudes towards women as the practical needs of the armaments industry increasingly triumphed over ideological considerations.[12] The first signs of this came in 1936–37, when a series of decrees effectively abolished the provision in the Marriage Loans scheme that prohibited the wives of recipients from taking up paid employment outside the home.[13] This was followed by further measures designed to encourage more married and single women into work, for instance through the expansion of part-time employment opportunities.

Nonetheless, by 1939 little progress had been made in addressing the main obstacles to the recruitment of more women into industry: low wages, poor promotion prospects and inflexible working hours. The women's section of the DAF, for instance, pushed for better working conditions for women and for equal pay for equal work, and was supported in this by Nazi papers like *Der Angriff*, which was concerned to protect male workers from cheaper female competition.[14] However, their efforts were continually thwarted by employers' organisations, who were anxious about rising labour costs, particularly as full employment led to more labour militancy and a demand for better wages for both women and men. Furthermore, private firms like Siemens had since the late nineteenth century been developing their own paternalistic welfare programmes and recreational facilities aimed at workers' families, and were reluctant to jettison these in favour of DAF schemes.[15] To some extent they had the backing of Hitler, who felt that too much state intervention in the labour market in favour of higher wages and better working conditions would distract women from the 'biological task' of motherhood.[16]

According to Dörte Winkler, the armed forces and the Ministry of Labour were more sympathetic to the DAF's case, especially as pressures grew to find more workers to feed the demands of the rearmament programme. Here too, though, concerns were raised about the implications of greater female participation in the workplace, particularly in relation to thorny issues like part-time working, protection for working mothers, and the maintenance of good discipline on the shopfloor. Interestingly, as Carola Sachse discovered, it was not the employers, but rather the DAF and its spokesmen within the party, like Robert Ley, who were most keen on the use of 'modern' industrial social work as a means of creating a motivated, 'rationalised' and politically reliable workforce in preparation for war. By contrast, big companies like Siemens continued to lay greater emphasis on providing their employees with material benefits in the form of cheap housing, medical care and schools – partly because they often viewed today's children as tomorrow's potential employees and therefore believed they had an important stake in their upbringing.[17] Franz Seldte, the old Stahlhelm leader and now Reich Minister for Labour, was unable to resolve this dilemma. On the one hand, he argued, women workers were 'indispensabl:' to the Four Year Plan and needed to be more disciplined and more aware of the great national importance of their labour in the factories. And yet he also believed that female labour should be used only as an 'emergency measure', so that managers of industrial plants had an obligation 'first of all to check whether technical modifications might lead to savings in terms of the workforce'. Furthermore, in his view, 'women should only work when it can be demonstrated that there are no health risks either to themselves or to the *Volk* as a whole'.[18]

Nonetheless, in spite of the contradictory and confused nature of Nazi labour policies, and the ongoing battles over areas of competency between state-sponsored agencies like the DAF and private employers, the absolute number of women in all branches of industry rose continuously throughout the 1930s, from 1.21 million in 1933 to 1.85 million in 1938. These figures are only partly offset by an even more rapid rise in the number of men working in industry too (see Table 7).

Table 7 Women workers in all branches of German industry, 1933–1938

Year	Number of women industrial workers	1933 = 100	% of women in all branches of industry
1933	1,205,000	100.0	29.3%
1934	1,408,000	116.8	27.0%
1935	1,463,000	121.4	25.5%
1936	1,549,000	128.5	24.7%
1937	1,749,000	145.1	25.3%
1938	1,846,000	153.2	25.2%

Source: Dörte Winkler, 'Frauenarbeit versus Frauenideologie. Probleme der weiblichen Erwerbstätigkeit in Deutschland, 1930–1945, in: *Archiv für Sozialgeschichte* 17 (1977), p. 126.
Copyright © Verlag J. H. W. Dietz Nachfolger, Bonn.

Particularly striking was the increase in female employment in some of the more producer-oriented industries: from 13 per cent to 19 per cent in iron, steel and engineering, for instance, and from 12 per cent to 29 per cent in the electro-technical industry.[19] However, for the most part women working on the shop floor were required to undertake monotonous 'gender-suitable' tasks at the assembly line and few ever made it into positions of responsibility or trust within the production process.[20] Other industries, like textiles, clothing and food processing, continued to rely heavily on women in unskilled positions, where they were paid, on average, somewhere between 25 per cent and 40 per cent less than men in equivalent positions.[21] The 1930s also saw a big increase in the number of women working in various kinds of clerical and white-collar jobs – from 1.6 million in 1933 to 1.9 million in 1939 – and wages in this sector were often closer to those of men.[22] Even so, women were not expected to establish a career out of such jobs, and they were generally still seen as a temporary break between school and marriage. As a result, opportunities for promotion into higher-salaried positions were rare.[23]

Overall, the number of women working in the wage economy in Germany increased from 11.5 million in June 1933 to 13.8 million in May 1939, and the number of married women in paid employment grew even faster, from 4.5 million to 6.4 million.[24] These statistics should be treated with some degree of caution, however. For one thing, the 1939 census figures refer not to the 'old Reich' of 1933 but to the new Greater German Reich – a territory somewhat enlarged by the incorporation of the Saar industrial region, Austria, the Sudetenland and Bohemia/Moravia into the 'old Reich'. In other ways, too, the increase in female employment was more apparent than real. For instance, in 1939, while over 90 per cent of all single women were in some kind of employment, two-thirds of married women of working age remained outside the workforce, indicating a relative (but by no means absolute) failure to mobilise female labour in the run-up to war.[25] Part of the reason for this, as Ulrich Herbert argues, is that the very notion of women as factory workers was still unpopular with both sexes in the 1930s.[26] Rising wages for skilled male workers also meant that many couples could now afford to survive on one pay packet only, particularly if they were also eligible for the marriage loan. Caution and restraint were necessary, as the Nazi authorities were well aware, especially as recruiting more women into the armaments sector could also lead to a shortage of labour in the consumer industries and to a corresponding rise in consumer prices, which could impact badly on the regime's popularity among the urban population.[27] This problem was compounded by the fact that the government and Nazi women's organisations were already doing their best to dampen consumer spending, especially on foreign imports, in order to serve the interests of the national economy.[28]

Nonetheless, an equally important factor in the failure to get more married women into work was structural: to put it quite simply, many married women were too busy acting as unpaid housewives and assistants in family businesses to consider taking on the additional burden of paid employment outside the home. The DAF was only partly successful in its efforts to persuade employers to take a more responsible attitude towards women workers, and even paternalistic firms like Siemens admitted that their own in-house plant welfare systems were incapable of boosting the number of married female employees in the long run because of the 'growing difficulty in placing children in day care centres or nurseries'.[29]

Furthermore, different parts of Germany were affected by changes in the economy in different ways, and much depended on regional as well as national factors. In agriculture, for instance, wages lagged well behind those paid in industry, and as a result thousands of farm labourers moved to the cities each year in search of better jobs and a higher standard of living. Already in 1933 a survey revealed that 84 per cent of the work on Bavarian farms was done by the farmer and his immediate family, and this figure must have risen as the labour shortages in the countryside reached crisis levels in the late 1930s.[30] By 1938 it was estimated that there was a shortfall of a quarter of a million agricultural labourers throughout the Reich, which in turn meant that many small and medium-sized farms were forced to rely to an even greater degree than usual on unpaid family members as their sole source of labour.[31] Other studies laid bare the disastrous impact of overwork and low wages on the health of rural women. One village in Saxony reported that over a quarter of pregnancies ended in miscarriage, while in Pomerania the opening of a paper factory attracted a large number of women labourers who were desperate to escape the burden of farmwork.[32]

In the meantime, while the DAF made ever greater efforts to improve conditions for women factory workers, the opposite was happening to women in agriculture. Increasingly they were seen as housewives and consumers rather than producers, even though they often worked for 16 hours a day and were involved in managing the tasks of milking cows, feeding poultry and collecting eggs, looking after kitchen gardens, baking bread, making cheese and so on, as well as in marketing their produce and purchasing animal feed and other vital resources. The women's section of the *Reichsnährstand* and the Vw/Hw section of the DFW both addressed women as housewives first and foremost, with discussion of ways to reduce the enormous burden of work they were also expected to carry outside the home. Not surprisingly, given all these difficulties, the proportion of women willing to stay and work in agriculture fell steadily throughout the 1930s. Indeed, such was the aversion to working on the land that from the end of 1938 both the Reich Agricultural Ministry and the *NS-Frauenschaft* were forced to issue regular appeals to young women not to migrate to the cities and leave their families in the lurch, especially at harvest time.[33]

The desperate conditions in the countryside by 1938–39 also had a knock-on effect on another area where women were traditionally the main source of labour: domestic service and ancillary housework. Nazi ideology had generally praised domestic service as a suitable occupation for young women between school and marriage, helping to create a new generation of obedient housewives willing and able to devote their lives to the care of their husbands and children. Indeed, by 1939 there were 1.5 million domestic servants in Germany, up from 1.2 million in 1933. Nearly all of them were female, and two-thirds were aged between 14 and 25, the ideal age range for this profession, as far as the Nazis were concerned.[34] Nonetheless, difficulties remained. The Nuremberg laws of 1935, for instance, forbade German maids of under 45 years of age from working in Jewish households, which meant temporary unemployment for some.[35] By the late 1930s, on the other hand, different kinds of pressures began to appear as domestic maids, like agricultural workers, were attracted into industrial jobs by the higher wages and better working conditions. For the rural economy, the loss of female helpers and domestic staff could be disastrous, increasing the burden on farmers and their wives to an even greater extent. For the Nazis, too, this was a cause for concern, not only because a healthy rural sector was vital to German success in the coming war, but also because the growth in the number of young women working in industry was also perceived to be having a negative effect on racial and population policy. Indeed, at the end of 1937 the government insisted that in spite of labour shortages, teenage girls leaving school should not be encouraged to go straight into factory work. Rather, they should first be given some kind of practical training and experience within the general field of domestic science so that they would not be lost forever to the 'biological task' of motherhood.[36]

The contradictory nature of Nazi labour policy can also be seen in the announcement of a year of duty (*Pflichtjahr*) in agriculture or housework for all single women under 25 who wished to go on to work in industry or in office jobs of various kinds.[37] The *Pflichtjahr* (to be distinguished from other labour service programmes discussed in Chapter 5) came into force in February 1938 and was amended 10 months later to broaden its scope to a greater number of women. Figures produced by the Reich statistical office indicate that between February and July 1938, 77,400 girls were registered to start their *Pflichtjahr*, and a year later the numbers had risen to 217,000.[38] Nonetheless, whether this scheme actually helped to ease the labour shortages in the countryside or to release more married women over 25 for work in factories is difficult to say; certainly some of the girls were seen more as a hindrance than an asset by their employers, especially if they had no previous experience of farming or childcare. In most cases, too, the girls were probably quite glad when their period of service was over and they could at last apply for better-paid and less onerous jobs in commerce, banking and industry.[39]

In general, the first attempts to use compulsion to make young single women work in areas deemed 'suitable' by the government were a failure;[40] and when war broke out in 1939 there was still no coherent strategy for mobilising female labour in the service of the German war effort. In fact, the government rejected all further proposals for the conscription of able-bodied women, even in the spring of 1940 when a rise in military-led demand revealed labour shortages in key industries essential to the war effort. Instead, government agencies of various kinds were planning to tap into another source of manpower: foreign labour drafted in from the areas of Europe that were now expected to fall beneath the overwhelming superiority of the Wehrmacht.[41]

2. Women and the wartime labour force

In Germany during the First World War, hundreds of thousands of women had worked in munitions factories and other areas of the industrial economy traditionally dominated by men.[42] By 1939, many people expected this practice to be repeated, perhaps on an even larger scale. The *Völkischer Beobachter*, for instance, warned in March 1939 that:

The concept of 'total war' ... demand[s] a broadening of the previous limits on women's participation in home defence. The deployment of experienced women workers can no longer be restricted to welfare work, red cross activities, air raid protection and simple office duties. A greater portion of them will have to be redirected into war industries, in particular into the armaments industry in a narrower sense, in order to replace men conscripted into the forces.[43]

Surprisingly, however, one of the consequences of the outbreak of war in September 1939 was not a sudden increase in female employment, but rather a slight decrease as half a million women withdrew from the labour market between May 1939 and May 1941. Even in 1942, according to Ulrich Herbert, the number of women working was still down on pre-war levels.[44] One of the reasons for this was that, as during the first two years of the First World War, there was a substantial loss of jobs in female-dominated industries like textiles and footwear, which were increasingly denied access to raw materials and spare parts for machinery in order to meet the priorities of armaments production.[45] Another reason was that the Nazi regime was reluctant to use coercion of any kind against married women whose husbands were serving in the Wehrmacht, for fear that this would undermine morale at the front.[46] Indeed, as early as 24 September 1939, an article in the *Berliner Lokal-Anzeiger* went to some length to reassure the population that the 'additional mobilisation ... of women who are not currently in work will not be necessary in the present war'. This was because 'the labour shortages which appeared at the beginning of the war are beginning to fade away since our rapid victory over Poland' and 'furthermore the adaptation to the demands of the war economy has led to a corresponding reduction of [the workforce in] non-essential industries'.[47] Labour shortages, in other words, would be dealt with partly by hiring foreigners and partly by transferring existing factory workers from civilian industries into munitions plants and other types of war-related production. In this way, approximately 250,000 women had been drafted into jobs in the armaments sector by June 1940, a surprisingly low figure for an economy of Germany's size and strength.[48]

In the meantime, it was women working in agriculture rather than industry who were most affected by the outbreak of war. In many areas of the countryside women were left behind to cope with the running of the family farm or small business while their husbands and grown-up sons were conscripted into the army. If they were lucky, they might receive a contingent of inexperienced land service girls or Polish agricultural workers to help them; otherwise they were on their own.[49] One woman, whose husband had been called up at the beginning of the war, wrote a letter to the deputy Führer's office in February 1940 pleading for him to be released from military service so that he could come home and rescue the dwindling fortunes of their farm:

I have two small children... After caring for them and doing the housework I have little time left, even with the best will in the world, to manage the family business. My father-in-law is 75 years old and therefore in no position to carry out the work previously done by my husband ... I regard it as my duty to report that the presence of my husband is absolutely necessary if one places value on the undiminished productivity of this farm ... I cannot imagine that it is the will of the Führer that vital businesses like ours should go to the wall simply for lack of sufficient manpower.[50]

As the war dragged on, the problems facing the rural economy were compounded by dwindling resources and the widespread requisitioning of grain, fats, dairy products, tractors, fuel and draught animals by the army. Occasionally help and advice were on offer from the local party office or the local branch of the *Reichsnährstand*, but not enough to compensate for the absence of a husband or the loss of experienced male staff to the Wehrmacht, which often led smaller farms and businesses to close.[51] Not surprisingly, by 1943 some farmers had ceased to cooperate with the authorities altogether, instead taking to hoarding food or distributing it through black market contacts. One security police, or SD, report from April 1943, for instance, noted an alarming growth in discontent in the rural areas of Lower Franconia, Bavaria:

... the general opinion is that they [the authorities] are playing fast and loose with the peasants. The local peasant leaders, mayors etc. are in a dreadful position ... Things have already gone so far that people make no secret of saying: 'it's immaterial to us what happens. If we get another government, we'll back it. Things can't get any worse'.[52]

At first, women working in urban occupations fared slightly better than their agricultural counterparts. The war generated a huge demand for female administrators of various kinds, not to mention thousands of new and quite well-paid posts in public transport, the postal service, the telephone exchanges, social work, child protection work, and so forth. All of these jobs were considered to be preferable to working on the assembly line in munitions plants, which added to the labour shortage problem. Partly in response to this, the women's section of the DAF made renewed efforts to improve working conditions for its members, including putting pressure on employers to set up more crèches for working mothers or offer part-time or flexible hours. In 1940 the DAF also announced the creation of a series of holiday homes where female munitions workers could relax and unwind for periods of up to two weeks. As an article in the *Berliner Lokal-Anzeiger* explained:

The operation of this scheme has been made possible at least in part by the requirement that all women students, by the time they have reached their fourth semester, are obliged to have completed at least one three-week stint as an unpaid factory assistant, so that the factory can continue to pay the wages of those workers who are given leave. Thanks to this measure at least 6,000 women have been able to take some form of holiday in the last year [1940].[53]

Initiatives like this were also strongly backed by the Wehrmacht and the Luftwaffe, since they offered a cheap and easy means of raising the morale of civilian women working for the armed forces while circumventing the pressure for higher wages. Keeping the workers happy remained a top priority, particularly as this was also considered to have an effect on productivity.[54]

Finally, in May 1942, after a period of intense lobbying from the DAF, the authorities agreed to pass a new 'Law for the Protection of Mothers in Gainful Employment', which built on existing factory legislation dating back to 1927 and went some way towards meeting the concerns raised by women workers themselves. For instance, the new law tightened up the regulations concerning the employment of expectant and breast-feeding mothers, including an all-out ban on overtime, night work and work during official holidays. It also called for a 'birth allowance' to be paid during the last six weeks before and the first six weeks after birth at a rate amounting to the average earnings of the previous 13 weeks. Last but not least, the Reich Labour minister, Seldte, was empowered to ensure that

> ... plants and offices ... contribute to the cost of crèches [built by] the National Socialist Welfare Organisation or [by] local government ... Where such crèches are not available or are not being established the Reich Labour Minister can also insist that crèches (cribs, kinder- gartens, or crèches) are established and maintained by the plants and offices.[55]

In spite of these additional welfare measures, however, the DAF's efforts to recruit more women into the factory labour force remained largely unsuccessful. Indeed, the size of the female workforce in Germany remained around the 14 million mark for much of the war and even in September 1944 stood at less than 14.9 million. In the same period the number of women in industry actually fell, from 3.8 million to 3.6 million (see Table 8).

Various explanations have been put forward for this. One of these was material: generous allowances for soldiers' wives and war widows, which in some cases amounted to 85 per cent of their husbands' former wages, dis- couraged many married women from seeking employment outside the home, especially if poorly paid shift work in factories was all that was on offer.[56] Another was ideological: Hitler was reluctant to conscript married women for 'biological reasons' and therefore resisted pressure from various

Table 8 The employment of 'Aryan' women in wartime Germany, 1939–1944
(in thousands)

Date	Agriculture	Industry, crafts, energy	Commerce, banking, insurance, transport	Domestic service	Administrative, clerical	Total
May 1939	6,049	3,836	2,227	1,560	954	14,626
May 1940	5,689	3,650	2,183	1,517	1,151	14,386
May 1941	5,369	3,677	2,167	1,473	1,284	14,167
May 1942	5,673	3,537	2,225	1,410	1,471	14,437
May 1943	5,665	3,740	2,320	1,362	1,719	14,806
May 1944	5,694	3,592	2,219	1,301	1,746	14,808
Sept. 1944	5,756	3,636	2,193	1,287	1,748	14,897

Source: Dörte Winkler, 'Frauenarbeit versus Frauenideologie. Probleme der weiblichen Erwerbstätigkeit in Deutschland, 1930–1945', in: *Archiv für Sozialgeschichte* 17 (1977), p. 126. Copyright © Verlag J. H. W. Dietz Nachfolger, Bonn.

quarters – from the DAF, from the armed forces and from Albert Speer and Fritz Sauckel, Minister for Armaments and Plenipotentiary for Labour respectively – to take a tougher line on the mobilisation of women.[57]

Neither of these explanations is entirely adequate, however. At the very least Hitler's ideological objections were compounded by his fear of producing a negative reaction among the middle classes if better-off women, including housewives and students, were forced into low-paid and 'degrading' factory work. Furthermore, as Tim Mason has persuasively argued, the Nazi leadership was ever mindful of the situation in Germany during the First World War, when striking women munitions workers had contributed greatly to the spread of anti-war feeling and the collapse of morale on the home front.[58] For all of these reasons, Hitler agreed to the conscription of women up to the age of 45 only in January 1943, and even then there were so many categories of exemption, on medical and other grounds, that few women were obliged to report for labour service if they really did not want to. In particular, as Martin Kitchen argues, 'the wives and daughters of prominent Nazis were noticeably unwilling to sacrifice any of their privileges and continued to lead lives of idle comfort [even after 1943]', a cause of much understandable resentment among ordinary working-class women.[59]

However, perhaps the most important reason for the failure to mobilise German women for war work was that the armaments firms themselves did not press too hard for extra female staff because they found it easier and cheaper to hire foreign workers instead. Indeed, foreign workers from Poland and the USSR could not only be made to work longer hours for less pay, but they were also exempt from the welfare legislation enacted by the German government in 1942. If they fell pregnant, for instance, they could be sent home or compelled to abort their babies; there was no question of giving them paid maternity leave or allowing them time out for breast feeding. If they were lax or ill-disciplined at work they could be dismissed without notice or even handed over to the Gestapo or SS for 're-education' in special punishment camps (*Polizeihaftlager* or *Arbeitserziehungslager*).[60] Certainly there would be less scope for problems with go-slows and absenteeism, especially if internal guards were allowed to operate on the shop floor and food rations were linked to performance, as they often were. Indeed, as Ulrich Herbert discovered, in many armaments plants managers achieved higher productivity rates among foreign workers 'solely by [offering] bonuses of extra food'.[61]

Unfortunately, as the war went on, the economic interests of the armaments industry coincided with the ideological priorities of the regime, which had become anxious to spare middle-class 'Aryan' women factory work while showing no concern whatsoever for the health and safety of foreign workers, especially those from the east. The organisation of armaments production, in other words, became a race issue as much as it was a gender or class issue, as we shall also see below.

3. Jewish women and forced labour

Beginning in the autumn of 1939, hundreds of thousands of Polish civilians were brought into the Greater German Reich in order to make good the acute labour shortages in German agriculture and industry caused by the outbreak of war. From July 1940 French workers and POWs also arrived in Germany in large numbers, and Russians and Ukrainians followed in the second half of 1941. On 9 June 1941, Victor Klemperer noted in his diary that a Dresden housewife sitting opposite him in a café had complained openly about the fact that her husband had been called up while at the same time there were 'nothing but foreigners running around the streets, Belgians, Italians, Serbs in the armaments factories ...'.[62] Evidence from security police reports indicates that this was a common cause of resentment among married women as the war continued.[63]

Before going on to look further at the treatment of the millions of forced labourers recruited from occupied countries during the war, however, it is first necessary to consider the plight of those German-Jewish women and men who were also compelled to register for war work in the early stages of the war. This, too, is an important, if little understood, aspect of the Nazi persecution of the Jews in Germany, forming the immediate background to the mass arrests and deportations of the early 1940s.[64] It also tells us much about the regime's attitude towards Jewish women in particular, for they too were now increasingly exposed to violence and physical intimidation, sometimes even replacing Jewish men as the main targets of Nazi brutality.[65]

Plans for the exploitation of Jewish forced labour had already been laid before the war in several important discussions between government departments and economic agencies, and were put into effect soon after the

German invasion of Poland in September 1939. Thus on 26 October 1939 the Reich Minister of the Interior gave his approval to measures 'for the deployment of Jews in communal factories and on building sites', and the Reich Minister of Labour agreed to the drafting of Jewish workers into armaments factories provided that they were clearly 'segregated from the rest of the workforce'.[66] By 1940 columns of forced Jewish labourers marching to work on building sites or shovelling snow in the streets was a common sight in many of Germany's cities. Nazi propaganda presented this as a further 'punishment' of the Jews for having allegedly started the war, although a *Sopade* report from Berlin presented a different picture of the reactions of 'ordinary' Germans:

> The sight of 'Jewish work battalions' being forced to shovel snow has not helped to raise the public mood here. These emaciated figures are enough to move a dog to pity. Jewish forced workers aged between 16 and 60 years are being used to carry out the heaviest tasks, such as building roads, unloading freight trains etc. There are many intellectuals among them, doctors, lawyers, writers.[67]

In March 1941 the Nazis went on to order that all Jews in the Reich, regardless of gender and with the exception only of those under 15 and over 65, should register for work.[68] Henceforth, Jewish forced labour was exploited to the full; even the 61-year-old former university professor Victor Klemperer, who was married to an 'Aryan', was obliged to report for 'labour duty' in 1942, and in the winter of 1944–45 there were also cases of half-Jews and 'Aryan' men married to Jewish women being drafted into compulsory war work.[69] Furthermore, in October 1941 the government decreed that Jews were to be denied all the rights and privileges afforded to 'Aryan' workers. In particular, they received the lowest pay, worked the longest hours, and had to pay the highest taxes. They could also be bullied and dismissed without notice by their 'Aryan' supervisors, a grave threat given that deportations of Jews to the East had already begun in the autumn of 1941 and continued at regular intervals almost until the end of the war.[70]

In respect to forced labour, the treatment of Jewish women now also differed little from the treatment of Jewish men. This in itself is significant, because before 1939 and even up until the early part of 1941 many Jews in Germany continued to believe (or hope) that in spite of the violence and hatred directed towards Jewish men, the Nazis would respect traditional social conventions and therefore do no harm to Jewish women and children.[71] In fact, things had now changed and conditions were gradually emerging in which it would be possible to contemplate first the physical maltreatment and ultimately the murder of women, children and the elderly as well as able-bodied men. No Jew, for instance, could expect to work in a safe environment and many were exposed to both verbal and physical abuse in the workplace. During night-time air raids (which frequently targeted munitions factories) they were often the last to be admitted into the underground shelters and had to wait until all 'Aryan' employees were accounted for. Husbands and wives naturally lived with the constant fear that their loved ones would not return home at the end of a night shift.[72]

The 19-year-old Inge Deutschkron, who worked briefly in the spring of 1941 at I. G. Farben's Lichtenberg plant in Berlin making parachutes for the army, remembered that Jewish women had to wear a yellow star to identify themselves on the shop floor long before this measure was formerly introduced for all Jews in Germany in September 1941. Furthermore, Jewish forced labourers were kept strictly segregated from the other women, being barred from using the staff toilets and canteen. On average the Jewish women at I.G. Farben had to work for at least 10 hours a day, often without a break and in an environment that was excruciatingly hot. Being absent from work was highly dangerous, as was seeking exemption from forced labour on medical grounds. Inge herself was lucky: she managed to get a sick note that allowed her to change jobs and work for a much more friendly employer, but not before the doctor at I. G. Farben had subjected her to a humiliating and unnecessary medical examination in order to satisfy his own perverse pleasures.[73]

Another account is offered by the then 50-year-old Else Behren-Rosenfeld from Munich, who held a doctorate in history and had previously worked as a teacher and academic. In 1941 she was forced to report for labour service in a flax factory in Lohof, despite being paralysed in one arm since birth. As she recorded in her diary:

> The work in the factory at Lohof was pretty hard ... The pulling straight and smoothing over of the fairly heavy bundles of flax required the strength of two arms and cannot be managed using just one. After a mere three-and-a-half days of doing this I began to feel regular pains in my nerve-endings, pains which returned after each period of over-exertion.[74]

In stark contrast to this, in 1942 Hitler personally intervened to ensure that German housewives who volunteered for war work would be given comfortable office and administrative jobs, thus saving them from the dangers of 'harsh treatment, molestation, common insults and moral outrage'.[75] In November 1943 the Nazi leader also rejected a proposal that German women between 45 and 50 should be made liable for labour conscription. This, he argued, would 'seriously affect the[ir ability to take] care of their husbands, some of whom are engaged in heavy manual work, so that whatever would be gained from the women in terms of a new labour service would be lost again through the depletion of the men's labour'.[76]

Of course, no such considerations were shown in the case of Jewish women or their husbands. On the contrary, forced labour meant that 'normal' family life for Jews was disrupted beyond all measure. Spouses working on different shifts, for instance, often found that they did not see each other for days on end. After work, women also had to attend to the extra duties of shopping, cooking, laundering and housekeeping, as well as looking after children or elderly relatives. Additional worries were caused by frequent Gestapo house searches, the step-by-step reduction of food rations for Jews, the removal of the right to use public transport except while travelling to work, and the forced relocation of Jews into overcrowded 'Jew houses' in order to separate them even further from the rest of German society. Finally, from October 1941, there were the deportations of Jews to the east, each wave of arrests bringing in its wake a rash of suicides among those who preferred to choose their own manner of death rather than place themselves at the mercy of the Gestapo. Camilla Neumann, for instance, recalled that amid all the confusion and anxiety she barely had any time left for a normal conversation with her husband, let alone a chance to enjoy the ordinary pleasures of life:

> ... from [the spring of 1942] we did not have a single happy moment. One transport after another left for Poland and there was always one of our friends on it, and little by little it also leaked out what awaited us there. The mass executions could not be kept secret in the long run. Above all, one already saw the bestial way in which the deportations took place in open cattle or freight cars, with a bucket for relieving oneself. No food. One awaited each new day with great anxiety. 'Who will it be this time?' was the fearful question. The sword of Damocles hung above us constantly, and that demanded all of our spiritual, emotional and physical strength.[77]

Eventually, Camilla's husband was arrested at his place of work and deported to Auschwitz during the notorious 'factory action' of 27 February 1943, which was intended to eliminate all those Jews still working in the armaments industry in Berlin (they were replaced by forced labour from occupied countries). She herself went underground and managed to survive, first by hiding with non-Jewish friends and later by obtaining false papers that allowed her to work on an agricultural estate on the edge of Berlin. In this way, she kept herself alive and fed until the liberation of 1945.[78] Camilla was one of the lucky few, however. At the beginning of 1943, to take another example, 293 Jewish women and men were still working at the Zeiss-Ikon plant in Dresden, making fuses for the German navy. They represented the last surviving members of the Dresden Jewish community, apart from one or two full Jews who were protected through marriage to 'Aryans'. All of the Zeiss-Ikon workers were deported to Auschwitz on 2 March, where most were gassed on arrival. Of the 50 or so who were selected as fit to enter the camp, only 10 were still alive in 1945, seven men and three women.[79]

4. Civilian deportees, prisoners of war, concentration camp inmates

While the last remaining members of the Jewish community in Germany were being rounded up and sent to their deaths in Poland, large numbers of foreigners, both civilians and POWs, were brought into Germany to work in armaments factories or on the land. Indeed, by August 1944 a total of 5,976,673 civilians from all over Europe had been deported to the Third Reich as forced labourers, among them nearly 2 million women, most of them from the east (see Table 9).

Table 9 Male and female civilian foreign workers in Germany according to nationality, 30 September 1944

	Men	Women	Total	% of women	% of all foreign workers
Belgium	170,058	29,379	199,437	14.7	3.4
France	603,767	42,654	646,421	6.6	10.8
Italy	265,030	22,317	287,347	7.7	4.8
Yugoslavia/Croatia	294,222	30,768	324,954	9.5	1.6
Netherlands	233,591	20,953	254,544	8.2	4.3
Slovakia	20,857	16,693	37,550	44.4	0.6
Hungary	17,206	7,057	24,263	3.0	0.4
Soviet Union	1,062,507	1,112,137	2,174,644	51.1	36.4
Poland	1,115,321	586,091	1,701,412	34.4	18.5

Source: Ulrich Herbert, *Hitler's Foreign Workers. Enforced Foreign Labor in Germany under the Third Reich* (Cambridge, 1997), p. 462.
Copyright © Cambridge University Press, Cambridge.

Conditions for civilian deportees and migrant workers varied widely, depending on local circumstances, but in general they were tough. French workers were valued as skilled factory labour and were often treated better than Italian workers – as Mussolini complained. Dutch, Flemish, Danish and Norwegian workers were also granted superior living conditions because of their alleged racial affinities with the Germans; like the French, they were paid at roughly the same rates as German workers and at least in theory were entitled to benefits such as paid holidays, maternity care, pension and sickness contributions, and days off to attend marriages and funerals.[80] Sometimes, too, male civilian workers from western Europe were allowed to bring their wives with them to Germany, and to live in married quarters.[81] By contrast, deportees from Poland and the occupied parts of the Soviet Union were forced to work in conditions barely sufficient to keep them alive and with little consideration for their dignity as human beings. One 18-year-old French girl, for instance, who was recruited to work in Germany at the beginning of 1944 and was sent to a camp near Frankfurt-am-Main, described how her employers, I. G. Farben,

... organised [everything] so that we foreigners should be separated off from one another and not show solidarity with each other. Thus, for example, the western workers in the Free Work Camp were given [bed] sheets to make it clear that we were regarded as human beings. The eastern workers, on the other hand, only got straw and a blanket; they were considered to be sub-human. The food was also different. A French woman, for example, was not allowed to go into a canteen for eastern workers. When on one occasion I passed such a canteen I smelt a horrible smell. I went in and tried something on a plate; the food was bad, rotten. When I complained about this to the Germans, they forbade me to visit the eastern workers' canteen again. I did go again. Then they said: if you're so concerned about the people from the east why don't you go and work with them.[82]

The fact that women accounted for 58 per cent of all Polish and Soviet civilian workers by May 1944 was also no accident; they were reckoned to be more productive and more docile than men, and there was also less fear of rebellions among them.[83] Furthermore, Slavs were considered sub-human and therefore the 'normal' standards of civilised conduct did not apply to them. Slav women could be treated just as harshly as Slav men, without inciting protests from the German public and without damaging Germany's reputation in the eyes of western collaborationist governments. It was only from the occupied territories in the east, for instance, that the Nazis forcibly deported women and children for work in industry; those women workers coming from western countries were mostly 'volunteers'.[84]

Furthermore, Russian, Ukrainian and Polish women who fell pregnant while in Germany were treated far more harshly than their counterparts from the west. Maternity provision in Germany was minimal, and pregnant eastern workers were actually forbidden to return home under an order issued by Himmler in July 1943.[85] Earlier, in 1942, Hitler had already given his express approval (via Martin Bormann) to measures designed to allow women from the east to terminate unwanted pregnancies; the Third Reich, he argued, had 'no interest in an increase in the non-German population'. Accordingly, the legal penalties for abortion were removed first from Russian and then from Polish women, and rudimentary medical facilities were made available to them.[86] Meanwhile, from 1943, children of 'good racial stock' born to eastern workers were separated from their mothers and placed in special SS-Lebensborn homes to be raised as Germans. The remainder were sent to so-called 'nursing homes for foreign children', where most died from malnutrition and neglect. A report written by SS Gruppenführer Hilgenfeldt, head of the NSV, to Himmler in the summer of 1943 made clear his own observations after visiting one of these homes:

On the basis of a decision by the state Food Office, the home is allocated a daily ration of only 0.5 litres of full cream milk and 1.5

pieces of sugar for each baby. With these rations after a few months the babies will die of malnutrition. I was informed that there are differences of opinion about the babies' treatment. Some people believe that the children of the eastern female workers should die; others believe that they should be raised. Since a clear statement of policy has not yet emerged, and – as I was informed – it was desirable to maintain our reputation in the eyes of the female workers, the babies are given insufficient nourishment, as a result of which, as already said, after a few months they inevitably die.[87]

In practice, though, there was some variation in the treatment of eastern women who fell pregnant. Some were classified by the SS Race and Resettlement Office as *eindeutschungsfähig* (capable of Germanisation), usually on the basis of physical appearance or 'racial' characteristics alone, and were therefore allowed to keep their babies. Others were simply fortunate to find themselves at the mercy of sympathetic German bosses who were prepared to bend the rules in their favour. Ulrich Herbert, for instance, discovered a case where a German supervisor at a Krupp-owned factory in Essen 'himself delivered six pregnant Russian women as they lay on the desk in the guard room'. Furthermore, he allowed the babies to stay with their mothers in the camp and even procured extra food for them.[88] Likewise, Jill Stephenson found that in some rural parts of Germany, especially the Catholic areas of the south, opposition to abortion was still very strong and few people were willing to cooperate with the Nazi authorities on these matters. Occasionally, too, a local priest, midwife or doctor might persuade a German woman to raise a foreign worker's child as if it were her own, at least until after the war. This was especially likely to happen if the child's father was a German.[89]

Finally, the deployment of millions of foreign men and women in the German armaments sector inevitably brought with it a vast increase in organised prostitution and pimping, which was officially encouraged by the Nazi authorities in order, as they saw it, to prevent foreign civilian workers from lusting after German women. Indeed, by late 1943 there were an estimated 60 'foreign' brothels in Germany, served by some 600 prostitutes. Most of the latter were young eastern European women who were very vulnerable and were often exploited mercilessly by their pimps. Some were forced to work as prostitutes through threats of physical violence, while others were given 'incentives', which might simply mean extra food rations for themselves or their babies. Those who fell pregnant were in particular danger; if they were discovered by the German authorities they could be compelled to have an abortion or be sent to a concentration camp. Worse still, they might be murdered by their pimps or clients before the Germans even got to them.[90] Other Russian and Polish women were raped or forced into prostitution by their German employers or plant managers; in most cases, however, they were too afraid to report this to the authorities and therefore suffered in silence.[91]

Meanwhile, aside from civilian workers, a further 1.9 million POWs (all men) were deployed in the German armaments industry and on the land between 1942 and 1945, even though this was prohibited under international law, as were hundreds and thousands of concentration camp inmates of all nationalities and both sexes. In the latter case, compulsory labour was indistinguishable from the organised terror of the SS, who quite literally 'owned' the prisoners and hired them out at a daily rate to companies like Flick, Krupp and I. G. Farben. According to the post-war testimony of the former deputy chief of the economic office of the SS, Karl Sommer, the deployment of concentration camp prisoners in German industry began in the late summer of 1942, largely at the behest of the armaments ministry under Albert Speer:

> In total, at the height of the labour mobilisation, about 500,000 concentration camp inmates were sent to work in German industry. At this time (in the spring of 1943) a firm would pay a standard rate of 4 RM a day for an unskilled labourer and 6 RM a day for a skilled worker, the monies being paid into SS funds.[92]

Many of the concentration camps themselves developed satellite camps (*Außenlager*) close to quarries and industrial plants. The most important of these was the massive I. G. Farben slave labour complex (known as the 'Buna') at Auschwitz in Poland, but there were countless others operating on a smaller scale in Germany itself. Thus by April 1945 approximately 3,077 women were imprisoned at the main camp at Ravensbrück and an additional 1,514 were held in the auxiliary camps. In the last 10 months of the war two women's labour camps were in operation in the city of Hanover: the Brinker iron works in Langenhagen was home to around 500 female slave labourers and the Continental rubber works at Limme held 266 women prisoners. Forced labour camps for women were also set up at Radeburg in Saxony, Deutz in Cologne and Hägerwelle in Pomerania.[93]

In all the SS-run work camps female and male prisoners were kept strictly segregated, and opportunities to meet with friends and family were extremely rare. The types of work given to female prisoners were especially severe and ensured that women had an even lower survival rate than men. The wife of the former German communist Heinz Neumann, Margarete Buber-Neumann, was a victim of both Nazi and Stalinist terror (she was forcibly repatriated from the USSR to Germany in 1940 and sent immediately to the women's camp at Ravensbrück, having first been imprisoned by the Soviet authorities for three years). She recorded her experiences as follows:

> One of the most dreaded institutions in Ravensbrück was the 'labor mobilization'. Every day labor gangs were formed to work in munitions or other war-connected factories or in the construction of

airfields. Every prisoner hoped to stay in the main camp and to avoid being shipped to the annexes, in most of which the food was much worse.[94]

Other women, especially those who survived the women's labour camp at Auschwitz, remembered first and foremost not the cold, the lack of food or the long hours of work, but rather the deliberate destruction of their female identities. This could be seen, for instance, in the practice of removing all body hair from prisoners and tattooing them on the forearm or shoulder, a particular (and very symbolic) humiliation for women, which reinforced their status as slaves. Fania Fénelon, a French Jew and resistance fighter who was sent to Auschwitz in January 1944, described her feelings at the end of the initiation process:

> For me everything is over; now I understand: the slogans on the walls, which a woman from Alsace translated for me: 'The block is your home'; 'A louse is your death'; 'Work makes you free'. This all hit me like a blow to the empty stomach. I am nothing any more, I have no rights or legal protection; I am alone, abandoned, at the mercy of the executioner! I have reached the final station: Hell![95]

Likewise, Olga Lengyel spoke of the devastating effect on morale caused by tattooing: 'A tattooed woman felt that her life was finished; she was no longer anything but a number.'[96] Furthermore, a tattooed and shaven-headed woman was easier for a male guard to beat because he no longer saw her as a woman or human being but merely as a Jew and a prisoner with a number:

> He (the SS officer) gazed at my bare skull, grew angry and slapped my face as hard as he could. Then he reprimanded the guard, and ordered him to give me a few lashes with his whip. That was the first time I was beaten in the camp. Each blow cut my heart as it did my flesh.[97]

Ultimately, though, as Sybil Milton writes, the women at Auschwitz 'faced the same brutal camp regime that the male prisoners did', being required to work from dawn until dusk without adequate clothing, food or shelter, and to stand to attention at roll calls every morning and every evening.[98] All inmates, in other words, were under a sentence of death and in the long run gender-specific humiliations appeared less relevant against this single, terrifying fact. No matter how hard a prisoner worked, she or he was almost certain to die eventually, alone and in a horrible, painful and degrading way. As one survivor of the women's camp at Auschwitz put it:

> One cannot describe this feeling if one hasn't experienced it ... but for a while I felt as if I were completely sexless, without gender. I cannot explain it exactly, but I know that I no longer felt like a woman.[99]

This, of course, was the ultimate purpose of SS slave labour policy: to destroy Jewish women as Jews and as women, before murdering them. And yet those few who survived also somehow found a way of reasserting their identity as human beings and as women, in spite of everything.

Notes

1 For a recent example of this approach see Götz Aly, *Final Solution. Nazi Population Policy and the Murder of the European Jews* (London, 1999).
2 *Das ABC des Nationalsozialismus* (Berlin, 1933). Cited in Erich Kasberger, *Heldinnen waren wir keine. Frauenalltag in der NS-Zeit* (Munich, 1995), p. 99.
3 Richard Overy, *War and Economy in the Third Reich* (Oxford, 1994), p. 304.
4 Ibid., pp. 308–9.
5 See e.g. Dörte Winkler, *Frauenarbeit im 'Dritten Reich'* (Hamburg, 1977); Mason, 'Women in Germany', *passim*; Herbert, *Hitler's Foreign Workers*, *passim*. Also Mason's rebuff to Overy in *Social Policy in the Third Reich*, p. 350, n. 208.
6 Heineman, *What Difference Does a Husband Make?*, pp. 59–71.
7 Mason, *Social Policy in the Third Reich*, pp. 109–28.
8 Heineman, *What Difference Does a Husband Make?*, p. 40.
9 Ibid.
10 'Frauen in der Arbeitsfront', in: *Berliner Tageblatt*, no. 381, 16 August 1933. Copy in: FZH, no. 256.
11 Ibid.
12 Mason, 'Women in Germany', p. 178.
13 Cf. Noakes and Pridham (eds), *Nazism, 1919–1945*, Vol. 2, p. 462.
14 See e.g. 'Männerlohn für Frauenarbeit, in: *Der Angriff*, no. 244, 18 October 1937. Copy in: BA Berlin, RLB-Pressearchiv, no. 7978, Bl. 53. Also Winkler, *Frauenarbeit im 'Dritten Reich'*, pp. 74–7.
15 On this issue see the essay by Carola Sachse, *Industrial Housewives. Women's Social Work in the Factories of Nazi Germany*, introduced and edited by Jane Caplan (London, 1987).
16 Cf. Martin Kitchen, *Nazi Germany at War* (London, 1995), p. 151.
17 Sachse, *Industrial Housewives*, p. 43.
18 Franz Seldte, 'Frauenarbeit ist unentbehrlich', in: *Königsberger Allgemeine Zeitung*, no. 593, 23 December 1937. Copy in: BA Berlin, RLB-Pressearchiv, no. 7978, Bl. 40. The newspaper article is a summary of the arguments put forward in Seldte's book *Sozialpolitik im Dritten Reich* (Berlin, 1936).
19 Overy, *War and Economy in the Third Reich*, p. 304.
20 Cf. Tröger, 'The Creation of a Female Assembly-Line Proletariat', *passim*.
21 See the figures in Mason, *Social Policy in the Third Reich*, p. 236, n. 202.
22 Stephenson, *Women in Nazi Germany*, p. 61. Cf. Mason, 'Women in Germany', pp. 182–3.
23 Mason, 'Women in Germany', p. 182.
24 Figures in Pine, *Nazi Family Policy*, p. 21; and Winkler, *Frauenarbeit im 'Dritten Reich'*, p. 198.
25 Heineman, *What Difference Does a Husband Make?*, p. 40.
26 Herbert, *Hitler's Foreign Workers*, p. 40.
27 Ibid., p. 41. Cf. Mason, *Social Policy in the Third Reich*, pp. 198–201 and 248–9.
28 Reagin, '*Marktordnung* and autarkic Housekeeping', *passim*.

29 Sachse, *Industrial Housewives*, p. 61.
30 Kershaw, *Political Opinion and Political Dissent*, p. 34.
31 Figure of a quarter of a million in Kitchen, *Nazi Germany at War*, p. 153. On the impact of rural migration between 1933 and 1939 in general see also John E. Farquharson, *The Plough and the Swastika. The NSDAP and Agriculture in Germany, 1928–1945* (London, 1976), pp. 183–202.
32 Farquharson, *The Plough and the Swastika*, p. 188.
33 Ibid., p. 189. Cf. the article 'Die Reichsfrauenführerin spricht zu den Landfrauen', in: *Nationalsozialistische Landpost*, 10 June 1939. Copy in: BA Berlin, RLB-Pressearchiv, no. 7979, Bl. 31, and a further article written in the same vein in: *NS-Frauenwarte*, 8/2 (1939–40), pp. 34–5.
34 Stephenson, *Women in Nazi Germany*, p. 66.
35 Cf. Noakes and Pridham (eds), *Nazism, 1919–1945*, Vol. 2, p. 536.
36 Stephenson, *Women in Nazi Society*, p. 100.
37 See e.g. *Berliner Tageblatt*, no. 88, 22 February 1938 ('Weibliches Pflichtjahr eingeführt'). Copy in: BA Berlin, RLB-Pressearchiv, no. 7978, Bl. 59.
38 Heineman, *What Difference Does a Husband Make?*, p. 41.
39 Stephenson, *Women in Nazi Germany*, p. 106.
40 Cf. Mason, *Social Policy in the Third Reich*, p. 235.
41 Herbert, *Hitler's Foreign Workers*, p. 41.
42 Daniel, *The War From Within*, pp. 278–9; Bessel, *Germany After the First World War*, pp. 18–21.
43 'Die Frau in der Landesverteidigung', in: *Völkischer Beobachter*, no. 66, 7 March 1939. Copy in: BA–Berlin, RLB–Pressearchiv, no. 7978, Bl. 188.
44 Herbert, *Hitler's Foreign Workers*, p. 257.
45 Cf. Frevert, *Women in German History*, p. 155.
46 Mason, *Social Policy in the Third Reich*, p. 329.
47 'Fraueneinsatz in der Kriegswirtschaft, in: *Berliner Lokal-Anzeiger*, no. 229, 24 September 1939. Copy in: BA Berlin, RLB-Pressearchiv, no. 7979, Bl. 60.
48 Winkler, *Frauenarbeit im 'Dritten Reich'*, p. 89.
49 This theme is explored extensively in Jill Stephenson, '"Emancipation" and its Problems. War and Society in Württemberg, 1939–1945', in: *European History Quarterly* 17 (1987), pp. 345–65, esp. pp. 351–61.
50 Münkel, *Nationalsozialistische Agrarpolitik*, pp. 150–1.
51 Ibid., p. 446.
52 Kershaw, *Popular Opinion and Political Dissent*, p. 294.
53 'Probleme der Frauenarbeit im Kriege', in: *Berliner Lokal-Anzeiger*, no. 43, 19 February 1941. Copy in: BA Berlin, RLB–Pressearchiv, no. 7979, Bl. 149.
54 Cf. Kitchen, *Nazi Germany at War*, p. 149.
55 The full text of the law is reprinted in Jeremy Noakes (ed.), *Nazism, 1919–1945, Vol. 4: The German Home Front in World War II* (Exeter, 1998), pp. 336–8.
56 Winkler, 'Frauenarbeit', p. 113.
57 Noakes (ed.), *Nazism, 1919–1945*, Vol. 4, pp. 304–5.
58 Mason, *Social Policy in the Third Reich*, esp. pp. 19–40.
59 Kitchen, *Nazi Germany at War*, p. 143. Cf. the evidence in Noakes (ed.), *Nazism, 1919–1945*, Vol. 4, p. 333.
60 Milton, 'Women and the Holocaust', p. 310.
61 Herbert, *Hitler's Foreign Workers*, p. 324.
62 Klemperer, *I Shall Bear Witness*, p. 371 (diary entry for 9 June 1941).
63 See e.g. the evidence in Schneider (ed.), *Frauen unterm Hakenkreuz*, pp. 158ff.
64 See e.g. Dieter Maier, *Arbeitseinsatz und Deportation. Die Mitwirkung der Arbeitsverwaltung bei der nationalsozialistischen Judenverfolgung in den Jahren 1938–1945* (Berlin, 1994).
65 Cf. Bock, 'Racism and Sexism in Nazi Germany', *passim*.

66 Maier, *Arbeitseinsatz und Deportation*, pp. 52–4.
67 Ibid., p. 57.
68 Kaplan, *Between Dignity and Despair*, p. 174.
69 See Klemperer, *To the Bitter End. Diaries, 1942–1945* (London, 1999), esp. pp. 15–27 and 261ff.
70 Kaplan, *Between Dignity and Despair*, p. 174.
71 Cf. Milton, 'Women and the Holocaust', p. 300.
72 Kaplan, *Between Dignity and Despair*, pp. 174–5. Cf. Carola Sachse, 'Zwangsarbeit für die Firma Siemens, 1940–1945', in: Christl Wickert (ed.), *Frauen gegen die Diktatur – Widerstand und Verfolgung im nationalsozialistischen Deutschland* (Berlin, 1995), pp. 140–53.
73 Inge Deutschkron, *Ich trug den gelben Stern* (Munich, 1985), pp. 72–3.
74 Else Behren-Rosenfeld, *Ich stand nicht allein. Leben einer Jüdin in Deutschland, 1933–1944* (Munich, 1988), pp. 97ff. Cited in Kastenberger, *Heldinnen waren wir keine*, pp. 112–13.
75 Winkler, 'Frauenarbeit', p. 116.
76 Noakes (ed.), *Nazism, 1919–1945*, Vol. 4, p. 335.
77 Camilla Neumann (née Selinger), 'Report of my Experiences from the Time of Hitler' (1946). Reproduced in Richarz (ed.), *Jewish Life in Germany*, p. 439.
78 Ibid., pp. 443–8. On the 'factory action' see also Maier, *Arbeitseinsatz und Deportation*, pp. 174–80.
79 Klemperer, *To the Bitter End*, pp. xiii–iv and 248–50.
80 Kitchen, *Nazi Germany at War*, p. 168.
81 Ibid., p. 158.
82 Cited in Noakes (ed.), *Nazism, 1919–1945*, Vol. 4, p. 326.
83 Herbert, *Hitler's Foreign Workers*, p. 324.
84 Stephenson, *Women in Nazi Germany*, p. 122.
85 For further details see Noakes (ed.), *Nazism, 1919–1945*, Vol. 4, pp. 327–9.
86 Ibid., p. 330.
87 Ibid.
88 Herbert, *Hitler's Foreign Workers*, p. 235.
89 Stephenson, *Women in Nazi Germany*, p. 123.
90 Ibid., p. 124; Herbert, *Hitler's Foreign Workers*, pp. 131 and 220.
91 Gellately, *Backing Hitler*, pp. 157–8.
92 Sommer's report as reproduced in: Schneider (ed.), *Frauen unterm Hakenkreuz*, pp. 132–3.
93 Milton, 'Women and the Holocaust', pp. 310–11. See also the information contained in the Historisches Museum Hanover, Abteilung Stadtgeschichte, no. 8: Gauhauptstadt im Dritten Reich – KZ–Außenlager in Hannover.
94 Margarete Buber-Neumann, *Milena* (London, 1990), p. 196.
95 Fania Fénelon, *Das Mädchenorchester in Auschwitz* (Munich, 1981), p. 23.
96 Lengyel, *Five Chimneys*, p. 116.
97 Ibid., p. 32.
98 Milton, 'Women and the Holocaust', p. 310.
99 Cited in Stefanie Schüler-Springorum, 'Verfolgung und Widerstand jüdischer Frauen in Osteuropa, 1939–1945', in: Wickert (ed.), *Frauen gegen die Diktatur*, p. 164.

|5|

Education, youth, opportunity

Like many other fascist movements in inter-war Europe, the Nazis placed a great deal of emphasis on youth and education as the key to the future of the empire and the race. Indeed, as Jill Stephenson writes, 'the totalitarian pretensions of the ... party leadership are nowhere better illustrated than in the belief that the entire German people could be "educated" to a sense of service to the *Volk*, that mythical community whose sum was allegedly infinitely greater than its parts'.[1] German girls and boys were placed at the centre of this process, since they were held to be less wedded to the class prejudices and social snobbery of the 'outlived bourgeois world';[2] consequently they could be moulded into something new, an 'heroic' youth for 'heroic' times, and could be encouraged to challenge conventional figures of authority, such as school teachers, priests or even parents. Much of Nazi education policy proceeded on the basis of this assumption.[3]

Hitler had already described his ideal educational system in great detail in *Mein Kampf*. In line with his racial thinking and Social Darwinistic beliefs, the primary focus would be on physical training and selection of the fittest in preparation for the wars of the future. At the same time, all alleged traces of pacifism, humanitarianism and sympathy for the weak were to be removed from the curriculum, which would emphasise instead the development of 'character', 'will-power' and 'determination'.[4] Jews and Marxists would be immediately removed from positions of influence over German youth, and 'intellectualism' in general would be eradicated, along with what Hitler contemptuously referred to as the 'upper class etiquette' which had led to 'cowardly, wretched indecision' on the part of Germany's past leaders.[5] First and foremost, however, 'no boy and no girl must leave school without having been led to the ultimate realisation of the necessity and essence of blood purity' since 'all physical and intellectual training would ... remain worthless if it did not benefit a being which is ready and determined on principle to preserve himself and his special nature'.[6]

After coming to power Hitler developed and refined his views on education to some extent, but the essentials were still there. In particular he continued to emphasise the importance of the 'national community' above that of the individual, and the mobilisation of youth outside the classroom in the form of physical and military drill. For this reason, much of youth policy was taken out of the hands of the Prussian (and from 1934 Reich) Education Minister, Bernhard Rust, and handed over to the Hitler Youth leader Baldur von Schirach. The aim was to ensure that young people were fully immersed in an organised network of indoor and outdoor activities which would take up most of their waking hours and remove them from the potentially harmful, 'softening' influence of family and teachers. Or, as Hitler put it in a conversation with Hermann Rauschning, the National Socialist chairman of the Danzig Senate, in 1933:

> I want an athletic youth. This is the first and most important thing. That is how I will eradicate thousands of years of human domestication. I don't want them to have an intellectual education. Knowledge would spoil my young people. I prefer that they learn only what they pick up by following their own play instinct. But they must learn self-control. I will have them master the fear of death through the most difficult trials. That is the stage of heroic youth. Out of it will grow the stage of free man, a human being who is the measure and the centre of the world.[7]

The question nonetheless remains: How were these ideas to affect the education of girls and young women in particular? In many previous studies the answer has been that girls were to be educated for motherhood and domesticity, while boys were to be trained for militarism and war.[8] As we shall see, there is much truth in this. Hitler himself, for instance, argued repeatedly that the 'goal of female education must invariably be the future mother'.[9] However, it is also important to recognise that the division of education along gender lines was never as clear-cut as some historians believe, and in fact began to unravel as soon as Nazi ideology was confronted with the realities of preparing for war and meeting the specific needs of a modern industrial economy. Furthermore, the very nature of Nazi youth organisations and labour service schemes – which took girls as well as boys away from their parents, providing some with opportunities for leadership and control over other girls – was bound, sooner or later, to come into direct conflict with traditional ideas about motherhood and domesticity. This became increasingly obvious during the war, when education for motherhood was overtaken by pragmatism and girls were required to fulfil their obligations to the state by undertaking agricultural labour, caring for evacuees and wounded soldiers, working in armaments factories, and even being sent to provide assistance in homes and schools for ethnic Germans in the occupied territories of the east. Before examining this issue further, however, it is first necessary to take a closer look at the impact of Nazi education policy on opportunities for girls and young women in the 1930s.

1. Education and opportunity

At first glance the sphere of education seems to be the one area in which Nazi policy most closely approximated to conservative views of women's 'nature' and special responsibilities within the domestic sphere. True, in 1933 the Nazis had no coherent plan for education, and reforms to the Weimar system were therefore introduced slowly and in piecemeal fashion, with much infighting between different government and party agencies. Nonetheless, by 1937–38 the key elements of the National Socialist curriculum were in place, including the abandonment of the co-educational experiments previously favoured by Social Democrat-controlled municipal authorities, the rewriting of school textbooks in key disciplines like biology and history in order to reflect Nazi racial views, and the systematic downgrading of intellectual and abstract subjects for pupils of both sexes.[10] Jill Stephenson describes the new system as it came into force in 1938:

> Four years at elementary school [from age six] were followed by five general senior school years [age ten to 15] and three years of specialisation [age 15 to 18]. In the general years, the difference between boys' and girls' curricula was that boys studied Latin while girls had needlework and music. In the final three years, however, there was a major difference: girls had no opportunity to specialise in science subjects or mathematics. Instead, they could choose between foreign languages and homecraft, which included nursing, social work, household management and childcare.[11]

A further characteristic of this system was that women, at least in theory, had fewer opportunities to go into higher education, especially as the homecraft stream in the school curriculum did not qualify them for university entrance at all until 1941, and having to catch up on Latin was also a serious hurdle even for brighter girls in the foreign language stream. Indeed, the number of women university students fell from an all-time high of 18,375 in the summer semester of 1932 to a mere 6,080 in the summer semester of 1939, a drop of over two-thirds, leading one historian to comment that the National Socialists had 'set back the development of women's education in Germany by thirty years'.[12] In fact, though, the number of men entering universities was also drastically reduced in the mid-1930s as part of the government's proposed cure for high rates of graduate unemployment. Thus in December 1933 the government decreed an annual intake of no more than 15,000 students per year, with the proportion of women limited to 10 per cent (in 1931–32 women had made up 18.9 per cent of the total student body).[13] This was entirely in line with the Nazis' anti-intellectualism in general and should not be seen as a specifically anti-feminist measure. Indeed, in the long run, the real victims of the Nazi educational reforms were not women but Jewish academics and students of both sexes; by the late 1930s they had been largely excluded from the university sector and, unless they were able to emigrate, had no prospect of a professional career in front of them.[14] In November 1938 Jewish children were also expelled from state schools. Henceforth they were obliged to attend separate schools run by the Jewish community until these were also closed down in June 1942.[15]

In spite of this, there were relatively few complaints from teachers about Nazi reforms to the education system; and there may have been some support from within the profession for the anti-Semitic measures and the move away from academic elitism. Like doctors and lawyers, many teachers felt threatened by the insecure job market of the 1920s and 1930s, and may therefore have welcomed the removal of Jews, socialists and other potential rivals for the top positions. Indeed, as Jeremy Noakes and Geoffrey Pridham note, teachers were 'heavily represented in the Party as a whole and in its leadership corps', so that roughly 25 per cent of the profession were members of the NSDAP by the end of 1934, compared to only 10 per cent of the population as a whole by the outbreak of war.[16]

True, some teachers resented having to attend compulsory ideological training courses run by the National Socialist Teachers League (NSLB, or *Nationalsozialistischer Lehrerbund*), which often meant spending several days away from home each year.[17] In the Catholic areas of the state of Oldenburg in north Germany most teachers (as well as parents) supported the long and ultimately successful campaign to keep the crucifix on classroom walls against the anti-clerical designs of over-zealous regional party officials.[18] Others disliked the heavy demands that extracurricular activities like those of the Hitler Youth and the BDM made on schoolchildren's time, leading to the disruption of conventional classroom teaching and a drop in academic standards.[19] Nonetheless, this was to some extent countered by vigorous propaganda that emphasised the innovative aspects of the Nazi educational programme, the importance of physical fitness and practical training in household skills, and the need to overcome the class divisions inherent in the Weimar educational system. What may have been lost in terms of academic excellence was, it seemed, to be made up for in terms of greater national cohesion and solidarity.[20]

In direct contrast to the de-intellectualisation of the school curriculum and the barriers created to female university entrance, however, the Nazi state was itself generating demands for increasing numbers of highly educated women, particularly in the 'caring' professions such as teaching, nursing, medicine and social work as well as in organisations like the DFW, the NSV, the BDM and the DAF. This conflict was never fully resolved and reveals, once again, how inconsistent the Nazis could be when it came to the 'woman question'. Thus, while between 1933 and 1936 the Prussian/Reich Education Minister Rust continually sought to reduce the number of women school teachers by restricting access to teacher training courses and giving preference to male applicants, by 1937 he was forced into a U-turn because of a predicted shortfall of over 5,000 teachers per year.[21] By this time, however, the damage had been done and there were not enough female or male students to meet government targets, at least in the short term. To make matters worse, many women graduates were being drawn away from teaching – traditionally seen by the Nazis as one of the few middle-class occupations suitable for women – towards better-paid jobs in engineering, medicine, veterinary science, pharmacy and scientific research, all of which were crying out for qualified personnel.[22] In fact, the Four Year Plan and the drive for rearmament had created new opportunities for almost anyone with a university degree, unless, of course, they were Jewish. Only politics, the judiciary and the military were still barred to women, as the Nazi Women's Leader Gertrud Scholtz-Klink noted in a speech before a group of journalists in 1937: 'Otherwise in every other profession it is the question of ability that comes first, not gender difference.'[23]

The increased demand for women with professional skills and training can also be seen in the proportion of female students admitted to universities and other institutions of higher learning in Germany, which was always much higher than the official 10 per cent ceiling set in 1933. In fact, as early as 1935 Rust abolished the ceiling altogether and in 1941 he also made it easier for women who had followed the homecraft stream at school to secure university places.[24] Whether or not the Nazis ever intended to expand the number of women students in the long run, the immediate effect was striking: whereas at the end of 1939 there were still only 5,815 female students in German universities, in the first trimester of 1940 this figure had grown to 7,378, in the second trimester to 8,509 and in the third to 12,639.[25] By the summer of 1942, with the war in full swing and most young men conscripted into the Wehrmacht, it was reported that women now formed a clear majority of the students in three of the faculties at the University of Berlin: in foreign languages, arts and mathematics/natural sciences. Furthermore, while women still showed a clear preference for the arts and medicine, there had also been a notable influx of women into the natural science departments of several universities, including Göttingen, Giessen and Würzburg as well as Berlin. At Giessen women students in arts subjects were 'twice as numerous as men' and in Freiburg the number was 'five times that of men'. At Würzburg 'in some lecture halls there [are] only about two male students out of an audience of forty or fifty ...'.[26]

If a small but growing minority of the academically more able middle-class girls were now being encouraged to attend university and establish careers, much energy was spent in denying that this would mean a return to the decadent individualism of the 1920s. Girls were to be educated to serve the state and the 'national community', not so that they could compete with men for jobs – and still less so that they could fritter away their time at university by flirting with their male peers or by engaging in other frivolous pastimes.[27] Furthermore, too much emphasis on intellect was also frowned upon, and marriage and motherhood were still presented as the ideal fulfilment of a woman's destiny, even by the official body for women students, the ANSt (*Arbeitsgemeinschaft Nationalsozialistischer Studentinnen*), which closely monitored the behaviour of all its members for signs of political and moral laxity.[28] It was in order to counter these perceived dangers to the nation's youth that the Nazis also expanded organisations like the Hitler Youth and the Reich Labour Service scheme (*Reichsarbeitsdienst*) to the point where membership for both sexes became compulsory by the end of the 1930s.

2. The BDM – League of German Maidens

In the 1920s Germany was known throughout the world for its multitude of youth movements. Indeed, by 1933 between 5 and 6 million young Germans of both sexes belonged to one organised youth group or another. Some of these had direct political or denominational affiliations, whereas others were geared solely towards sport and gymnastics, and others still adhered to the idealistic but non-political outlook of the *Bünde* or free youth movement.[29] Within this diverse environment, the Hitler Youth movement for boys (*Hitlerjugend* – HJ) was established in 1926, and the League of German Maidens (*Bund deutscher Mädel* – BDM) was set up four years later, in 1930, as an amalgamation of a number of groups previously organised at local level.[30] Both movements, the HJ and the BDM, came under the direct control of the Reich Youth Leader, Schirach, who jealously guarded his empire against attempted encroachments from rival agencies, most notably the *NS-Frauenschaft* and the *Deutsches Frauenwerk*. From 1934 onwards, indeed, Scholtz-Klink was forced to watch from the sidelines and had no real influence over Nazi policy in the area of youth education, even when this affected her own work with women and families. Nonetheless, she was able to establish children's groups within the NSF for the under-10 age group.[31]

After 1933, membership of the HJ and the BDM was still voluntary, but from 1935 onwards there was increasing pressure to conform to the requirements of the new regime. Indeed, while the number of boys joining the HJ continued to rise steadily after 1935, the number of girls entering the BDM grew much more quickly, so that by the beginning of 1939 there were almost as many girls as boys within the entire Nazi youth movement. According to the Hitler Youth law of 1936, girls were to join the *Jungmädel* (JM) at age 10, and the BDM itself from age 14 to 18. At the same time, all non-Nazi youth groups – whether or not religious or political in nature – were either to be taken over by the HJ or dissolved, a move that caused particular problems in Catholic areas because Catholic youth groups had hitherto been protected by the 1933 Concordat between the Vatican and the Nazi regime. By the end of 1936, membership of the entire Hitler Youth (including the BDM and the JM) had climbed from 3.9 million to 5.4 million, and by March 1939, when membership was made compulsory for all German youth of 'Aryan' blood, it had risen to almost 7.3 million (see Table 10).

Table 10 Membership figures for the entire Hitler Youth Organisation, 1933–1939

Year	HJ (boys aged 14–18)	DJ (boys aged 10–14)	BDM (girls aged 14–18)	JM (girls aged 10–14)	Total
End 1932	55,365	28,691	19,244	4,656	107,956
End 1933	568,288	1,130,521	243,750	349,482	2,292,041
End 1934	786,000	1,457,304	471,944	862,317	3,577,565
End 1935	829,361	1,498,209	569,599	1,046,134	3,943,303
End 1936	1,168,734	1,785,424	873,127	1,610,316	5,437,601
End 1937	1,237,078	1,884,883	1,035,804	1,722,190	5,879,955
End 1938	1,663,305	2,064,538	1,448,264	1,855,119	7,031,226
Beginning 1939	1,723,886	2,137,594	1,502,571	1,923,419	7,287,470

Source: Jeremy Noakes and Geoffrey Pridham (eds.), *Nazism, 1919–1945. A Documentary Reader, Vol. 2: State, Economy and Society, 1933–1939* (new edn) (Exeter, 2000), p. 227. Copyright © University of Exeter Press, Exeter.

For many young girls, joining the BDM represented an act of rebellion against their parents and their school teachers. It enabled them to take part in out-of-school activities which, under the 'separate spheres' model of gender and education, were previously reserved for men and boys, such as physical training, competitive sports and military-style parades, as well as lessons in politics and racial awareness. Cleanliness and an orderly appearance were part of the requirement too.[32] There was indeed nothing passive or submissive about being in the BDM; girls, like boys, were required to become 'tough as leather, hard as Krupp steel, swift as greyhounds', and the use of cosmetics and feminine beauty products was strictly condemned as 'unGerman'.[33] The emphasis, as usual, was on the promotion of instinct over intellect, as well as the strict separation of the sexes, with girls being afforded 'different, but equal' treatment from their male counterparts. However, whereas this sometimes meant preparation for domestic and housewifely duties, greater attention was paid to the development of healthy bodies and minds which would be ready to serve the *Volk* in myriad ways, not just through having babies. As the *Völkischer Beobachter* put it in an article in March 1938:

> The times are finally gone when bourgeois prejudices grant to girls the dubious privilege of idleness. Certainly they should prepare themselves for their later roles as housewives and mothers. But they must combine this with a simultaneous or additional input of their labour into the *Volksgemeinschaft*. Of course, they cannot fulfil this obligation if they

lead a more or less useless existence as so-called 'house daughters' in their parents' or other people's homes for years on end.[34]

Membership of the HJ also offered new opportunities for social recognition, and training in leadership skills for both boys and girls. According to one estimate, by 1935 the BDM alone must have required some 33,000 leaders to continue functioning at all levels, ranging from the *Mädelschaft*, or team, (about 10 girls) to the *Schar*, or company (comprising four teams), right up to the sub-regional and regional divisions (*Untergaue* and *Obergaue*).[35] Jutta Rüdiger, who herself rose to become national organiser of the BDM at the age of 27, described the qualities needed to hold a position of responsibility over other girls:

> Character and the ability to perform, not useless knowledge, but an all-round education and an exemplary bearing are the distinguishing personality traits of the leader.[36]

Perhaps the most important aspect of the BDM, however, was the emphasis on comradeship between girls from different parts of Germany and from all social classes. According to Inge Scholl, members of the BDM 'sensed that there was a role for them in a historic process, in a movement that was transforming the mass into a *Volk*'.[37] Likewise, Renate Finkh, a former *Jungmädel* leader interviewed by Heike Mundzeck in the 1980s, remembered how some of her school friends were quite happy to develop their interests and talents within the home environment:

> ... however, I needed a group outside my parents' house, since there was nobody at home who really had any time for me. True, I also felt to some extent like an outsider even in the Hitler Youth, but slogans like: 'Jungmädel, the Führer needs you too!' affected me deeply. To be actually needed for a higher goal filled me with happiness and pride.[38]

There were problems here, too: for instance, the generational conflict that sometimes arose between parents and their daughters over membership of the BDM and participation in its activities, especially when this interfered with normal family life. Ilse Koehn remembered how her father, a socialist and half-Jew, 'looked at me as if I were a ghost, then yelled: "Join an organisation of those pigs?"' But later he calmed down and explained to her why he had been so angry.[39] Likewise, complaints were heard from teachers about lapses in discipline, disruption to school lessons and the alleged tendency of BDM leaders to belittle the authority of adults. Indeed, Gestapo records show that teachers were frequently denounced by their pupils for refusing to allow Nazi emblems to be hung in the classroom.[40] On the other hand, older girls, especially those who were beyond the school leaving age of 14, were sometimes put off by the youth movement's emphasis on military-style uniforms and outdoor pursuits. Instead they yearned for opportunities to express their femininity and to meet members of the opposite sex, normal teenage pastimes denied to them in the all-girl environment of the BDM.[41]

In spite of these obvious conflicts and tensions, however, most girls were happy to take part in the Hitler Youth movement, including even those who came from non-Nazi backgrounds or who were able to identify themselves as opponents of National Socialist ideology. It was only during the war, for instance, that alternative illegal youth movements began to emerge in some of the larger German cities, such as the Edelweiss pirates in Cologne and the Swing Youth in Hamburg, both of which openly defied Nazi conventions.[42] Before 1939, however, the Hitler Youth itself may have functioned as a kind of 'counter-authority', providing an outlet for young people to break out of the stuffy conventions of the past and express themselves in ways that had not been open to previous generations. This was especially the case, as Detlev Peukert argues, for those who lived in less populated rural areas; here the arrival of the BDM and the HJ often revolutionised the type and scope of leisure activities available to young people.[43]

Parents, too, were reassured by Nazi propaganda films such as *Der Stammbaum des Dr. Pistorius* (Dr Pistorius's Family Tree, 1939) which told the story of a family coming to terms with and even welcoming the involvement of its younger members in the Hitler Youth movement.[44] Horror stories, for instance of daughters returning home from BDM camps pregnant or with sexually transmitted diseases, circulated in private, but were rarely discussed in public. Even so, sexist jokes were often told by men about BDM girls. The initials 'BDM' were thus said to stand for *Bund deutscher Milchkühe* (League of German Milk Cows), *Baldur Drück mir* (Baldur [von Schirach] take me) or *Bald Deutsche Mütter* (German mothers-to-be), although in reality preparation for marriage and motherhood was surprisingly low on the list of priorities for the BDM.[45]

3. Labour service schemes

In the meantime an even more total and all-encompassing experience for young women than the BDM was provided by the various residential labour service schemes run by organisations like the Reich Education Ministry, the *Reichsnährstand*, the NSF, the Land Year programme, the women's section of the Reich Labour Service (*Reichsarbeitsdienst der weiblichen Jugend*, or RADwJ) and the ANSt. Although there were sometimes differences in detail, the basic pattern of all labour service schemes was the same: to bring together a group of young single men or women aged 17 to 25 for a period of six months to a year to work on farms or on projects beneficial to the rural community, such as road-building or canal-building, in return for board and lodging, and perhaps a little pocket money. Accommodation was in sparse military-style barracks, usually situated on the edge of small villages and towns, and all schemes operated a strict policy of segregating the sexes; this meant that for men labour service was often combined with military training of some sort, while women were encouraged (but not forced) to sign up for projects which involved an element of cooking, cleaning and childcare duties. In dairy farm areas girls on the Land Year scheme (*Landjahr*) were expected to learn how to milk cows and perform other basic farm duties.

The typical day on a labour scheme would begin at 5.30am and finish at 9.30pm. During this time there would be seven hours of manual labour, out in the fields or in a household, as well as periods devoted to 'political education', sports, singing and other group activities. At first, labour service for both women and men was voluntary except for those who wished to go on to university after leaving school, for whom it became compulsory in 1934; this was in order to impress upon students the importance of non-intellectual pursuits and was also a way of reducing the overall numbers in the university system. However, due to changing economic and military priorities labour service became compulsory for all men in June 1935 and for all women in September 1939.[46]

Like the youth movements, the service schemes had their antecedents in the 1920s when they were put forward as a solution to the problem of long-term unemployment, especially among young men.[47] Middle-class feminists from the BDF were also active in promoting voluntary schemes for women and saw this as part of their contribution to the promotion of female equality, as well as to the recovery of the German nation after the defeat of 1918.[48] For the Nazis, who continued these schemes into the 1930s and beyond, labour service had many purposes, not all of which were compatible. Thus the Reich Labour Service leader, Konstantin Hierl, emphasised first and foremost the educational aspects of the scheme, in particular the development of a 'correct attitude to work' and the fostering of a sense of community between Germans of all classes. To this, the *Völkischer Beobachter* added a further objective of providing 'a bridge between town and country'.[49] Others, however, had different priorities. In particular the *Reichsnährstand* wished to use Hierl's scheme to reduce labour shortages in the countryside and alleviate the huge burden of work shouldered by the farmer and his family, while Goering went so far as to create his own scheme in 1938, the so-called *Pflichtjahr* for girls wishing to work in industry, in order to meet targets set by the Office for the Four Year Plan (see also Chapter 4). Finally, and perhaps most importantly, the army high command regarded women's labour service as the female equivalent of military conscription, and hoped that it could be used to create a reserve of skilled labour – particularly in the field of nursing and air raid protection – for use in the event of war.[50] As one retired army general wrote in 1935:

Closeness to nature and a mind for sports should also be cultivated among women. And this all the more as the urbanisation of the population continues and as the struggle to make ends meet ties women to the typewriter and the shop counter, and brings them into the lecture halls and the factories. The old Greek saying, that a healthy mind requires a healthy body, is particularly relevant to women. And certainly they too should experience joy at their own strength.[51]

As with the BDM, labour service brought together single women of the same age but from different backgrounds and classes, and was therefore intended to have a political and ideological as well as an educational function. According to Hierl, the camps would become 'fortresses in the countryside' in which a 'conscious *Deutschtum* and a practically applied National Socialism can be fostered and carried from there into the family'.[52] For this reason great importance was attached to early morning exercises in the fresh air and the cultivation of traditional folk songs around the campfire in order to provide a counterweight to the 'asphalt culture ... of the big city'.[53] For women, much emphasis was also placed on the development of household management skills, including cooking, sewing and gardening, as well as welfare work with the needy.[54] Alcohol, smoking and cosmetics were strictly banned and early morning exercises promoted in order to create a 'female race which is strong and heroic'.[55] Finally, the camps also provided new opportunities for the development of leadership skills, especially after 1934, when the occupation of 'labour service leader' was designated a fully fledged profession, with three years' training. In selecting recruits for this course, preference was given to those with a 'clear National Socialist conviction' and a high degree of physical fitness, while academic achievement was placed low down on the list of priorities.[56] Jews and other racial 'inferiors' were of course not considered at all for any involvement in labour service schemes.[57]

In spite of the massive recruitment campaigns, however, the numbers of women joining voluntary service schemes remained relatively low before 1939. At the end of 1935, for instance, there were 200,000 men working on labour service projects, but only just over 10,000 women.[58] In 1937 there were two six-month cohorts of 25,000 girls each, and in the second half of 1939 there was one single cohort of 36,219 girls, but again these figures lagged well behind those for the men's camps.[59] This can be contrasted with the relative success of Goering's *Pflichtjahr* for girls wishing to take jobs in industry, which had mobilised over 300,000 by the end of 1939 and also had the advantage of being more practical and much cheaper to run than the labour service schemes.[60] Complaints were often heard from farmers, for instance, that labour service girls spent too many hours on non-productive activities such as sports and 'political education' and not enough time actually working on the land. All too often they were seen as a financial liability to the countryside, and Hierl's self-professed aim of using the Reich Labour Service to a create self-sufficient economy in food seemed even further off in 1939 than it had done in 1934.[61]

Attitudes towards labour service among the girls themselves also varied, especially in the period before it became compulsory in September 1939. One sceptical American observer could not help wondering whether the girls were really as happy and content as her Nazi guide claimed, especially after she had been shown the rather spartan living quarters:

> For each girl there was a tin wash-basin, a cake of soap and a tooth-brush in a glass and that was all. No mirror or powder or any of the feminine foibles. Was it not possible to overdo this emphasis on health and hardiness? After all, girls are essentially feminine creatures and to deprive them of their femininity is in the last analysis to make them unattractive to men. And the Nazis claim they want wives and mothers![62]

Some young women also disliked the work they were expected to perform. Melita Maschmann, a labour service leader, complained about 'the unbelievably filthy underwear' of the family she was assigned to and the table manners of the grandfather who used to 'spit against the kitchen wall'.[63] An even worse experience was had by Irmgard Lotze, who was forced to abandon both her *Pflichtjahr* and then her Land Year after some of the farmers made sexual advances towards her.[64] Nonetheless, other women regarded their labour service as a great adventure that took them away from the narrow confines of middle-class domesticity and allowed them to see the world in a new light. The American sociologist Clifford Kirkpatrick, by no means pro-Nazi, praised what he saw as a 'genuine [attempt] to break down the barriers of education and class by an ultimately universal labour service' and compared this positively with the social snobbery that still prevailed 'in so-called democratic countries'.[65] Another American visitor, a woman doctor, wrote that the girls she saw were 'all rosy and energetic and full of vigour' in spite of their 'rough clothes' and simple way of living:

> I thought of William James' vision of each youth and maiden giving a year of service to the country [the USA] and though I could not possibly imagine American girls doing work such as these German girls are capable of, still it would be a beautiful thing to see the same spirit over here.[66]

In the final analysis the most that can be said about women's labour service is that it was part of a broader trend evident since the 1920s which recognised – and yet sought to control and manipulate – the brief period of independence between leaving school and getting married, which increasing numbers of young women were experiencing.[67] For Hitler, as for Hierl, it is likely that the educational and ideological aspects of labour service were more important than the material benefits. In this sense it is also significant that in 1938 Hitler personally approved measures for the expansion of the scheme, so that by April 1940 at least 50,000 places would be available for women in each six-month cohort. This was in spite of the massive labour shortages that were beginning to appear in many different sectors of the economy and despite demands from the army and the munitions industry for more women workers.[68]

4. German youth at war, 1939–1945

The outbreak of war in September 1939 changed the face of the Hitler Youth movement and the labour service schemes beyond recognition and led to a massive mobilisation of girls and single women under 25 in the service of the Nazi state. Little emphasis was now placed on training for motherhood or domesticity; rather, everything was geared towards winning the war. This meant a broader economic function for the youth schemes and the increasing militarisation of teenage girls as well as boys. As early as 4 September 1939 it was announced that the girls' labour service (RADwJ) would become compulsory for all single girls aged 17 to 25 who were not in full-time employment or full-time education, so that an estimated 100,000 girls would be called up every six months.[69] These numbers were expanded in July 1941 when, in the wake of the invasion of the Soviet Union, Hitler ordered that the six months served with the RADwJ should be augmented by a further six months' auxiliary war service (*Kriegshilfsdienst*). This meant drafting girls into auxiliary nursing and social work, or into clerical work with the civilian authorities and armed forces.[70] Finally, another decree in 1941 made all schoolchildren aged 10 years and over available for war work (*einsatzfähig*). By this time many 10- to 14-year-olds were already spending their summer holidays working on the land under the government's child evacuation scheme (*Kinderlandverschickung* or KLV) run by the Hitler Youth; and their teachers were expected to accompany them.[71]

In total over 14.5 million girls and young women were estimated to be contributing to the German war economy in some way by 1942–43, performing the equivalent of 151 million work hours per year.[72] Important as this work was, however, it could not in itself compensate for the loss of young men to the army, especially in the countryside, which experienced ever worsening labour shortages as the war continued.[73] At best it can be said that those children over 10 who were evacuated from the cities under the KLV scheme were less frequently exposed to the danger of bombing and under-nourishment than their counterparts who chose to stay behind with their parents. Sometimes the evacuees were ruthlessly exploited as cheap labour, however, and all of them faced serious disruption to their school education. Ilse Koehn from Berlin, who had joined the BDM in 1940 despite her father being half-Jewish, spent time in three KLV camps between 1941 and 1944, the first at Radoczowitz in Czechoslovakia, the second on the island of Ruegen off the Baltic coast, and the third at Harrachsdorf in the

Sudetenland, 'a small mountain village miles away from everything'. On Ruegen, which was famous in pre-war Germany for its luxurious beaches and holiday resorts, she and the other girls from her school lived in a military-style camp surrounded by barbed wire, with a pole and Nazi flag in the centre. They got up at 6.15 in the morning and after drill were expected to work for eight hours in the fields under the supervision of carefully selected BDM leaders who were themselves aged only 16. As Ilse noted in her diary:

> All is *Scheisse* here. The toilets and showers are army-type and unpartitioned. The dormitories, two of them with fifty beds in each, contain nothing else, not even a chair. And they have no doors. Eva and Anita, standing in the open doorways, order us to go to bed. And a command is the last thing we hear at night. 'Eyes closed! Everyone face the door!'. We do. Who wants to stand barefoot on cold cement for an hour? Uschi and I already experienced twelve hours of this punishment for nothing worse than a giggle or a whisper.[74]

Life in the other two camps was not much better. The girls had to stand up and salute whenever one of the BDM leaders came into the room, and were subject to regular inspections of their dormitories, with punishments for any form of untidiness or uncleanliness. Their letters home were also read and sometimes torn up, especially if they contained any complaints about their treatment or living quarters. ('How dare you write such hogwash, such nonsense? You will sit down right now and write again ... You will write only pleasant things!').[75] Even the teachers who had accompanied the group from Berlin had to accept the petty rules and regulations of camp life, and the rank of *Lagermädelführerin* (BDM camp commandant) was held to be higher than that of any qualified teacher. Some kind of formal education nonetheless continued in an ad hoc manner, interrupted as it was by military drill, sports, political instruction and endless singing.[76] Undoubtedly many of the children and teenagers sent on KLV evacuation programmes were bored and homesick, and some were deeply traumatised by their experiences, which included widespread physical and mental bullying. Others, however, like the former BDM functionary Jutta Rüdiger, continued even after the war to extol the patriotic idealism and self-sacrificing spirit of the KLV camps, in which there was allegedly 'no hard work and no corporal punishment'.[77]

Meanwhile, much greater status was afforded to those BDM leaders and women students who were selected for periods of work experience in the occupied territories of the east under the so-called *Osteinsatz* programme. The girls chosen usually represented the elite of the BDM and were sent out on short-term assignments to develop their skills as teachers, childcare assistants and social workers. According to one report, by April 1944 some 110 to 140 *Osteinsatz* camps were in existence and over 18,000 girls had taken part in the scheme.[78] Typical tasks included helping to set up kinder-gartens, youth groups and motherhood classes for German settlers in specific localities; in addition, 500 village schools were created in the period to April 1944.[79] In areas selected for large-scale expulsions of non-Germans, BDM girls were also expected to clean and tidy up confiscated houses in preparation for the arrival of new families. They were instructed to lend moral support to ethnic German settlers only and not to show any sympathy to the Polish and Jewish victims of 'ethnic cleansing', who were in turn accused of having committed atrocities against Germans.[80] As the *Ostdeutscher Beobachter* put it in 1940: 'We desire a coming together of all forces and a decisive, clear-cut separation between German and Pole; after the victory of arms we shall bring about a final victory. National Socialist women can and will make a contribution to this struggle.'[81]

Elizabeth Harvey, in her study of the post-war recollections of German girls sent out to work in occupied Poland, found that most of them remembered only the positive features of their involvement in Nazi Germanisation policies, as well as the beauty of the Polish countryside, while choosing to forget all about the Jews and the Poles they saw. Nonetheless, she also discovered that it was not uncommon for girls to be present during forced expulsions and to witness scenes of racially motivated violence. Her conclusion, that German women 'were by no means operating in a different world or with a necessarily different perspective on Poland than men' is significant when considering the extent of women's complicity in Nazi war crimes.[82]

While 'going east' turned some young German women into perpetrators, others felt a greater sense of unease about the role they were expected to play in the occupation regime, even if very few spoke openly about their misgivings.[83] Some later became victims of ethnic violence themselves, especially those who stayed for longer periods in the east and were thus caught up in the acts of revenge carried out by Polish civilians and Red Army units between 1944 and 1947 (see also Chapter 7). Making up another group exposed to the terrifying violence of war were the thousands of single women drafted into auxiliary military duties on the home front after 1943, with 13,000 girls participating in air raid protection duties and a further 25,000 working on anti-aircraft batteries by the spring of 1945.[84] The number of girls actually killed or seriously injured in the course of these duties is difficult to estimate, but is likely to have been quite high, especially in the closing stages of the war. One girl who was conscripted into anti-aircraft work later remembered:

> We each had ten hours on duty and ten hours free. First we were stationed in a barracks. After it was destroyed by bombing, we lived in a huge tent ... In January 1945 fate overtook us. There was a massive British air-raid by low-flying craft. One fired at our gun so that every-thing was mown down by machine-gun bursts. The NCO took a direct

hit ... his stomach ripped open, and his intestines were hanging out. I stood in front of him, unable to move. 'Lisa, take my pistol and shoot me dead!'. I couldn't do it.[85]

Other young single women were called up to work as auxiliary nurses and social workers, or agreed to help out in the 'Neighbourhood Aid' section of the NSV, which provided food and emergency shelter for bombed-out families and refugees.[86] Here too they were likely to witness traumatic scenes, and to suffer from overwork and stress. Indeed, as Elizabeth Heineman has pointed out, wartime labour policy aimed to spare not only German women at the expense of foreign workers but also married women at the expense of single women.[87] In the autumn of 1944 even certain categories of women students were made liable for labour conscription, and university life virtually ground to a halt. One student in Munich recalled: 'I was assigned immediately to the tram company ... [where I] worked [as a conductor] through the worst air-raids of 1944 and 1945 ... I got to know bunkers and shelters of good and bad quality, waded barefoot through flooded streets strewn with rubble and broken glass in order to get home, and no longer cared whether I lived or died.'[88]

Even so, residual resentments continued to exist against students who were granted exemptions or partial exemptions from war work. Much of this resentment was directed against single women from middle-class backgrounds, who made up 49.5 per cent of the total student body by 1943–44 and were seen, generally, as loafers and idlers.[89] Sometimes, too, SD reports noted that women students were showing 'insufficient regard for the seriousness of the times', for instance by organising illicit dance evenings where jazz music was played.[90] None of this was reported in the press, however. Instead, in February 1943 the *Frankfurter Zeitung* leapt to the defence of students, BDM leaders and other 'privileged' young women who were still exempt from labour conscription, declaring in an editorial:

> Wherever there are still 'house daughters', for instance in the country-side, they are ... mostly indispensable assistants in the family household. The same goes for the women students and pupils at institutions of higher learning. One should not demand their conscription into factory work with that form of malice which derives from resentment against educated women in general, and against educated women in wartime in particular. In any case, the woman student is doing her duty in the same spirit of cooperation and with the same degree of readiness as her male comrade who has been called up into active military service.[91]

In general it is difficult to quantify the experiences of girls and young women in Germany during the war. A small minority, especially those con-scripted to work in the east, became fanatical Nazis who enthusiastically supported the racial policies of the regime. Most, however, became frustrated by the increasing regimentation of everyday life, the lack of personal freedoms and the limited opportunities to engage in romantic adventures with members of the opposite sex, even if few moved over into explicit opposition to the state (see also Chapter 6). In particular, as Dagmar Reese has argued, the BDM, like the Hitler Youth, was less popular in city environments like Berlin, where there were alternative forms of entertainment and night life with a much greater attraction for working-class adolescent girls.[92] Some of the young people arrested in Hamburg in January 1942 and sent to concentration camps for being members of the non-conformist 'Swing Youth' (a group of jazz enthusiasts known for their extravagant dress and alternative lifestyles) were also female.[93] However, for those young women who were drafted into war work of one kind or another, it was probably a combination of hunger, exhaustion and concern over mounting casualty figures at the front, rather than principled opposition to Nazism, that accounted for much of the disillusionment with the regime by the end of the war.[94]

Notes

1 Stephenson, 'Women's Labor Service', p. 241.
2 Hitler, *Mein Kampf*, p. 351.
3 On the National Socialist educational system in general see Geert Platner (ed.), *Schule im Dritten Reich – Erziehung zum Tod? Eine Dokumentation* (Munich, 1983). Also the chapter on education in Grunberger, *A Social History of the Third Reich*, pp. 362–85; and the chapter on youth in Burleigh and Wippermann, *The Racial State*, pp. 201–41. Lisa Pine is currently preparing a new book on education and socialisation in Nazi Germany for Palgrave.
4 Hitler, *Mein Kampf*, p. 371.
5 Ibid., p. 373.
6 Ibid., p. 389.
7 Cited in Jost Hermand, *A Hitler Youth in Poland. The Nazis' Program for Evacuating Children During World War II* (Evanston, Illinois, 1997), p. xvii.
8 See e.g. Pine, *Nazi Family Policy*, esp. pp. 47–87.
9 Hitler, *Mein Kampf*, p. 377.
10 On school curricula see Brigitte Kather, 'Mädchenerziehung – Müttererziehung?', in: Schmidt and Dietz (eds), *Frauen unterm Hakenkreuz*, pp. 27–34. On school textbooks see Pine, *Nazi Family Policy*, pp. 58–72; and *idem*, 'The Dissemination of Nazi Ideology and Family Values Through School Textbooks', in: *History of Education* 25 (1996), pp. 91–110.
11 Stephenson, *Women in Nazi Germany*, p. 73.
12 Irmgard Weyrather, 'Numerus Clausus für Frauen – Studentinnen im Nationalsozialismus', in: Frauengruppe Faschismusforschung (ed.), *Mutterkreuz und Arbeitsbuch*, pp. 131–62. The statistics on numbers of women students are taken from Winkler, *Frauenarbeit im 'Dritten Reich'*, p. 196.
13 Jill Stephenson, 'Girls' Higher Education in Germany in the 1930s', in: *Journal of Contemporary History* 10 (1975), p. 43.
14 Bock, *Frauen in der europäischen Geschichte*, p. 287.
15 Kaplan, *Between Dignity and Despair*, p. 235.

16 Noakes and Pridham (eds), *Nazism, 1919–1945*, Vol. 2, p. 433.
17 Ibid., pp. 431–3.
18 Jeremy Noakes, 'The Oldenburg Crucifix Struggle of November 1936. A Case Study of Opposition in the Third Reich', in: Stachura (ed.), *The Shaping of the Nazi State*, pp. 210–33.
19 Noakes and Pridham (eds), *Nazism, 1919–1945*, Vol. 2, pp. 429–30.
20 Stephenson, 'Girls' Higher Education', p. 45.
21 Ibid., pp. 50–2; Noakes and Pridham (eds), *Nazism, 1919–1945*, Vol. 2, p. 431.
22 McIntyre (i.e. Stephenson), 'Women and the Professions', pp. 198–9. On the acceptance of women as engineers see also the article 'Frauen als Ingenieure', in: *Der Angriff*, no. 224, 19 September 1938. Copy in: BA Berlin, RLB-Pressearchiv, no. 7978, Bl. 127.
23 Gertrud Scholtz-Klink's speech to an audience of journalists at the 'Haus der deutschen Presse', as reported in the *Völkischer Beobachter*, no. 114, 24 April 1937. Copy in: FZH, no. 256. In fact, women could still study law and work in private practice as lawyers, especially in civil cases involving family law. What they could not do was practise at the bar, i.e. in the courtroom. I would like to thank Jill Stephenson for this information.
24 Weyrather, 'Numerus Clausus', p. 160.
25 Winkler, *Frauenarbeit im 'Dritten Reich'*, p. 196.
26 See the report 'The position in German universities in the summer semester of 1942', reproduced in: Stephenson, *Women in Nazi Germany*, pp. 161–3.
27 Weyrather, 'Numerus Clausus', p. 161.
28 On the ANSt see Stephenson, 'Girls' Higher Education', pp. 61–4, and Haide Manns, *Frauen für den Nationalsozialismus. Nationalsozialistische Studentinnen und Akademikerinnen in der Weimarer Republik und im Dritten Reich* (Opladen, 1997), esp. pp. 151–88.
29 Noakes and Pridham (eds) *Nazism, 1919–1945*, Vol. 2, p. 417. Cf. Walter Z. Laqueur, *Young Germany. A History of the German Youth Movement* (London, 1962).
30 For further details on the origins of the BDM see Dagmar Reese, 'Bund Deutscher Mädel – Zur Geschichte der weiblichen deutschen Jugend im Dritten Reich', in: Frauengruppe Faschismusforschung (ed.), *Mutterkreuz und Arbeitsbuch*, pp. 163–87; and Reese, '*Straff aber nicht stramm*', pp. 31–4.
31 Cf. Stephenson, *The Nazi Organisation of Women*, p. 91.
32 Cf. Pine, *Nazi Family Policy*, pp. 47–58.
33 Ilse Koehn, *Mischling, Second Degree. My Childhood in Nazi Germany* (London, 1981), p. 84.
34 'Warum immer neue Forderungen an die Mädel?', in: *Völkischer Beobachter*, no. 69, 10 March 1938. Copy in: FZH, no. 256.
35 Kirkpatrick, *Woman in Nazi Germany*, p. 83.
36 Reese, '*Straff aber nicht stramm*', p. 75.
37 Haste, *Nazi Women*, p. 136.
38 Charles Schüddekopf (ed.), *Der alltägliche Faschismus. Frauen im dritten Reich* (Bonn, 1982), p. 71.
39 Koehn, *Mischling, Second Degree*, p. 40.
40 Pine, *Nazi Family Policy*, p. 157; Gellately, *The Gestapo and German Society*, p. 156.
41 Stephenson, *Women in Nazi Germany*, p. 77; Frevert, *Women in German History*, p. 247.
42 On the alternative youth movements see Peukert, *Inside Nazi Germany*, pp. 154–69.
43 Ibid., p. 151. Cf. Wilke, 'Village Life in Nazi Germany', *passim*.
44 Pine, *Nazi Family Policy*, p. 57.

45 Haste, *Nazi Women*, p. 139.
46 On the service schemes see Stefan Bajohr, 'Weiblicher Arbeitsdienst im "Dritten Reich". Ein Konflikt zwischen Ideologie und Ökonomie', in: *Vierteljahrshefte für Zeitgeschichte* 28 (1980), pp. 331–57; and Stephenson, 'Women's Labor Service', *passim*. Also Kirkpatrick, *Woman in Nazi Germany*, pp. 84–91.
47 Lore Kleiber, '"Wo ihr seid, da soll die Sonne scheinen!". Der Frauenarbeitsdienst am Ende der Weimarer Republik und im Nationalsozialismus', in: Frauengruppe Faschismusforschung (eds), *Mutterkreuz und Arbeitsbuch*, pp. 188–214.
48 Bajohr, 'Weiblicher Arbeitsdienst', p. 333.
49 Stephenson, 'Women's Labor Service', p. 243. Cf. 'Der Arbeitsdienst wurde zur Brücke zwischen Stadt und Land', in: *Völkischer Beobachter*, 8 September 1933.
50 Bajohr, 'Weiblicher Arbeitsdienst', p. 350.
51 Generalleutnant a.d. v. Metzsch, 'Frau und Wehrkraft', in: *NS-Frauenwarte* 4 (1937/8), p. 98.
52 Bajohr, 'Weiblicher Arbeitsdienst', p. 340.
53 Ibid., p. 341.
54 Stephenson, 'Women's Labor Service', p. 246.
55 Bajohr, 'Weiblicher Arbeitsdienst', p. 341.
56 Stephenson, 'Women's Labor Service', pp. 254–5. Cf. Bajohr, 'Weiblicher Arbeitsdienst', pp. 345–7.
57 See here the Reichsarbeitsdienst-Gesetz of 26 June 1935, §7 (1), which reads as follows: 'Zum Reichsarbeitsdienst kann nicht zugelassen werden, wer nichtarischer Stammung ist oder mit einer Person nichtarischer Abstammung verheiratet ist ...'. Cited in Schneider (ed.), *Frauen unterm Hakenkreuz*, p. 54.
58 Stephenson, 'Women's Labor Service', p. 251.
59 Kirkpatrick, *Woman in Nazi Germany*, p. 86; Bajohr, 'Weiblicher Arbeitsdienst', p. 347.
60 See article '300,000 Mädchen kommen ins Pflichtjahr', in: *Deutsche Allgemeine Zeitung*, 29 November 1939. Copy in: BA Berlin, RLB-Pressearchiv, no. 7979, Bl. 67. Also Stephenson, 'Women's Labor Service', p. 253.
61 Ibid., p. 259. Cf. Farquharson, *The Plough and the Swastika*, pp. 200–1.
62 Kirkpatrick, *Woman in Nazi Germany*, p. 89.
63 Stephenson, 'Women's Labor Service', p. 261.
64 Stephenson, *Women in Nazi Germany*, p. 81.
65 Kirkpatrick, *Woman in Nazi Germany*, p. 87.
66 A. Hamilton, MD, 'Women's Place in Germany' (1934). Cited in ibid., pp. 164–5.
67 Cf. Sneeringer, *Winning Women's Votes*, p. 121.
68 Bajohr, 'Weiblicher Arbeitsdienst', pp. 347–8.
69 Stephenson, 'Women's Labor Service', p. 256.
70 Ibid., p. 260.
71 Farquharson, *The Plough and the Swastika*, p. 234. On the KLV programme see also the documents and commentary in Noakes (ed.), *Nazism, 1919–1945*, Vol. 4, pp. 421–40.
72 Reese, 'Bund Deutscher Mädel', p. 175.
73 Cf. Farquharson, *The Plough and the Swastika*, p. 235.
74 Koehn, *Mischling, Second Degree*, pp. 81–2.
75 Ibid., p. 47.
76 Ibid., p. 107.
77 See Jutta Rüdiger (ed.), *Die Hitler-Jugend und ihr Selbstverständnis im Spiegel ihrer Aufgabengebiete* (Lindhorst, 1983), pp. 297ff. Rüdiger's glowing account nonetheless needs to be set against Jost Hermand's far more damning report, *A Hitler Youth in Poland*, *passim*.

78 *Zeitungsdienst des Berliner Nachrichtenbüros*, 20 April 1944. Copy in: BA Berlin, RLB-Pressearchiv, no. 7980, Bl. 103.
79 Ibid.
80 Cf. Harvey, '"We forgot all Jews and Poles"', p. 451.
81 Helga Thrö, 'Die deutsche Frau im Osten', in: *Ostdeutscher Beobachter*, no. 142, 24 May 1940. Copy in: BA-Berlin, RLB-Pressearchiv, no. 7979, Bl. 101.
82 Harvey, '"We forgot all Jews and Poles"', p. 460.
83 Ibid., p. 461. Harvey is currently preparing a larger study of this subject for publication by Yale University Press.
84 See the article 'Frauen an der Front. Luftwaffen-Helferinnen bei Terrorangriffen', in: *Der Angriff*, no. 209, 28 August 1943. Copy in BA-Berlin, RLB-Pressearchiv, no. 7980, Bl. 76. Also 'Frauen am Scheinwerfer', in: *Münchner Neueste Nachrichten*, no. 169, 19 June 1944. Copy in ibid., Bl. 113; and Stephenson, 'Women's Labor Service', p. 263.
85 From Gerda Szepansky's account, 'Die Flakhelferin im Café. Über Lisa G.', reproduced in: Stephenson, *Women in Nazi Germany*, p. 165.
86 Cf. Schneider (ed.), *Frauen unterm Hakenkreuz*, pp. 176–8.
87 Heineman, *What Difference Does a Husband Make?*, p. 45.
88 Kasberger, *Heldinnen waren wir keine*, p. 122.
89 Weyrather, 'Numerus Clausus', p. 159; Stephenson, '"Emancipation" and its Problems', p. 348.
90 Weyrather, 'Numerus Clausus', p. 161.
91 'Mobilmachung des Zivils', in: *Frankfurter Zeitung*, no. 70, 7 February 1943. Copy in: FZH, no. 256.
92 Reese, '*Straff, aber nicht stramm*', p. 218.
93 Noakes (ed.), *Nazism, 1919–1945*, Vol. 4, p. 460. See also the evidence in Michael Hepp, 'Vorhof zur Hölle. Mädchen im "Jugendschutzlager" Uckermark', in: Angelika Ebbinghaus (ed.), *Opfer und Täterinnen. Frauenbiographien des Nationalsozialismus* (Frankfurt/Main, 1996), pp. 239–70.
94 See e.g. the documentary evidence in Schneider (ed.), *Frauen unterm Hakenkreuz*, esp. pp. 166ff.

|6|

Opposition and resistance

Few issues in historical writing on Nazi Germany are as controversial as that of the German resistance to Hitler. For one thing, as Ian Kershaw notes, in both East and West Germany after 1945 'the history of the resistance ... played a pivotal role in the [formation of national] self-image ... and in the attempt to mould the political consciousness and values of the population'. In other words, it was intimately bound up with ideological differences emerging out of the Cold War and the arms race between the capitalist and communist blocs.[1] For another thing, even 50 years and more after the end of the Third Reich, historians still cannot agree on an accepted definition of the term 'resistance'. In particular, while some believe that resistance is synonymous with conspiratorial action designed to overthrow the Hitler regime, others feel strongly that it cannot be studied in isolation from the wider problem of the relationship between the state and society during the Nazi era. In the latter case, it is further argued that the boundaries between conformity, dissent, opposition and outright resistance are too difficult to pin down and that individuals could find themselves moving between all four categories at different points during the 12 years of Nazi rule.[2]

In addition to these general points of contention, attempts to place women within the framework of historical discussions of German resistance have thrown up a number of historiographical, methodological and ethical problems of their own. The earliest accounts of the home-grown opposition to Hitler, for instance, tended to assume that the role of women was either insignificant or at best of minor importance. This reflected both the prejudices of Allied wartime propaganda, which portrayed all German women as loyal Nazis and avid Jew-haters and, later on, the emphasis placed by West German historians on the patriotic self-sacrifice of German army officers and aristocrats involved in the failed July 1944 plot to assassinate Hitler.[3] Even in East Germany, where considerably more attention was given to 'ordinary' working-class people who opposed Nazism, the face of the 'anti-fascist' was almost invariably that of a disciplined, fanatical, battle-hardened warrior fighting on the front line (in Spain, in Moscow, in the concentration camps) against fascist oppression. There was indeed little room for women within the anti-fascist canon, unless they conformed to the masculine image of the class-conscious patriotic German worker put forward in the propaganda of the KPD, and its successor party, the SED, after 1946.[4]

Secondly, even if it is accepted that women were actively involved in resistance, it is by no means clear that their motivations were self-consciously female/feminist, as opposed to socialist, communist, Zionist or German nationalist. On the contrary, most women resisters were members of clandestine networks and subcultures led by men and guided by a particular ideology or set of beliefs that the defeat and overthrow of the Nazi regime was more important than any other contemporary political goal, including progress towards the emancipation of women or the over-throw of the capitalist economic system. As Antonia Grunenberg has written of the German Communist resistance (and this might also apply to other groups as well):

> What on the surface looked like genuine emancipation – women were to fight alongside men against National Socialism/fascism – trans-formed itself when the going got tough into rivalry and resentment.[5]

Indeed, to pull women resisters out of this historical context and suggest that they were fighting for a specifically female/feminist agenda would necessarily skew our understanding of their motivations and experiences, as well as of the broader significance of resistance in general.

Finally, in contrast to other parts of Nazi-occupied Europe, such as Italy or France, the German resistance to Hitler was very small-scale and frag-mented, which ultimately doomed it to a very minor role indeed in the Allied–Soviet military victory of 1945. For instance, it failed to prevent the Nazi invasion of the USSR in June 1941 and the deportation of Jews from German soil after October 1941. It also failed to create the basis for a popular mass anti-fascist movement of the type that appeared in northern Italy in the dying days of Mussolini's puppet fascist state, the Salo republic, between 1943 and 1945. For this reason, even left-wing and feminist historians of Nazi Germany have tended not to dwell so much on the issue of resistance, and instead have focused their efforts on explaining why Hitler was able to command so much loyalty from the German population, even in the final phase of the Third Reich.[6]

Against these objections to studying women's resistance from a gendered perspective, however, two points can be made. Firstly, even if the different resistance movements were never a serious threat to the regime, the Gestapo and the party nonetheless saw them as such and spent much time and energy seeking to infiltrate them. For this reason, Gestapo files and court records can be very revealing about the attitudes of the regime towards the thousands of German and German-Jewish women involved in resistance activities and about the different roles played by both sexes in anti-Hitler organisations.[7]

Secondly, over and above the attitudes of the Gestapo, some historians have argued that women – because of their upbringing and socialisation – brought specific skills and expectations to resistance movements that made their contribution and experiences significantly different to those of men. This is particularly the case, as we shall see, with women's resistance in the concentration camps and forced labour camps of Germany and occupied Poland, where the struggle to survive (itself a form of resistance) was aided by women's more highly developed bonding skills and their greater concern for issues of bodily and food hygiene.[8]

Before going on to consider these issues in more depth, however, it is first necessary to consider the various types of resistance and opposition in which German and German-Jewish women could become involved.

1. Types of opposition and resistance

Older studies of the Third Reich often proceed from the assumption that resistance was possible only among those who were active anti-Nazis before 1933 or who became members of small-scale conspiratorial groups during the war years, such as the communist *Rote Kapelle* (Red Orchestra), the conservative group around Ludwig Beck and Carl Goerdeler, or the more heterogeneous Kreisau circle, which included both Christian-conservative and social democratic elements. Once again, this meant that resistance was seen as a largely male affair. Statistics reveal, for instance, that women made up only 5 to 10 per cent of all those convicted of belonging to an illegal political organisation in Nazi Germany,[9] although it should not be forgotten that the institutions of state terror (Gestapo, SD, SS) were more likely to target men than women because of their own prejudices and assumptions about gender.[10]

Another group of women drawn into opposition to the regime at a later stage (post-1933) were those with strong religious views, such as the various Catholic and Protestant women who came to reject National Socialism as an 'ungodly' phenomenon. The proportion of women among those imprisoned for religiously motivated acts of resistance is estimated to have been between 20 and 25 per cent, significantly higher than for political groups.[11] Part of the reason for this is that much of the care of the mentally and physically handicapped continued to be carried out by religious orders, who were thereby drawn into Nazi schemes for compulsory sterilisation and 'euthanasia'. Some Catholics, of course, enthusiastically participated in the killing process, but others expressed varying degrees of disquiet, and some went even further, protesting openly against the 'euthanasia' programme in the wake of Bishop von Galen's sermon in Münster in August 1941. An example here would be Maria Terwiel, a young Catholic woman from the

Rhineland, who was arrested and sentenced to death along with her fiancé Helmut Hippel in 1943 after being caught distributing illegal copies of von Galen's sermons. Maria had also provided Jews with false passports in order to help them escape from Germany.[12]

Finally, during the Second World War, even basic acts of humanity, such as giving a few cigarettes to a French prisoner of war or speaking to him in his own language, were outlawed and therefore became by definition an expression of political or moral defiance against a regime that, as Claudia Koonz argues, required the confinement of all motherly feeling to the private sphere in order to implement its brutal racial policies.[13] Gestapo records and other evidence indeed indicate that not all Germans were willing to conform to such petty-minded rules, even if violation carried the risk of denunciation or worse. For instance, in the town of Oberhausen, Wilhelmine Haferkamp, the wife of a local party member, was caught on several occasions engaged in the act of 'feeding the enemy', i.e. giving food to prisoners of war working in the fields near her home. Even after her husband was called into party headquarters and threatened with loss of his membership card, she refused to stop: 'I kept on doing it. Always had something different. Came from the baker, got two big breads lying there on the table. And there stand the [foreign] workers.'[14] Other examples of deliberate kindness towards the victims of Nazi persecution can be found in the diaries of Victor Klemperer, the Dresden philologist mentioned earlier in this book. On 4 October 1941, for instance, a few weeks after Klemperer and other German Jews were forced to wear the yellow star in public, he recorded the following incident, which took place in a busy Dresden street:

> Elderly woman selling from a handcart. 'Can I have some of the large radishes?' – 'But of course!' – I glance longingly at the tomatoes, forbidden 'goods in short supply'. 'They're not to be had without a card, are they?' – 'I'll give you some, I know how things stand'. Makes up a pound. Then reaches under her cart, pulls out a handful of onions, which are very rare: 'Hold out your bag – so that's 60 pfennigs altogether'.[15]

On another occasion, Frau Reichenbach, one of Klemperer's Jewish neighbours, told him how she had been greeted by a complete stranger in the street, a fact that surprised her because nobody now talked to Jews in public:

> Had he not mistaken her for someone else? – 'No, I do not know you, but you will be greeted frequently from now on. We are a group "who greet the Jew's Star"'.[16]

Whether such actions, brave as they are, could ever be described as 'resistance' is nonetheless controversial. Ian Kershaw, for instance, has argued that everyday instances of non-conformity or individual protest cannot be classified as 'resistance' because they were not directed towards overthrowing the regime itself but were merely a sign of opposition to certain 'wholly unnecessary aspects of [Nazi] policy', such as the requirement that Jews and foreign workers live in strict isolation from the rest of society.[17] On the other hand, as Jill Stephenson points out in her recent study, if people could be executed during the war simply for listening to foreign radio broadcasts or for spreading 'false rumours' about German defeats on the eastern front, then such activities might be considered a form of resistance in the sense that they 'threatened the totalitarian claims of the Nazi leadership' and allowed for the development of alternative views of the war.[18]

Another, more straightforward, case would be that of the Munich students Sophie and Hans Scholl, leaders of the non-political but broadly Christian 'White Rose' movement, who were sentenced to death in February 1943 after distributing a series of home-made leaflets denouncing the crimes being committed in their name by the leaders of the Nazi state. Their aim, according to Hans Rothfels, was to 'bear witness to their faith in the existence of another, more decent Germany' and thereby make a contribution to the building of a 'new spiritual Europe' in which the values of tolerance and respect for human life would be paramount. After they had been executed along with four of their fellow conspirators, the slogan 'the spirit lives' appeared painted on the walls of many houses and public buildings in Munich. The threat of capital punishment, it seemed, was no deterrence to such activities.[19]

There are of course numerous other instances like this, of young women and men who risked their lives, sometimes recklessly and sometimes naively, but always with great bravery, in order to make a stand against National Socialism and to lead by example. Furthermore, even if it is accepted that not all of those who were arrested for criticising the regime or for spreading 'defeatist' ideas can be classified as 'resisters' in the formal sense, they still took up a great deal of the Gestapo's time and therefore tied up resources that could have been used elsewhere. By 1943, for instance, the Gestapo alone numbered 40,000 officers whose main task was to root out dissent and opposition among the civilian population as a whole rather than to hunt for underground conspiratorial groups.[20] This statistic in itself indicates that the more organised forms of resistance progressed 'through the people' and not in isolation from them, at least in the latter stages of the war.

In the remainder of this chapter, I have decided therefore to follow a number of other historians in making a distinction between 'resistance' – defined as politically organised action aimed at the overthrow of the National Socialist system – and 'opposition' – defined as any type of behaviour that was intentionally non-conformist or that showed contempt for the Nazi regime and its policies.[21] Thus 'resistance', under this definition, would include activities like giving shelter to the victims of Nazi persecution, helping to set up escape lines for people on the run, establishing contacts with foreign intelligence agencies or maintaining underground anti-Nazi movements in preparation for the time when the regime finally fell. 'Opposition', on the other hand, might be expressed in less complex and time-consuming forms of social action like a simple refusal to give the Nazi salute or a private decision to boycott local events being put on by the DAF or other Nazi organisations. However, it is important to remember that the boundaries between organised resistance on the one hand and opposition or non-conformity on the other, were never fixed; rather, in the words of Detlev Peukert, 'they represent the two end points of a sliding scale of dissident behavior in the Third Reich'.[22]

2. Organised resistance

For the purposes of simplicity, organised resistance may be divided into four main categories: communist and socialist; Catholic and Protestant; Jewish and Zionist (by no means the same thing); and aristocratic/military. In this section, each category will be examined in turn, with particular emphasis on the opportunities and experiences they offered to the women within their ranks.

By far the largest and best organised of the anti-Nazi groupings in Germany before 1933 were the left-wing political parties, the Social Democrats and the Communists, whose combined support still amounted to 13 million votes (or one-third of the electorate) in the Reichstag elections of November 1932. Ideological and tactical differences between them, however, had prevented any effective joint action against the Nazi seizure of power, and the period between February and December 1933 saw a mass wave of arrests and 'preventative detentions', which largely destroyed both organisations. By the end of 1933 most of the top Communist and Social Democrat functionaries were dead, on the run, in concentration camps or living in exile, and those who still lived in freedom in Germany were reluctant to engage in reckless acts of heroism, which – as they had now learned through brutal experience – would result only in pointless sacrifice of life and liberty. Instead they tended to meet in small groups for orientation, mutual support and political education, often using the camouflage of gardening clubs or hiking associations. This form of small-scale organisation also had the advantage of minimising the danger of betrayal through informers. At first, few socialists and communists believed that the Nazi regime would remain in power for long, certainly not longer than a few years; later they resigned themselves to sitting out the war until the moment when Hitler was defeated or overthrown, at which point they could emerge from the shadows in order to make their own contribution to the democratic reconstruction of Germany.[23]

In the meantime, women were given an important role in left-wing resistance groups by the need to maintain some kind of underground structure in order to look after the families of imprisoned, murdered and exiled comrades, and prepare for the period after the liberation from Nazi tyranny. They acted as couriers for underground communist groups and for the Prague-based *Sopade* (Social Democratic Party in exile), helped to type up and distribute illegal pamphlets, and offered solace to men whose world had fallen apart since the Nazis came to power. At even greater risk to themselves, they allowed their homes to be used for clandestine meetings, or as hideaways for political fugitives or Allied airmen on the run. Annie Kienast, a Social Democrat and trades union activist from Hamburg, for instance, began working for the resistance after a chance meeting on the street with former comrades at the turn of the year 1934–35:

> They knew that I had a flat of my own. So they came with a typewriter hidden under blankets and put up heavy curtains, so that the noise would not force its way out of the flat. We did some experiments to see if anything could be heard since my neighbour was a convinced Nazi. But my neighbour didn't notice anything.[24]

Occasionally, too, women took over leadership positions within the illegal SPD or KPD following the arrest and imprisonment of men. An example here would be Elli Schmidt, who became leader of the Berlin section of the KPD in November 1935 after the cover was blown on her predecessor, Anton Ackermann.[25] Gestapo records reveal, however, that women's contributions were still considered of secondary importance by the agents of state terror. In other words, most of the high-profile Gestapo investigations were against men, and most of those arrested for political offences, especially in the early years of the regime, were men. To quote from Annie Kienast again:

> The Nazis saw women as stupid and only fit to be good housewives and mothers. So my neighbour [an SA man] could not imagine me to be anything else than a stupid, insignificant little woman.[26]

This does not mean, however, that women too did not suffer harassment and torture at the hands of the SA and Gestapo. Claudia Koonz, for instance, is quite wrong when she says that 'in the Third Reich, the second sex was beneath suspicion'.[27] Numerous examples from the year 1933 alone suggest otherwise. In March of that year former SPD Reichstag deputy Minna Cammens was arrested for distributing anti-Nazi leaflets in Breslau and murdered while in Gestapo custody, making her one of the first women anti-fascists to be killed by the Nazis. In the same month SA thugs beat up the SPD Berlin city councillor Marie Jankowski. After Jankowski's friend Clara Bohm-Schuch sent a complaint directly to Reichstag president

Hermann Goering, she herself was subjected to frequent Gestapo house searches and was held in custody for 15 days in April 1934. She died in May 1936, partly as a result of the harrassment she had suffered. Several other prominent left-wing women were murdered or died after being tortured during the first few years of Nazi rule, including the former communist Reichstag deputies Franziska Kessel (found hanged in jail in April 1934) and Helene Fleischer (died in 1940 of 'natural causes' after years of brutal mistreatment at Moringen concentration camp for women), and the former SPD deputy in the Prussian Landtag, Leni Rosenthal (killed by the Gestapo in October 1936).[28]

Hundreds of lesser-known women also fell victim to the Nazi terror system. Some faced savage beatings and even summary execution, while others spent months or even years in special ad hoc concentration camps set up by the Gestapo after 1933, often in former workhouses or disused factories. Later the SS established its own camp for women at Ravensbrück in Mecklenburg; some 1,415 'politicals' and a further 260 Jehovah's Witnesses were transferred here when it first opened in May 1939.[29] More frequently, anti-Nazi women were placed before Nazi special courts and given long sentences in the normal prison system, usually for the crime of sedition. They would then be transferred to a concentration camp on release. Meanwhile, between August and November 1933 three communist women were executed by guillotine at Ploetzensee jail in Berlin – the first women to be sentenced to death by a German court since the end of the First World War.[30] This was followed, in 1938, by the trial and execution of Liselotte Herrmann, a 29-year-old communist from Stuttgart who was charged with conspiracy to commit high treason after being caught in possession of illegal KPD pamphlets and secret information pertaining to German rearmament plans, which she had passed to contacts in Switzerland. Unlike the previous cases from 1933, this one caused a storm of national and international controversy, perhaps because Herrmann was a young mother with a four-year-old son. In spite of this, the Nazi authorities showed no mercy and even tried to use her son as a tool to persuade her to inform on her comrades. She refused.[31]

The Gestapo also frequently took the wives, daughters and sisters of suspected political opponents into custody as hostages or for purposes of interrogation and intimidation. Refusal to reveal the whereabouts of male relatives could lead to lengthy periods of solitary confinement, combined with frequent beatings and torture. Gerda Ahrens, for instance, a member of a communist youth organisation in Hamburg who was arrested in December 1934 for distributing an illegal communist pamphlet, 'The Truth About the Reichstag Fire', remembered a telling incident during her first days at the Gestapo prison at Fühlsbüttel:

> Next to my cell was a girl who was interrogated and beaten every night, we heard her screams ... and also the blows, and one day, when

I was brought back from the courtyard, I found a pencil stump in my cell, with a piece of paper wrapped around it, and on the paper was written: 'I am 17 years old and they want me to tell them where my brother is. I have no idea where my brother is. I cannot stand anymore of this, I want to kill myself' ... What was I to do? Now, we were given newspaper to use as toilet paper, and every day I tore off a strip and used the pencil to write something to her ... The young girl eventually survived and later thanked me, since, as she said, she was given hope through these clandestine communications which she received from me every day.[32]

Gerda herself was released after three months, but was re-arrested in 1937, together with her mother, after a bungled attempt to help a fellow German communist cross the border into Denmark. This time she was sentenced to five years' imprisonment, only to be arrested again in 1943 for similar offences. During the war, meanwhile, the death penalty was frequently used against those convicted of assisting escape attempts or of harbouring political opponents of the regime. Johanna Kirchner from Frankfurt-am-Main and Irene Wosikowski from Hamburg are just two examples of anti-fascist women who provided assistance to German exiles in France and later worked for the French resistance. Both were handed over to the Gestapo by the French Vichy authorities in 1942, and both were later put on trial and executed at Ploetzensee jail. Maria Juchacz, a former SPD Reichstag deputy, helped fellow German refugees in France during the war, but despite several close calls she managed to escape arrest and deportation, returning to an active role in West German public life after 1945.[33]

While socialist and communist women had at least some kind of structure to turn to, women who resisted Nazism out of their own consciences or from religious conviction faced an even lonelier struggle. Indeed, neither the Catholic nor the Evangelical (Protestant) churches in Germany accepted illegal forms of resistance as a possible course of action for Christians. Thus Protestant churchmen made regular reference to the tradition of 'throne and altar' based on Romans Chapter 13 ('there is no power but that of God; the powers that be are ordained of God'), in order to emphasise the separation of temporal and spiritual powers on earth, while in August 1935 the Fulda Bishops' conference passed a resolution reaffirming that Catholic associations in Germany would continue to 'reject all subversive attitudes and conduct, refrain from any political activity and ... resolutely repel all attempted approaches of Communism'.[34] The closeness of many leading representatives of the Christian churches to the Nazi regime is of course a matter of continuing and very painful controversy, especially when it is remembered that even Bishop von Galen of Münster had known of the Nazi 'euthanasia' programme for a least a year before he chose to speak out in August 1941, and that even then his protest was considered ill-judged by other senior figures in the Catholic hierarchy.[35]

Nonetheless, pockets of 'Christian' resistance to Nazism did exist and should not be forgotten. The case of the Jewish-born Catholic nun Edith Stein (murdered at Auschwitz in August 1942) is relatively well known, as are the activities of the 'White Rose' group in Munich, some of whose members tried to establish links with the Protestant theologian Dietrich Bonhoeffer and his circle in Berlin, with the aim of establishing a broader anti-fascist Christian front. Bonhoeffer himself was arrested in April 1943 and murdered at Flossenbürg concentration camp in April 1945; before his imprisonment, though, he had organised a number of illegal discussion groups for Christian men and women at his house in Berlin and had also made contact with members of the Kreisau circle.[36]

Finally, there is the example of the group of German wives who braved savage threats of reprisal from the Gestapo to mount a week-long vigil in protest at the arrest and probable deportation of their Jewish husbands, who had been picked up during the 'factory action' in Berlin on 27 February 1943 and were being held in a building on the Rosenstrasse, in the heart of the old Jewish quarter. This was the only mass demonstration against the deportation of Jews known to have taken place in Nazi Germany, eventually bringing together as many as 6,000 protesters. It ended in success: on 6 March the Gestapo decided to release around 1,500 men from Rosenstrasse and others were even brought back from Poland, so that in total the lives of between 1,700 to 2,000 intermarried Jews were saved. At this point, shortly after the great reversal at Stalingrad, the Nazi regime was very concerned about morale on the home front and did not want to make things worse by deporting Jews who had close 'Aryan' relatives. Some of the senior government officials and legal experts in charge of Jewish policy were also anxious that 'Aryan' family members might pursue inheritance or child custody claims through the courts. This would create many difficulties, especially if family lawyers demanded to see death certificates for husbands or fathers who had 'disappeared' after being sent to the east.[37]

With the exception of the Rosenstrasse protest, however, the Jews in Germany received little help or support from non-Jewish Germans, even during the latter stages of the deportations, when knowledge of the mass gassings in Poland became fairly widespread. The same can also be said for the secular Jewish and Zionist resistance groups, which operated not only in isolation from German society at large, but often without the backing of Jewish religious and civic leaders, who, like their Catholic and Protestant counterparts, were willing to tolerate legal forms of opposition only.[38] Thus approximately 2,000 German Jews are estimated to have fought against Nazism by taking up arms against their own country – for instance, as anti-fascist volunteers in Spain between 1936 and 1939, or as members of the British, American, Free French and Soviet armed forces during the Second World War.[39] Other German Jews engaged in political work on behalf of the Allied or Soviet cause.

It was only after 1942, however, that a Jewish-Communist cell was encouraged to take up active resistance inside Germany: the Herbert Baum group, made up of a small number of Jewish forced workers in the Siemens plant in Berlin, who were organised along communist lines but were kept entirely separate from the main Berlin KPD group for security reasons. In May 1942, after some members of the Baum group attempted to burn down the Nazi propaganda exhibition 'Soviet Paradise' in the Berlin Lustgarten, the Gestapo moved in to take revenge. A total of 18 members of the Baum group, 12 of whom were women, were eventually tried by a special court and sentenced to death, and a further 500 Berlin Jews (all of them entirely unconnected to the Baum group) were arrested and shot as a warning to others.[40]

Meanwhile, by the winter of 1942–43, with the ruthless crushing of underground resistance networks like the communist 'Red Orchestra' and the Baum group, and the evident failure of the left to mobilise German workers against the war, it had become increasingly evident to all resistance groups that only the assassination of Hitler could bring an end to the National Socialist regime. It was also clear, however, that only those with regular access to the person of Hitler – disaffected elements within the army leadership – had a chance of pulling off such a coup. It was from such considerations that the Stauffenberg plot of July 1944 emerged, involving a small group of army officers acting in total secrecy and without the knowledge even of the Wehrmacht High Command. Their aim to kill Hitler at Führer Headquarters in East Prussia was foiled at the last moment, when a briefcase containing a bomb was moved from one side of a table leg to another, thus sparing the Nazi leader from the immediate impact of the blast. Even so, several other people who had been in the room with Hitler at the time of the explosion were killed or seriously injured.[41]

Those directly involved in the conspiracy were all men: on the military side they included Colonel Claus Schenck von Stauffenberg, the man who placed the bomb, Lieutenant Werner von Haeften, his adjutant Major-General Friedrich Olbricht, Colonel Albrecht Ritter Mertz von Quirnheim, Colonel Henning von Tresckow, General Karl Heinrich von Stülpnagel and General Ludwig Beck, and on the civilian side Carl Friedrich Goerdeler, Ulrich von Hassell, Peter Graf Yorck von Wartenberg, Adam von Trott zu Solz, Hans-Bernd von Haeften, Fritz-Dietlof von der Schulenburg, Alfred Delp, Adolf Reichwein and Julius Leber. Nonetheless, their wives also played an important, if sometimes overlooked, role. As Michael Burleigh writes, 'they shouldered duties uncommon to their class and time' including running 'wartime households, which in this case often meant supervising considerable agrarian enterprises, [and] sometimes taking part in clandestine meetings or helping the conspiracies along'.[42] In this sense, the failure of 20 July 1944 also marked a key turning point in their lives, and in particular the beginnings of a determined campaign to uphold their honour and dignity in the face of what seemed like almost certain torture and death.[43]

In the end, nearly all of the wives were arrested, interrogated and threatened for several weeks, but none was executed, whereas all the male conspirators were. Stauffenberg's wife, Nina Schenck von Stauffenberg, for instance, who was pregnant at the time of her arrest, was held in custody from July 1944 to April 1945, and during this time gave birth to her fifth child at a heavily guarded clinic at Frankfurt-an-der-Oder. Her other four children were taken from her and placed in a special home at Bad Sachsa under new names. A similar fate befell many other relatives of the conspirators. When Ida Vermehren arrived at Buchenwald concentration camp in August 1944, for instance, she met there no fewer than 10 Stauffenbergs and eight Goerdelers.[44] In total 5,000 people were arrested in connection with the plot, most of them members of the old aristocratic elite, who now faced a savage purge of their ranks in order to satisfy Hitler's desire for revenge. According to Ian Kershaw, only the end of the war prevented SS leader Himmler from fulfilling the promise made in his speech to a group of Gauleiters in Posen in August 1944 to wipe out 'the family of Graf Stauffenberg ... down to its last member'.[45]

Another example of the resistance of an aristocratic woman would be that of Freya von Moltke, whose husband, Helmuth James von Moltke, the leading figure in the Kreisau circle, had already been arrested in January 1944, some months before the July plot, for having warned another anti-Nazi that the Gestapo were watching him. Freya immediately went into action in support of her husband, visiting him regularly in jail with gifts of food and books, and using various contacts to try and secure his release. After the failure of the bomb plot, however, her tactics changed: henceforth she tried to have her husband granted a pardon on the grounds that he had not been directly involved in the assassination attempt and was a dreamer rather than a politician.[46] This reflected the general despair and gloom in resistance circles after July 1944: now the only choice was to sit and wait until Hitler was finally overthrown by the military power of the Allies. In the meantime, in spite of Freya's efforts, Helmuth James von Moltke was executed at Ploetzensee on 23 January 1945, one of the last of those connected with the conspiracy to go to the gallows.

3. Opposition and non-conformity in everyday life

It is now time to turn to the second category of anti-Nazi activity outlined above, namely opposition in the broader sense of the word, including various forms of active non-conformity and private non-compliance with the regime. Here we are dealing with a diverse range of activities that are not easy to categorise and did not always involve serious risk of arrest and imprisonment. In some cases opposition could take the form of single-issue protests, which did not seriously challenge the principles of National Socialism and might even have stabilised the regime by providing a 'safety valve for the expression of dissent'.[47] On the other hand, court records also reveal that 'ordinary' Germans could be sentenced to death or to long periods of imprisonment for relatively trivial offences, especially in the final years of the war.[48]

One group of women who were prepared to defy the Nazi regime openly without seeking to overthrow it were the members of the German branch of the Jehovah's Witnesses. During the period 1933–35 Jehovah's Witnesses faced various forms of persecution, including loss of employment, business boycotts and violence from the SA. When this failed to produce the desired results the sect was banned in 1935 and many members were imprisoned in concentration camps. Men who were Jehovah's Witnesses refused military service and therefore were at first more likely to be persecuted than women. Up to 1,000 of them were executed and a further thousand died in concentration camps between 1933 and 1945.[49] Nonetheless, as we have seen, at least 260 women were transferred to the Ravensbrück concentration camp in 1939 and were kept there as long as they refused to sign a statement renouncing their religious views. Later reports indicate at least 575 *Bibelforscherinnen* at Ravensbrück by 1940, all of them German 'except for a few Dutch women'.[50] Paradoxically, although imprisoned for anti-war activities, they were among the most trusted inmates, because they did not believe in violence of any kind and were willing to do menial work like cleaning the houses of SS guards. What they refused to do was to take any oath of loyalty to the Nazi state or even give the Nazi salute. Margarete Buber-Neumann, the above mentioned former communist and Ravensbrück inmate, later recalled her impressions of the women Jehovah's Witnesses she came across as the *Blockälteste* of block 3:

> The 'Jehovah's Witnesses' were in some senses 'voluntary prisoners'. All they had to do, in order to secure their release, was to go to the senior guard and declare their willingness to sign an undertaking [to renounce their religion] ... [They] all, without exception, had a very low level of education. Most of them came from small towns and villages, from farming or working class families, or from the lower middle classes, but all had had some schooling ... I once asked one of the Jehovah's Witnesses: 'I cannot understand why you don't sign. How can that stop you from continuing your religious beliefs and agitating in private? By securing your release you would probably be much greater help to your movement than if you allow yourself to perish in a concentration camp'. 'No,' was the answer, 'we cannot square that with our conscience. To sign the statement for the SS would be like making a pact with the Devil'.[51]

From the summer of 1942, about 90 of the more dedicated Jehovah's Witnesses suddenly refused to work in the wool detail any more, because they discovered that the wool was being used for military purposes. They also refused to appear at the daily roll calls since 'we pay our respects to Jehovah, not to the SS'. For this they each received 75 lashes with the whip followed by 40 days of confinement in a darkened cell with food brought to them only every fourth day:

> After 40 days I saw them in the shower. They had turned into skeletons and were covered in weals. They all had dysentery and seemed to have developed mental illness. Many of them were taken straight to the [camp] hospital.[52]

In spite of this, they still refused to work or to stand to attention at roll call. Eventually they were sent on to the Auschwitz death camp, where their fate is unknown, although it seems likely that they were all killed within days or weeks of arrival.[53]

As far as is known, no other oppositional group sought martyrdom to the same extent as the Jehovah's Witnesses. Many women from communist underground organisations nonetheless braved torture and long periods of imprisonment rather than reveal the whereabouts of their comrades to the Gestapo. In communist historiography much is also made of the opposition of 'ordinary' working-class women in the workplace and especially in the armaments factories. There is some evidence for this, especially in the mid-1930s, when women in various parts of Germany, including Munich, Leipzig and Berlin, are known to have organised protests against low wages.[54] Complaints about long hours and hard working conditions also mounted in 1938 and 1939. A KPD flysheet that circulated in a Berlin armaments factory in the summer of 1939 sought to capitalise on this:

> Fellow women workers! ... the more the factory management succeed in forcing us to take on men's work, crazy production targets, the ten hour day and starvation wages, all the more easily will Hitler continue his unscrupulous campaign of conquest and thereby bring the catastrophe of war onto our people. If we want to avoid contributing to this, we cannot afford to remain silent. Therefore we must defend ourselves ... every pfennig added to our wages is a pfennig less for the war. We women belong at the side of our men, our fellow workers, in the great people's front for peace and freedom.[55]

However, after 1939 things began to change here. There was less evidence of resistance in the workplace because more women left the labour market than entered it, and those who remained in employment were often able to secure relatively well-paid jobs, for instance as typists and secretaries, who were in high demand. Furthermore, use of foreign labour tended to take the edge off the exploitation of German women, who were encouraged to place themselves above foreigners in the factory hierarchy. Figures produced by Detlev Peukert, for instance, show that the vast majority of those arrested by the Gestapo in 1942 for the crime of *Arbeitsverweigerung* (refusal to work) were not German communists but rather foreigner workers, especially Poles, who were among the worst paid and most poorly treated of all factory employees.[56] By contrast, German women could evade labour registration quite easily if they wanted to, by changing their names upon marriage, reverting to their maiden names or even by moving house and leaving no forwarding address. Only very rarely did Nazi bureaucrats or the Gestapo bother to pursue such cases.[57]

In the end, ordinary German women were most likely to show their opposition to and contempt for National Socialism when defending their own families against the intrusion of the Nazi state, and it is here too that they achieved their greatest successes. Thus families stood up to the Nazis against the 'euthanasia' programme in the summer of 1941, forcing Hitler to back down and announce the official termination of the 'T-4' programme, and German women in mixed marriages successfully rescued their Jewish husbands from the Gestapo as a result of the Rosenstrasse protests of February 1943. Such protests were of course partly motivated by self-interest and therefore do not fit easily into the traditional resistance paradigm with its stress on martyrdom in the cause of a noble ideal (for instance, communism, or the idea of the 'other Germany'). Nonetheless, the actions of women in attempting to save their families, while self-interested, were certainly not selfish. As Nathan Stoltzfus rightly points out, the selfish thing would have been for families to abandon handicapped relatives to their fate (which sometimes happened) or for German women to divorce their Jewish spouses (which, again, was a choice some made). The fact that most of the families affected by these policies refused to take the easy option, and the fact that several thousand women were prepared to take to the streets to protest in spite of Gestapo threats and intimidation, are matters of no small significance, especially as they caused the regime to make some rather uncharacteristic (and life-saving) compromises in the field of racial policy.[58] They are also an important corrective to Claudia Koonz's argument that adherence to traditional family values predetermined German women to play a diversionary role in the Third Reich that helped make the Holocaust possible.[59]

Occasionally German women without Jewish relations also helped Jews. Some belonged to groups who greeted the 'Jew's star', for instance, even though such behaviour was criminalised by a law of 24 October 1941 forbidding all public contact between 'Aryans' and Jews.[60] Others were prepared to hide Jews in their houses, or to look after the property of Jewish neighbours in order to save it from confiscation by the Gestapo during house searches. Helene Jacobs, for instance, a Berliner with strong Christian beliefs, helped to hide Jews and supply them with false papers. An anonymous denunciation led to her arrest in August 1943. Fortunately, however, the Gestapo was unable to discover the full extent of her 'crimes' and she was sentenced to only two and a half years in jail for trading on the black market and falsifying documents. In July 1946 a special sitting of a Berlin court overturned her conviction on the grounds that:

> The accused carried out this deed solely in order to help those perse-cuted on political and racial grounds and to supply them with food and passes. She did this on the basis of her religious convictions and without demanding or obtaining any financial advantages for herself. It thus seems that the accused acted justifiably and in self-defence.[61]

Examples of Jewish rescue by German women were relatively rare, how-ever. More common – at least as would appear from the records – were cases of women leading protests against the interference of Nazi officials in local and communal affairs. Thus in the summer of 1941 women in several towns and villages in southern Germany led a 'mothers' revolt' against a series of anti-clerical decrees issued by the Bavarian Minister of Education, Adolf Wagner. As with the crucifix campaigns in the state of Oldenburg in 1936–37 and the Rosenstrasse protest in Berlin in February 1943, the Nazi authorities felt it necessary to bow to such grassroots pressure from women acting in unison to protect the perceived interests of their children and families. According to Ian Kershaw, 'the [crucifix] issue was all the more emotive since, as the mothers never tired of pointing out, their husbands were away fighting ... against "godless Bolshevism", while the "Bolsheviks" at home were removing the crosses from schools'.[62] Indeed, in many cases women persuaded their soldier husbands and sons to help them bring the crosses back into the schools during periods of army leave, having informed them in advance of the situation in letters sent to the front. In other instances, the school crucifixes were replaced by the women themselves, usually after a mass to celebrate the life of a fallen soldier from the local area. Eventually Wagner backed down and permitted the crucifix to return to all schools under his jurisdiction, thus signalling what Kershaw describes as 'a clear defeat for the Nazi administration in Bavaria', even if it is true that the broader 'parameters of Nazi rule' were hardly touched by these events.[63]

4. German-Jewish women in hiding and in the concentration camps

While for non-Jews a decision to disobey particular Nazi laws and decrees was to some extent a question of personal choice (although often deter-mined by strong political or religious conviction), for Jews it was a matter of life and death. Even official representatives of the German-Jewish community eventually came to recognise this, agreeing in 1938 to open illegal bank accounts for the purpose of financing escape attempts for those many thousands whose applications for visas had been turned down.[64] In the autumn of 1941, however, the Nazis banned all further emigration from occupied Europe, and this meant that efforts to sponsor would-be emigrants also had to cease.

After 1941, officials from the *Reichsvertretung der Juden in Deutschland* (Reich Association of Jews in Germany) were charged by the Gestapo with sending out registration forms and ensuring that the deportation of Jews to the east ran smoothly. This meant, among other things, that the *Reichsvertretung* was unable or unwilling to offer protection to those who were considering refusing to comply with a deportation order; indeed, it advised strongly against any form of civil disobedience.[65] In spite of this, between 10,000 and 12,000 Jews opted to go into hiding, most of them in Berlin, and about three in ten of them survived without being caught. Among them were Inge Deutschkron and her mother, who moved between various hiding places in Berlin between 1943 and 1945, eventually ending up in Potsdam by the end of the war.[66] Another example was the artist Valerie Wolffenstein, who was forced to change her place of residence no less than 18 times in order to avoid capture.[67]

Living underground, as Konrad Kwiet writes, 'required courage, endurance, social adaptability and financial resources'.[68] In particular, the ability to obtain ration cards, money and counterfeit papers was essential, as was the ability to find reliable protectors within the non-Jewish community. Whether women were better equipped socially to perform these tasks is difficult to say, but the kind of contacts Inge Deutschkron made during her period underground would perhaps suggest this was the case. Inge and her mother changed hiding places no less than 22 times between 1943 and 1945, and were forced to rely on the support of ordinary Berliners who could provide false papers, food, employment and the next hiding place. At times this meant negotiating with people who were not especially sympathetic to their situation or who were outright Nazis. Jewish women also found it easier to hide their Jewishness than Jewish men because they did not carry the mark of circumcision on their bodies and because any man under 45 years of age aroused immediate suspicion if he was not in the military or in a reserved occupation. One is reminded here of the story of the Polish Jewish woman who visited Oskar Schindler's enamelware factory in Cracow one day in order to beg him to employ her elderly parents, who were inmates of the Plaszów forced labour camp. She herself was living on forged South American papers in Cracow, which by then was a 'Jew-free' city.[69]

Historians are also beginning to explore the possible advantages women had in the forced labour camps and extermination camps of Germany and German-occupied Poland as a result of gender socialisation. Thus tales abound of camp inmates who formed themselves into little groups of surrogate families for the purposes of 'organising' food and looking out for each other's welfare and safety. Within each group, some women would take on the role of adults, or organisers, and some the role of children or dependants.[70] Sometimes, though, these roles might be reversed, especially if an older group member suddenly fell ill or suffered a beating that left them unable to fend for themselves. Particular attention was also paid to issues of personal hygiene, since a healthy appearance was crucial to surviving the 'selections'. Thus group members would goad each other on to eat properly and to wash themselves as best they could. Fania Fénelon, the French resistance fighter who was transported to Auschwitz in January 1944 and ended up as a member of the orchestra within the women's camp, remembered how on her birthday she had to report herself as sick.

> They didn't send me to the camp hospital. Alma feared that I would be gassed. During the night I thought to myself, nobody cares about me in the entire world. I am so ill and so alone and nobody even knows that I exist. And suddenly the girls came to me in their night shirts, they brought me presents and gave me bread, bread was so important to me. The girls started to sing, my resistance songs. Such an experience only happens once in a lifetime. To this day I still feel very strange when I think of this wonderful solidarity.[71]

On the other hand, it is important to acknowledge that alongside the stories of mutual assistance from fellow inmates, there are also memories of physical violence, theft and bullying, as well as the constant fear of sexual assault from male guards and prisoners, which weakened the will of most women to resist or even to stay alive. The whole camp system was indeed designed to isolate the prisoner and leave her or him standing totally alone and in total despair. Furthermore, as Atina Grossmann has recently pointed out, the supposed advantages arising from women's nursing, bonding and housekeeping skills turned out in practice to be a double-edged sword. There were indeed many instances where 'staying together was more dangerous than splitting up', such as when mothers accompanied their children to the gas chambers or when friends took huge risks to help each other during 'selections'.[72] Family units that lost one of their members – as a result, for instance, of a 'selection' or transfer to another camp – were also often racked by guilt and recriminations, which could undermine the cohesion of the group. Some group members became so fearful of separation from their real or adopted families that they could scarcely function at all and became a liability to the other members.[73]

As for the role of Jewish women in active resistance networks in the camps and ghettos of eastern Europe, information remains sparse; but the general impression is that here they were a more or less 'invisible' and unacknowledged force. True, there were also some important exceptions, like Gisi Fleischmann who helped to organise an underground escape route for Jews in occupied Poland, and Franceska Mann, who shot dead two SS men in the crematorium at Auschwitz-Birkenau before herself being killed.[74]

Nonetheless, according to Judith Tydor Baumel not one woman was appointed to serve on the *Judenräte* or Jewish councils that administered the ghettos on behalf of the German authorities. Nor were women accepted as leaders of clandestine resistance committees within the slave labour camps of Poland.[75] This made female solidarity even more important if the special concerns of women were to be taken into account within the Jewish resistance as a whole. Or, as Ami Neiberger puts it, 'building relationships with fellow prisoners allowed women to reclaim their humanity and to forge a living link to the present ... [It] was an act of resistance at the personal level, because it gave life meaning and offered support and hope.'[76] The same can also be said for the women's support groups that sprang up within the DP (Displaced Persons) camps in the aftermath of the war, when many Jewish families were waiting for permission to emigrate to Palestine or the USA. Here too, women had to struggle to make their voices heard, since few were appointed as leaders of organisational committees within the DP camps and many became 'involved in marriage, childbearing and childrearing during the first post-war years, leaving little time for official communal duties'.[77]

German-Jewish women, like their non-Jewish counterparts, thus brought special skills to the various opposition and resistance movements, including a greater degree of adaptability to changing circumstances and a greater resilience in the face of short-term adversity. Women were also better than men at pooling scarce resources and looking out for each other.[78] They were less interested in individual acts of heroism and more interested in collective or family survival. Ultimately, though, there was no resistance movement that could have united all German women against Nazism. Rather, the fragmented nature of opposition to the Hitler regime highlights once again the salience of other factors like class, religion, political affiliation, marital status and above all race in determining the different experiences of women in the Third Reich.

Notes

1 Kershaw, *The Nazi Dictatorship*, p. 185.
2 On the problems of definition see in particular the excellent collection of essays edited by David Clay Large, *Contending with Hitler. Varieties of German Resistance in the Third Reich* (Cambridge, 1991).
3 For an example of Allied wartime propaganda see Katherine Thomas, *Women in Nazi Germany* (London, 1943). For a classic West German account of resistance in the conservative mode see Gerhard Ritter, *Carl Goerdeler und die deutsche Widerstandsbewegung* (Stuttgart, 1954).
4 For a critique of the totalitarian ideology behind the KPD version of 'anti-fascism' see e.g. Burleigh, *The Third Reich*, p. 667, and Antonia Grunenberg, *Antifaschismus – ein deutscher Mythos* (Reinbek bei Hamburg, 1993), esp. pp. 76–87. For a brief summary of East German historiography on the resistance see Tim Mason, 'Der antifaschistische Widerstand der Arbeiterbewegung im Spiegel der SED-Historiographie', in: *Das Argument* 43 (July 1967), pp. 144–53.

5 Grunenberg, *Antifaschismus*, p. 83.
6 See e.g. Mason, *Social Policy in the Third Reich*, *passim*; Mason, 'The Containment of the Working Class in Nazi Germany', *passim*; Frevert, *Women in German History*, pp. 240–52.
7 Gellately, *The Gestapo and German Society*, *passim*; Johnson, *Nazi Terror*, *passim*.
8 Cf. Milton, 'Women and the Holocaust', pp. 311–16.
9 Christl Wickert, 'Frauen zwischen Dissens und Widerstand', in: Wolfgang Benz and Walter H. Pehle (eds), *Lexikon des deutschen Widerstandes* (Frankfurt/Main, 1994), p. 154.
10 Cf. Stephenson, *Women in Nazi Germany*, p. 110.
11 Wickert, 'Frauen zwischen Dissens und Widerstand', p. 154.
12 On Maria Terwiel see the entry in Annedore Leber (ed.), *Conscience in Revolt. Sixty-Four Stories of Resistance in Germany, 1933–45* (Oxford, 1994), pp. 123–6.
13 Koonz, *Mothers in the Fatherland*, *passim*.
14 Owings, *Frauen*, pp. 20–1.
15 Klemperer, *I Shall Bear Witness*, p. 419 (diary entry for 4 October 1941).
16 Ibid., p. 426 (diary entry for 24 November 1941).
17 Kershaw, *Popular Opinion and Political Dissent*, pp. 176–7.
18 Jill Stephenson, '"Resistance" to "No Surrender". Popular Disobedience in Württemberg in 1945', in: Francis R. Nicosia and Lawrence D. Stokes (eds), *Germans Against Nazism. Nonconformity, Opposition and Resistance in the Third Reich. Essays in Honour of Peter Hoffmann* (Oxford, 1990), pp. 351–67. Cf. Stephenson, *Women in Nazi Germany*, p. 109.
19 Hans Rothfels, *The German Opposition to Hitler. An Assessment* (London, 1961), pp. 13–14.
20 Ibid., p. 15.
21 This is the position taken by most of the contributors in Large (ed.), *Contending with Hitler*. See in particular the essays by Konrad Kwiet, Detlev Peukert and Claudia Koonz.
22 Peukert, 'Working Class Resistance', in: Large (ed.), *Contending with Hitler*, p. 36.
23 Burleigh, *The Third Reich*, p. 672.
24 Schüddekopf (ed.), *Der alltägliche Faschismus*, p. 28.
25 On Schmidt see Heinz Habedank *et al.*, *Geschichte der revolutionären Berliner Arbeiterbewegung*, 2 vols (East Berlin, 1987), Vol. 1, pp. 397–400. Schmidt went on to play an important role in the foundation of the communist regime in post-war East Germany, serving as the leader of the DFD (*Demokratischer Frauenbund Deutschlands* – Democratic Women's League of Germany) between 1947 and 1953.
26 Schüddekopf (ed.), *Der alltägliche Faschismus*, p. 28.
27 Koonz, *Mothers in the Fatherland*, p. 335.
28 Information on all the above in Milton, 'Women and the Holocaust', pp. 298–9.
29 Ibid., p. 306.
30 Richard Evans, *Rituals of Retribution. Capital Punishment in Germany, 1600–1987* (London, 1996), p. 646. Christl Wickert, 'Frauen zwischen Dissens und Widerstand', p. 142, wrongly gives 1935 as the date of the first execution of a woman; Claudia Koonz, *Mothers in the Fatherland*, p. 336, suggests 1938, as do Martha Schad, *Frauen gegen Hitler. Schicksale im Nationalsozialismus* (Munich, 2001), p. 204, and Irmgard Weyrather, *Muttertag und Mutterkreuz*, p. 10.
31 On Herrmann see Schad, *Frauen gegen Hitler*, pp. 204–12.
32 Gerda Ahrens, 'Vortrag im Rahmen der "Sonntagsgespräche" in der KZ-

Gedenkstätte Neuengamme', 26 June 1988. Copy of transcript in: FZH, WdE, no. 327 T.

33 On Kirchner, Wosikowski and Juchaz see Koonz, *Mothers in the Fatherland*, pp. 319–20.

34 Burleigh, *The Third Reich*, pp. 721–3.

35 Ibid., p. 723. On von Galen's protest see also the documentation in Noakes and Pridham (eds), *Nazism, 1919–1945*, Vol. 3, pp. 1036–9.

36 On Bonhoeffer see the study by Eberhard Bethge, *Dietrich Bonhoeffer* (London, 1970).

37 On the Rosenstrasse protest see Stoltzfus, *Resistance of the Heart, passim.*

38 Konrad Kwiet, 'Resistance and Opposition: The Example of German Jews', in: Large (ed.), *Contending with Hitler*, pp. 65–74.

39 Ibid., p. 69.

40 On the Baum group see Habedank *et al.*, *Geschichte der revolutionären Arbeiterbewegung*, Vol. 2, pp. 468–9.

41 On the July plot see the account in Ian Kershaw, *Hitler. Nemesis, 1936–1945* (London, 2000), pp. 655–84.

42 Burleigh, *The Third Reich*, p. 706.

43 On the wives' of the conspirators see also the series of interviews conducted by Dorothee von Meding, *Mit dem Mut des Herzens. Die Frauen des 20. Juli* (Berlin, 1992).

44 Rothfels, *The German Opposition to Hitler*, p. 159.

45 Kershaw, *Hitler, 1936–1945*, p. 691.

46 Schad, *Frauen gegen Hitler*, pp. 280–3. On Helmuth James von Moltke see the study by Michael Balfour and Julian Frisby, *Helmuth von Moltke. A Leader against Hitler* (London, 1972).

47 Koonz, 'Courage and Choice', p. 50.

48 Cf. Klaus Marxen, *Das Volk und sein Gerichtshof. Eine Studie zum national-sozialistischen Volksgerichtshof* (Frankfurt/Main, 1994).

49 Koonz, *Mothers in the Fatherland*, p. 331.

50 Margarete Buber-Neumann, *Als Gefangene bei Stalin und Hitler*, reprint (Munich, 2002), pp. 250–66.

51 Ibid., pp. 253, 255.

52 Ibid., p. 286.

53 Ibid., pp. 316–17. On the persecution of Jehovah's Witnesses in Nazi Germany see also Detlev Garbe, *Zwischen Widerstand und Martyrium. Die Zeugen Jehovas im 'Dritten Reich'* (Munich, 1994).

54 See the examples in Kuhn and Rothe (eds), *Frauen im deutschen Faschismus*, Vol. 2, pp. 188–9.

55 Habedank *et al.*, *Geschichte der revolutionären Berliner Arbeiterbewegung*, Vol. 2, p. 432.

56 Peukert, *Inside Nazi Germany*, pp. 135–6.

57 Cf. Wickert, 'Frauen zwischen Dissens und Widerstand', p. 144; Kitchen, *Nazi Germany at War*, pp. 137–9.

58 See Stoltzfus, 'Protest and Silence', esp. pp. 161–5.

59 Koonz, *Mothers in the Fatherland, passim.*

60 Cf. Gellately and Stoltzfus (eds), *Social Outsiders*, p. 9.

61 Cited in Gerda Szepansky, *Frauen leisten Widerstand, 1933–1945* (Frankfurt/Main, 1983), p. 83.

62 Kershaw, *Public Opinion in Nazi Germany*, p. 349.

63 Ibid., pp. 353, 355.

64 Kwiet, 'Resistance and Opposition', p. 67.

65 Ibid., pp. 72–3.

66 Deutschkron, *Ich trug den gelben Stern, passim.*

67 Milton, 'Women and the Holocaust', p. 320.
68 Kwiet, 'Opposition and Resistance', p. 73.
69 The story is retold in Thomas Keneally, *Schindler's Ark* (London, 1982), pp. 200–3; and also features as one of the scenes in Steven Spielberg's film *Schindler's List* (USA, 1993).
70 On this theme see e.g. Baumel, *Double Jeopardy*, esp. pp. 67–99; and Ami Neiberger, 'An Uncommon Bond of Friendship. Family and Survival in Auschwitz', in: Rohrlich (ed.), *Resisting the Holocaust*, pp. 133–50.
71 Fania Fénelon interviewed in *Die Zeit*, 3 October 1980, p. 64. Reproduced in: Kuhn and Rothe (eds), *Frauen im deutschen Faschismus*, Vol. 2, pp. 201–4.
72 See Grossmann's review article, 'Women and the Holocaust. Four Recent Titles', in: *Holocaust and Genocide Studies* 16 (Spring 2002), pp. 94–108.
73 Neiberger, 'An Uncommon Bond', p. 141.
74 On Fleischmann see Yehuda Bauer, 'Gisi Fleischmann', in: Ofer and Weitzman (eds), *Women in the Holocaust*, pp. 253–65. On Mann see Carol Rittner and John K. Roth (eds), *Different Voices. Women and the Holocaust* (St Paul, Minnesota, 1993), p. 31.
75 Baumel, *Double Jeopardy*, p. 239.
76 Neiberger, 'An Uncommon Bond', p. 143.
77 Baumel, *Double Jeopardy*, p. 239.
78 Cf. Milton, 'Women and the Holocaust', pp. 311–12.

|7|

From total war to defeat and
military occupation

How did German women experience the war years on the home front and the transition from early victories through 'total war' to defeat and military occupation? We have already provided a partial answer to this question by looking at the impact of war on women's employment patterns and on single women's involvement in the BDM and labour service schemes. However, the war had an enormous influence not only on women's work but on all aspects of everyday life. Thus women living in cities faced a significant decline in their standard of living as rationing grew ever tighter after 1942 and facilities such as shops, cinemas, theatres and crèches were destroyed in bombing raids.[1] The evacuation of women and children from urban areas also led to tensions in the countryside. Often their rural hosts had families of their own to support and understandably resented the additional burden of looking after tired and hungry migrants from the big cities, especially when they 'seemed to think that they should be waited on hand and foot, as in a hotel'.[2]

Conversely, many single women who left rural areas in search of factory work and the 'freedom' of big city life found that the value of their wages was eroded by rising food prices and the development of a black market in goods and services, especially from 1943 onwards. On top of this, factory work itself was increasingly militarised, with armed guards sometimes patrolling the shop floor in massive industrial plants like the Krupp works in Essen, especially if Russian or Polish civilian workers were present. In some cases German women even found themselves locked up during the day with forced workers of various nationalities, as the rules about the racial segregation of the workforce fell apart towards the end of the war.[3] Meanwhile, in rural areas, as Gerhard Wilke writes, wartime rationing and labour conscription meant that 'for the first time village women experienced the full force of undisguised State power'.[4]

Above all, millions of women in both the cities and the countryside had to fill the gap left by conscripted male relatives, 1.9 million of whom were confirmed dead and 1.7 million taken prisoner or missing in action by the end of 1944.[5] This put increasing, almost intolerable, burdens on many women, especially those responsible for bringing up small children or those forced to manage farms and small businesses on their own, without adequate supplies of labour or raw materials.[6] At the same time, the increasing intrusion of the state into the home in the form of labour conscription, rationing and forced evacuations caused great resentment, especially when rumours also arose that better-off women, the wives of senior party officials, mayors and other *Prominenten*, were being allowed to evade most of the wartime restrictions.[7] Occasionally there were even open expressions of discontent. In Dortmund in April 1943, for instance, a crowd of 300 to 400 women assembled in the Hörde district to protest against the alleged ill-treatment of a local soldier by a Wehrmacht officer. According to an SD report written several weeks later, the women were heard to cry: 'We want our sons, we want her husbands back!'. Furthermore: 'the anger of the crowd grew by the minute and took on such a threatening manner that the officer had to make good his escape in a tram'.[8]

Despite incidents such as this, however, there was nothing to parallel the food riots and mass strikes witnessed on the German home front during the First World War. This failure of underground left-wing groups to ignite the forces of opposition and resistance has often been put down to the fact that even during the final stages of the war most Germans had enough to eat, albeit at the expense of foreign workers and people in the occupied territories. Indeed, it was only in the period 1945–48 that shortages of food and fuel became seriously life-threatening in Germany itself, especially for the elderly. Or, as one woman Berliner later remembered: 'During the war we were bombed, but had assurance of food supplies; when the war ended, there was no more bombing raids, but there was also nothing to eat.'[9]

Nonetheless, even if the availability of food was a crucial determinant of wartime morale, the ruthless nature of Nazi rule and the regime's determination to crush all signs of overt political opposition should not be underestimated. Between 1940 and 1943, for instance, the number of judicial executions per year rose from 926 to 5,326, and by 1944 death sentences were even being passed on children aged 14 to 16 years of age.[10] This is on top of the hundreds of thousands of 'ordinary' Germans who were sent to concentration camps and forced labour camps, often for minor breaches of discipline at work or petty offences against the law. Indeed, Annemarie Tröger, in her study of women's recollections of the war after 1945, found that the threat of the concentration camp allowed some urban working-class women to perceive a link between their own experiences and those of forced foreign workers, since they were both 'victims' of the 'big bosses' and Nazi officialdom.[11]

Even so, the differences between 'them' (the foreign workers) and 'us' (German women) remained quite striking, particularly in relation to the distribution of food and the allocation of housing. While German housewives and war workers disliked having to eat turnips instead of carrots, they were also well aware that Russian workers were given the worst food of all and were forced to steal just to keep themselves alive. In the chaos of the closing stages of the war there was also a fear that the Russian workers in big industrial cities would take their revenge on 'ordinary' German civilians when the Red Army or the Allies arrived. Little therefore remained of the traditional proletarian internationalism that had characterised the outlook of some sections of the German working class before 1933.[12]

Under these circumstances the lack of mass protest against falling living standards and increasing food shortages becomes more understandable. As Jill Stephenson argues, 'individuals could see that official propaganda diverged sharply from their own reality'. However, instead of protesting 'they turned in on themselves, insensitive to the sufferings of others and sceptical about officially-managed news media'.[13] In other words, most people were simply concerned to keep their heads down and survive the war as best they could, in spite of the enormous additional burdens placed on themselves and their families. How this affected women in particular will be discussed in greater depth below.

1. War on the home front: rationing and its impact

When war broke out in 1939 German housewives were already used to dealing with shortages caused by the import restrictions and currency exchange regulations introduced under Goering's Four Year Plan. The Vw/Hw section of the DFW, for instance, had started its own campaign against excessive spending on consumer goods as far as back as 1934, and from 1939 onwards it redoubled its efforts, dispensing leaflets, and organising classes and radio programmes on themes like mending old clothes, darning socks, repairing broken furniture, and conserving energy and food. Likewise the RMD was active in promoting greater awareness of breast-feeding and dietary issues, and also helped to organise schemes for the exchange of second-hand prams, cots and children's clothes.[14] In this sense, the transition to a wartime economy was smoother than would otherwise have been expected. Indeed, rationing was treated in a somewhat light-hearted manner at first. Marie Vassiltchikov, a white Russian who worked in Berlin during the war as a translator for German radio, recorded how in April 1940 her bosses became concerned at the huge quantity of toilet paper being consumed by the staff in her office:

> At first they concluded that the staff must be suffering from some new form of mass diarrhoea, but as weeks passed and the toll did not diminish, it finally dawned on them that everyone was simply tearing off ten times more than he (or she) needed and smuggling it home. A new regulation has now been issued: all staff members must betake

themselves to a Central Distribution Point, where they are solemnly issued with the amount judged sufficient to meet their daily needs.[15]

On another occasion, shortly afterwards, she complained of feeling

... desperate at having to queue up after the office, just for a piece of cheese the size of one's finger. But people in the shops remain friendly and seem to take it all still smilingly.[16]

The Nazi regime had of course always been very sensitive to any signs of social discontent, and as early as 1938 Hitler refused to countenance a rise in food prices because of its potential negative impact on the living standards of the average urban housewife and consumer.[17] The rationing system introduced in September 1939 was intended to avoid the same problems, with pregnant women and workers in heavy manual jobs assigned the highest allowances, and Jews and foreign workers from the east the lowest. Indeed, in most women's memories, it was only from 1942 that the shortages and time spent queuing became really bad, worsening further after the surrender of 1945 and not really improving until 1948 onwards.[18] Before then, extensive plundering of occupied territories, combined with the development of substitute foodstuffs and the partial restructuring of the domestic agricultural sector, guaranteed a reasonable standard of living for civilians on the home front, with some provision made even for the supply of 'luxury' items like tobacco, alcohol, cosmetics and 'foreign' fashion accessories.[19] After the defeat of France in 1940, for instance, French beauty products – lipsticks, powders, paints and silk stockings – were among the most highly valued presents sent home by soldiers serving in the occupation army, despite the earlier emphasis on the creation of a 'Germanic' fashion. In June 1942, when Gauleiter Albert Förster of Danzig complained at a meeting in the Reich Chancellery about the 'Modepüppchen' or fashion-conscious ladies seen hanging around and smoking in Berlin cafés, Hitler leapt to their defence, claiming that they were probably women factory workers who were relaxing at the end of their shifts. Besides which, the Führer continued, 'if we were to drive the fashion-conscious girls from the cafés, we would also be taking away one of the greatest pleasures for the common soldier on leave'.[20]

Still, reports drawn up by the SD revealed a rapid deterioration of domestic morale during the war, especially after the defeat at Stalingrad in the winter of 1942–43. The single most important cause of discontent and grumbling was the steady rise in prices for essential items like food and children's clothing. The government made some effort to control inflation through the appointment of a Reich Prices Commissioner, but without much success.[21] By the middle of the war potatoes and other home-grown vegetables had become the staple diet of poorer urban Germans, as bread, meat and fat became increasingly difficult to get hold of (see Table 11).

Table 11 Weekly food rations for the 'normal' urban German consumer, 1939–1945 (in grams)

Time period	Bread	Meat	Fat
End September 1939	2,400	500	270
Mid-April 1942	2,000	300	206
Beginning June 1943	2,325	250	218
Mid-October 1944	2,225	250	218
Mid-March 1945	1,778	222	109

Source: Wolfgang Schneider (ed.), *Frauen unterm Hakenkreuz* (Hamburg, 2001), p. 126. Copyright © Hoffmann und Campe Verlag, Hamburg.

Shortages of food bore particularly heavily on urban women with children and on factory women working shifts. Indeed, the latter often had to queue for hours in front of shops at the beginning or the end of a long working day. Occasionally the preferential treatment given to pregnant women and to the mothers of young children, who were given extra points on their ration cards and were allowed to jump food queues, led to scenes of public unrest requiring police intervention.[22] Often, too, it was volunteer activists in the DFW who were sent out to placate angry women workers and housewives, fending off complaints about inadequate price controls and attempting to dissuade local people from abusing the system.[23]

In general, however, the Nazi regime managed to prevent a repeat of the huge shortages of the years 1916–19. Although foreign workers, especially Russians and Poles living in urban areas, were often housed and fed very badly, and Jews living in Germany after 1941 faced cuts to their food allowance that bordered on starvation levels,[24] the average German did not suffer to the same extent as in the First World War. In other words, Hitler's aim of avoiding unrest on the home front was achieved: even if urban consumers were far from content with the amount they received with their ration cards, there was little they could do about it apart from turning to the black market or taking 'hamstering' trips into the countryside in order to exchange goods for food. In the meantime, the harsh new penalties introduced for those caught handling or trading in stolen goods, including the use of capital punishment for theft of poultry and other livestock, acted to some extent as a deterrent against others.[25]

2. Marriage, divorce and sexual relations at time of war

As we saw in Chapter 2, the outbreak of war in September 1939 led to a sudden increase in the number of marriages, particularly in cases where the husband was about to be called up into the armed forces. Ironically, as Elizabeth Heineman points out, socially 'undesired' elements benefited from the marriage boom of the early war years at least as much as the 'socially desirable'. For instance, concern about the likely demographic impact of war led the regime to relax its requirements regarding proof of genealogy and hereditary health for those couples applying for the marriage loan.[26] Growing numbers of women who were of only 'average' racial worth, or even 'asocial' in the Nazi definition of word, were also awarded Motherhood Crosses in the years 1939 to 1944.[27] Conversely 'Aryan' women married to Jewish men were subject to increased levels of harassment from the Gestapo, with divorce as the desired outcome. Indeed, persecution of the Jews now took priority over all other aspects of Nazi racial policy.

Women who married during the war often found that there was little to separate them from single women in experiential terms. Thus married women were given precious little time to spend with their husbands, except during brief periods of military leave, but many more opportunities for extra-marital liaisons, for instance through contacts made at work or through the practice of hiring foreign workers to help out on family-run farms. In 1943 the most senior social worker in Hamburg, Dr Käthe Petersen, indeed reported an alarming decline in moral standards among soldiers' wives:

> Many previously respectable wives have been alerted to the existence of other men through going out to work. In many firms – the tram company is a particularly good example – the male workers seem to have acquired the habit of going after the soldiers' wives. In many factories too soldiers' wives have been led astray by the corrosive influences of some of their ruder female co-workers. Women who previously devoted themselves to their household chores, and were good mothers, have been led by such influences to neglect their housework and children, and to interest themselves only in night-time adventures and the quest for male company.[28]

Often, too, married women as well as single women were forced to live with their parents or to sublet rooms from other families for lack of a suitable marital home, which may have increased their sense of boredom and isolation and thus their inclination to look around for other, more available men. Some 'war brides' hardly got to know their husbands at all, contributing to a sharp rise in the divorce rate immediately after the war.[29] Similarly, the large number of casualties at the front meant that many women became widows without ever having experienced 'normal' married life. Indeed, 40 per cent of the nearly 4 million German soldiers killed during the Second World War were married.[30] Meanwhile, longer working hours made it difficult for women in employment to meet members of the opposite sex, and left little time for the traditional forms of courtship. Working women who married after the outbreak of the war were not allowed to leave their jobs, unless they became pregnant, which meant that they had more in common with single women than with women who had married before September 1939.[31]

Intervention by the regime, which was anxious, as always, to boost birth rates among 'healthy' 'Aryans', also led to a blurring of the legal and social differences between married and single women. For instance, a government decree of November 1941 allowed women who had borne children by soldiers killed at the front to enter into 'post-mortem' marriages which in effect made widows out of unmarried 'Aryan' mothers. Approximately 18,000 women had taken advantage of this scheme by 1945.[32] An earlier measure introduced by the Reich Ministry of Interior in 1940 also allowed unmarried mothers to carry the designation 'Frau' instead of 'Fraulein', thus in effect removing the stigma of illegitimacy from 'Aryan' children.[33] Alongside this, the state sponsored a number of match-making schemes to bring together unmarried women and soldiers on leave in 'appropriate' settings. In 1944 a broader letter-writing programme was also introduced by representatives of the League of German Families (*Reichsbund Deutscher Familien*), which was aimed at finding suitable wives for wounded ex-servicemen lying in hospitals and convalescent homes. Neither of these schemes was particular successful, however, especially as women investigating the possibility of marrying wounded veterans 'often lost interest once they understood what was meant by "severely wounded"'.[34]

Finally, the SS Race and Resettlement Office began its own experimental breeding project in 1940, known as the *Lebensborn* programme, which involved the establishment of special maternity homes for the racially 'valuable' brides and wives of young SS men and also for unmarried mothers of 'good blood' who had fallen pregnant by soldiers serving at the front.[35] As Himmler later explained in a conversation with his masseur Felix Kersten in 1943:

> I have made it known privately that any young woman who is alone and longs for a child can turn to *Lebensborn* with perfect confidence. I would sponsor the child and provide for its education. I know this is a revolutionary step, because according to the existing middle-class code an unmarried woman has no right to yearn for a child ... Yet often she cannot find the right man or cannot marry because of her work, though her wish to have a child is compelling. I have therefore created the possibility for such women to have the child they crave. As you can imagine, we recommend only racially faultless men as 'conception assistants'.[36]

Alongside these apparently 'enlightened' (but actually deeply chauvinistic and racist) attempts to encourage procreation and remove the stigma from illegitimacy, however, there was a male backlash against what was perceived to be a breakdown in conventional morality during the war, or rather a breakdown in the mechanisms by which society sought to control female sexuality. Thus in 1941 Himmler ordered a complete ban on the importation, production and sale of all contraceptive devices, with an exception made only for condoms, which were distributed freely to soldiers because of their role in protecting men from contracting sexually transmitted infections (STIs).[37] Women who sought an unauthorised abortion, and those who helped them, could face the death penalty from 1943 onwards, especially 'if the perpetrator through such deeds continuously impairs the vitality of the German *Volk*'.[38] Women who knowingly passed on STIs to soldiers could also face severe punishments, including the possibility of incarceration in a concentration camp for repeat offenders. In 1940 one Nazi doctor justified these harsh measures on the grounds that 'about 50 per cent of infertile marriages are due to a sexually transmitted disease', so that preventative action was no longer a matter for individuals but had become a 'priority for the race' [*eine Volksfrage*].[39]

Finally, women (unlike men) could also be classified by Nazi social workers as 'asocial' simply because they engaged in actual or alleged extra-marital heterosexual activity of a kind deemed harmful to the 'national community'.[40] Orphaned, abandoned or neglected teenage girls found hanging around military barracks were a particular cause for concern, and were frequently blamed for the rising incidence of STIs among soldiers. Some were placed in foster care or were subject to the supervision of social services, while others were able to slip through the net due to the increasing chaos caused by the war. Those unlucky enough to be caught more than once were sent to a special youth detention centre (*Jugendschutzlager*) for 'wayward' girls at Uckermark in Mecklenburg, often on the recommendation of a police official or social worker, where they were subject to forced labour and various kinds of physical and mental cruelty.[41]

In an act of supreme hypocrisy, the police and local authorities agreed to tolerate official army brothels where prostitutes were subject to regular health checks, while continuing to come down very heavily on all forms of unlicensed prostitution.[42] This meant, among other things, that women and girls who were not prostitutes were often caught up in police raids on bars and nightclubs and forced to undergo humiliating medical examinations in accordance with a revamped version of the 1927 Reich Law for the Combating of Venereal Diseases. Sometimes this led to embarrassing episodes, for instance when the wives and daughters of prominent local party officials were netted in police raids. Interestingly, similar events took place in the western occupation zones of Germany after 1945, but the main targets of police raids were teenage girls and young women deemed to be at risk of spreading STIs to American and British soldiers.[43]

Married women suspected of committing adultery while their husbands were away at the front presented a different problem, especially if pregnancy resulted. On the one hand, there was the 'honour' of the husband to consider, but on the other hand, the Nazi state was also interested in encouraging the birth of more 'racially valuable' children, whether legitimate or not. A rise in the divorce rate during wartime might also have a detrimental effect on morale, a matter of particular concern to the Reich

Ministry of Interior. In most cases, therefore, the state did not encourage husbands to initiate divorce proceedings but tried to find other ways of settling marital disputes. For instance, in 1942 a new crime of 'insulting husbands at the front' was introduced, allowing married soldiers to claim compensation from male interlopers through the courts while leaving the marriage intact.[44] Nonetheless, errant wives could be punished in other ways too. In May 1942, for instance, the Reich Ministry of Interior granted local authorities the discretionary right to remove state benefits from wives found to be engaging in 'dishonourable or immoral conduct'.[45] Also, from 1943 war widows who were considered to be leading immoral lives could be faced with retrospective divorce proceedings instituted by the state.[46]

Meanwhile, much more effort was put into policing sexual relations between German women and foreign workers, mainly because this came into conflict with the regime's obsession with maintaining the 'purity' of the nation's blood. Indeed, fraternisation with 'the enemy' was a matter of growing concern to the Nazi authorities, as can be seen in numerous SD reports from the war years. One such report, from the year 1943, read as follows:

> Women who have relations with prisoners of war come into constant contact with them through their work in agriculture or in factories. They are by no means all of them women of loose morals. Among the accused there are respectable farmers' daughters from good families with no sexual experience, the wives of soldiers who have been happily married for many years, many of them women with several children. As soon as Frenchmen are found in more responsible positions, typists, housekeepers and members of the intelligentsia appear as the accused. With the little supervision and considerable freedom enjoyed by French prisoners of war it is possible for many instances of sexual relations to pass unreported. On the other hand it seems that in the course of a relationship both the prisoners of war and the women become increasingly carefree, so that in time they are discovered, often as a result of a spiteful denunciation.[47]

Those who were caught faced dire punishments, especially in cases that involved Polish or Russian men having sex with German women. In such instances, the men were often put to death by public hanging while the women were first humiliated by having their heads shaved and then sentenced to terms of imprisonment ranging from six months to several years. This form of on-the-spot justice was actively encouraged by senior Nazis and local party functionaries. Indeed, in a directive issued on 31 January 1940 Himmler explicitly instructed the police forces under his control 'not to intervene' in cases where the 'sound instincts of the people' were crying out for revenge against local women who had brought shame on their communities by developing forbidden contacts with POWs. He also called for the women in question to be taken into protective custody 'for at least one year'.[48] Instances where German men were discovered to have had sexual relations with (or forced themselves upon) Polish women were generally dealt with in a more lenient fashion, however. At worst, the man might lose his job or be taken into custody for a few weeks as a warning, while the woman might be arrested for up to three weeks and – unless more serious charges were pending – sent to a new place of work after her release. Here again, gender inequalities had an important impact on the way Nazi racial laws were enforced in practice.[49]

3. Denunciations and their consequences

Despite the various risks involved, thousands of German women from all walks of life, both single and married, widowed and divorced, had casual relationships with foreign labourers during the war. Their motives varied. Some were undoubtedly subject to varying degrees of coercion ending in the threat of violence and rape, while others were responding to a genuine sexual attraction or instinctive need for intimacy and emotional comfort at a time of great uncertainty about the future. As Jill Stephenson has shown, there were other factors at play too. In particular women left to run farms on their own in the absence of husband and sons often felt unable to spurn the advances of their Polish workers in case they threatened to leave the farm. The Polish workers in turn sometimes expected and demanded sex as a reward for their labour, and, at a time of acute manpower shortages, they had considerable leeway in persuading their female bosses to bow to their wishes.[50] Sex, in other words, became a commodity long before the end of the war, and the boundaries between rape, prostitution, fraternisation and casual sexual arrangements became increasingly blurred as time went on.[51] After the military surrender in 1945 it was the turn of Allied soldiers to offer German women material benefits, such as ration cards, cigarettes and chocolate, in exchange for sex. One Ruhr metalworker, for instance, later recalled his memories of the spring of 1945 as follows: 'A Negro said: "The German soldier fought for six years, the German woman for only five minutes!". That's a fact from beginning to end. I was ashamed.'[52]

Before 1945, the danger facing women who embarked upon relationships with foreign workers was the threat of denunciation. Indeed, according to Elizabeth Heineman, 'most women were found out only when their neighbors or co-workers denounced them'.[53] Again motivations for denunciation varied. Sometimes a husband or lover wanted revenge. Sometimes the local population deplored such relationships and wanted the culprits to be severely punished. Only very rarely was a denunciation made for purely political reasons, however. In other words, the phenomenon of denunciation cannot be used as evidence of widespread support for Nazi racial views.

Rather, in at least some cases the underlying motive was the resolution of conflicts and disputes within families and marriages or between neighbours and colleagues. In this sense, the Gestapo did not simply force its will onto the people; 'ordinary' women and men might also use the Gestapo in order to solve their marital problems or to settle an old score.[54]

There were also, it must be said, instances of women informing on relative or complete strangers, sometimes with terrible consequences. In Düsseldorf in 1942, for instance, a 34-year-old woman reported a foreman at a local factory whom she had observed meeting up with a Polish woman outside her house on each Sunday for several weeks. Even though the Gestapo could find no evidence of a sexual relationship, the foreman was sacked from his job and was sentenced to 21 days in 'protective custody'.[55] In another case, in October 1944, a Frau Frank-Schulz from Berlin was denounced by a Red Cross nurse for having expressed her regret that the assassination attempt on Hitler had failed; she was also alleged to have said that a few years of Anglo-Saxon occupation would be a small price to pay for the ending of National Socialist rule. In passing the death sentence on her, Roland Freisler, the President of the People's Court, declared that the accused had 'made common cause with the traitors of July 1944' and had thus shown herself to be 'forever without honour'. This was in spite of the fact that nothing could be found to link Frau Frank-Schulz to the actual events of July 1944, and the only evidence against her was the testimony supplied by the Red Cross nurse.[56]

In less serious cases women and men were denounced and put on trial for violation of currency regulations or for black market offences. Those convicted generally received a jail sentence in a 'normal' criminal prison, while second- or third-time offenders might have to go into 'protective custody', which usually meant a spell inside a concentration camp. Nonetheless, as the war continued, the number of 'crimes' for which people could be sentenced to death increased significantly, as did the number of women and men executed for seemingly minor offences like spreading news obtained from foreign radio broadcasts or criticising the war in public. For instance, in 1944, the last year for which statistics are available, nearly half of all those defendants brought before the People's Court (2,097 out of 4,379) were sentenced to death.[57] This figure can be compared with the grand total of 'only' 644 death sentences carried out in Nazi Germany before 1939.[58] Meanwhile, the population of concentration camps like Ravensbrück and Uckermark soared in the final years of the war. Hundreds of thousands of petty criminals, prostitutes and 'asocials' were imprisoned without trial and required to work for the German war effort in truly murderous conditions, as were hundreds of thousands of anti-Nazis, POWs and resistance fighters from across occupied Europe.[59]

Sometimes the mere threat of denunciation could play havoc with people's lives. Inge Deutschkron and her mother, for instance, who as Jews were living in hiding in Berlin in a house belonging to a friend, Walter

Rieck, received a terrible shock one day in 1944 when they received a threatening letter with the words: 'Rieck-Deutschkron-Jews' written on it using letters cut out of a newspaper. At first they were beside themselves with worry and believed, at the very least, that they would have to find another hiding place. Their anxiety grew when they heard that Rieck, who lived in another part of town, had been called in for questioning by the Gestapo. However, it later transpired that the message had been written by Rieck's wife, who had discovered that her husband was having an affair with an actress, and wished to frighten and punish him because she was afraid of losing him. Her motives were entirely non-political and she had no real intention of endangering the Deutschkrons or leading the Gestapo to them. Fortunately for Inge and her mother, the Gestapo also believed Rieck's explanation that his wife was merely trying to get revenge for his sexual transgressions, and did not pursue the matter further.[60]

As this case shows, denunciation (or the threat of a denunciation) often came from those who were in a weak position vis-à-vis their potential victims and were looking for a means of making themselves more powerful. Furthermore, while the Gestapo always investigated cases that involved Jews, they were more reluctant to intervene in domestic or marital disputes between 'Aryans'. For instance, men who were denounced by their wives for alleged minor political offences were often released without formal charge, even if there was a history of repeated domestic violence.[61] Even when cases were brought to court, the Nazi state considered it had a higher interest in maintaining marriages, unless the accused had committed very serious (i.e. capital) offences, such as murder, high treason, arson or attempting to undermine the German military effort. Judges, for instance, were under strict instructions that false or substantiated denunciations of one spouse by another did not necessarily constitute adequate grounds for divorce unless there were aggravating factors. Nor did the temporary incarceration of a spouse in a concentration or forced labour camp automatically result in the granting of a divorce. The aim here was to deter the use of denunciations as a means of resolving marital disputes or achieving quick divorce settlements, thus freeing up time to concentrate on what the Gestapo considered to be the more important task of hunting down Jews in hiding and terrorising political or racial enemies of the regime.[62]

Gestapo case files and records from the Nazi special courts in Würzburg, Düsseldorf, Munich, Hamburg and Bielefeld confirm that it was generally the urban poor who informed on the urban poor, especially in cases involving allegations of domestic violence, sexual crimes or illegal black market trading.[63] Petty jealousies at work and disputes between neighbours over noise levels and anti-social behaviour were also often the underlying cause. While denunciation was usually a crime of the weak against the strong, however, it would be wrong to see it as a crime committed primarily by women. True, when women used the Gestapo to punish their violent or wayward husbands they not only challenged their traditional role as subservient wives, but also helped to turn 'the very notion of the family as a "safe haven" ... upside down', so that even the most intimate sphere of sexuality and family life was opened up, by mutual agreement, to the scrutiny of the Nazi terror state.[64]

It is this two-way politicisation of the domestic sphere that makes the phenomenon of women denouncers so interesting to scholars of Nazi Germany.[65] Nonetheless, the fact remains that at all stages of the Third Reich men were far more likely to become Gestapo informants than women. Indeed, Eric Johnson, Gisela Diewald-Kerkmann and Klaus Marxen, in three separate studies of Gestapo case files, have all come to the same conclusion, that women accounted for only 17 per cent of denunciations and men for 83 per cent. During the war years, the percentage margin between male and female denouncers did narrow somewhat – to 69 per cent men and 31 per cent women – but the difference itself remains striking, especially given that millions of younger men had by then been called up to serve in the armed forces.[66] Denunciation in other words, was a predominantly male rather than a predominantly female phenomenon, even if some women also turned to the Gestapo to secure advantages for themselves or in order to hurt others.

4. The bombing of German towns

Even before the war had started, German women were being prepared for the possibility of bombing raids. As early as May 1935, for instance, an agreement was drawn up between the *NS-Frauenschaft* and the *Reichsluftschutzbund* (Reich Association for Air Raid Precautions) for the training of women's leaders as air raid wardens, and in June 1935 a new government decree made all German citizens liable to be called up for civil defence duties in the event of war.[67] The bombing of the Spanish town of Guernica by the Luftwaffe and of Shanghai by the Japanese air force, both in 1937, had also illustrated the horrific impact of aerial bombardment on non-combatants. Fear of the possible use of chemicals led to the mass distribution of gas masks to German civilians in the summer of 1939, and families living in Baden near the border with France were temporarily evacuated to Württemberg as a precautionary measure in the opening months of the war.[68] Finally, in the autumn of 1939 well-stocked hotels and boarding houses in south German resorts were overwhelmed by a sudden influx of wealthy women and couples from the northern and western industrial districts of the Reich; here they might expect to live out the war in relative luxury, especially since hotel owners often turned to the black market to meet their customers' demands.[69] Nonetheless, while rationing, food shortages and labour mobilisation in 1939–40 helped to reveal the importance of class differences in determining the wartime experience of German women, the Allied bombing campaign, once begun in earnest in the second half of 1940, tended to have more of a social levelling effect. Or as Joseph Goebbels noted, with ill-disguised enthusiasm: 'the bomb terror spares the dwellings of neither rich nor poor'.[70]

In spite of this, it was only in the last three years of the war that the total inadequacy of German civil defence precautions was revealed for all to see. The use of incendiary bombs by the RAF and the American air force was first tried out in a raid on Lübeck in north Germany in March 1942 and soon extended with devastating effect to the city of Cologne and other towns in the Rhineland and Westphalia, beginning to have a serious effect on morale by 1943.[71] On 22 July 1943, for instance, the SD noted in a 'Report on the terror raids on Cologne and Aachen' that the inhabitants of these two Rhineland cities no longer believed in victory, although most people were still keeping a 'remarkable composure' in the face of adversity. Furthermore, there was a strong feeling:

> that the Rhineland ha[s] ... been written off by Berlin ... One could see this best from the way the evacuees were treated in the reception Gaus. The necessity – because of the suspension of public transport – of having to go to work over piles of rubble and through clouds of dust; the impossibility of washing oneself properly or of cooking at home because there was no water, gas or electricity; the sudden value acquired by a spoon or a plate which had been rescued; the difficulty of shopping for food because most of the shops had been destroyed or had closed on their own accord; the continual explosions of delayed action bombs or duds or the blowing-up of parts of buildings which were in danger of collapsing; the delay in postal deliveries, the stopping of newspapers; the impossibility of listening to the radio because the electricity had been cut off; the disappearance of every means of relaxation such as the cinema, theatre, concerts etc. – these are aspects of a life which is being lived as if on the front line and of which people in the rest of the Reich have no idea.[72]

Towns in the Ruhr like Dortmund, Essen and Duisburg were likewise repeatedly hit, sometimes in broad daylight but mostly at night, with the local inhabitants facing 'little sleep and shattered nerves'.[73] Berlin, Hamburg and Hanover were also seriously affected, as were many other towns and cities. Indeed, by 1943 an estimated 4.5 million German civilians had been made homeless, rising to 12 million by the end of the war.[74] Among them, women 'standing alone', whether as workers or as housewives and mothers, formed a disproportionately high number. After 1943 mothers with small children were often forcibly evacuated to rural areas, while those left behind – mostly single women and mothers with older children – continued to eke out a precarious existence in burned-out apartments and underground cellars. However, while everybody who lived through the air raids suffered from constant stress and anxiety, those women working in factories now at least had somewhere warm to go to for part of the day or night, unless their factories were bombed out too. Getting to and from work was of course even more difficult if bombs had destroyed public transport networks.[75]

Meanwhile, the distrust of official news propaganda inevitably meant that the number of people rumoured to have been killed during bombing raids on northern towns and cities swelled to enormous levels in the popular imagination. For south Germans, who did not experience bombardment on a large scale until 1944–45, the story of the terrible firestorm that raged in Hamburg in July and August 1943, killing around 34,000 people and destroying 255,691 homes, served as a frightening portent of things to come.[76] With the war evidently now lost, rural populations also took an increasingly tolerant attitude towards fraternisation with foreign workers and POWs.[77] Denunciations to the Gestapo in the area of racial policy tailed off significantly after 1943,[78] as did the number of incidents in which women were publicly shamed if they were caught having sex with foreigners.[79] On the other hand, bitter criticism was frequently heard of the inadequacy of civil defence measures and the slow pace of rehousing schemes for bombed-out families. Many rural communities also disliked evacuees from urban areas and often blamed them, rather than their trusted foreign workers, for the growing food shortages and rising crime rates.[80]

Surprisingly, though, the blanket bombing of German cities did not lead to any significant increase in hatred for the British or Americans. Whereas in 1940 the pages of the *NS-Frauenwarte* and other magazines had been full of invective against the 'pirate state England',[81] after 1943 what was more striking was the growing number of 'ordinary' Germans who secretly listened to BBC radio broadcasts despite the dire punishments awaiting those who were caught.[82] More palpable still was a fear of communism as the Soviet army moved slowly but inexorably towards Berlin, on its way capturing vast swathes of territory in the eastern provinces of the Reich. A decade and more of Nazi propaganda against the 'Asiatic' Russian hordes, combined with gruesome stories of mass rape and mutilation told by German women refugees fleeing westwards to escape the advancing Red Army soldiers, and the sheer terror that the thought of a Soviet occupation inspired, perhaps explain the reluctant acceptance of Hitler's call to hold out to the bitter end.[83]

The anti-Nazi journalist Sebastian Haffner, a Berliner who lived in exile in Britain from 1938 onwards, also had a theory on this. In his view, one of the effects of the First World War and the economic crises of the 1920s and 1930s had been to accustom the Germans to under-nourishment. It was therefore a mistake to believe that they could be starved into submission. Indeed:

> the Germans will scarcely give up Nazism or a second world war out of hunger. Today they consider hunger almost as a moral duty and anyhow, it is not hard to bear. They have become rather ashamed of

their natural needs. Paradoxically, the Nazis have acquired a new, indirect propaganda weapon by giving the people too little to eat.[84]

In fact, though, the cities were kept reasonably well fed throughout the latter stages of the war, while it was the largely unbombed rural areas that felt most resentful at the compulsory requisitioning of their machinery and grain, and therefore wished for a rapid end to the war.[85] Furthermore, as the Prussian noblewoman and journalist Ursula von Kardorff noted in her diary in April 1944, while many older Berliners were now resigned to the worst – the arrival of the Russians and the collapse of all civilised values – the attitude of younger city dwellers, herself included, was much more hedonistic:

> At the moment life is still worth living. People keep behaving as if the threat is not really there. We make ourselves beautiful, go to the Adlon [the most exclusive hotel in Berlin], are pleased when we find ourselves in the company of good-looking men, especially if we arouse the envy of others, and drink wine and cognac in order to forget. It is so much easier to enjoy life than to grumble.[86]

Fear of the SS and the Gestapo, and demoralisation following the collapse of the July plot in 1944, may also have played a role in persuading people not to resist orders to defend each town and village down to the last house. By the end of the war Goebbels and other senior Nazis were even welcoming the destruction of the Reich's historic cities on the grounds that this would finally destroy the remnants of 'decadent' bourgeois culture and lead to the rebuilding of a harder, more proletarian Germany in years to come.[87] In any event, the big cities in western and central Germany, which were now largely inhabited by women, children and the old, held out to the end and there was no sudden collapse in support for the war effort. This was the case even after the ninth armoured division of the US army crossed the Rhine at Remagen on 7 March 1945, and the Soviets came within striking distance of Berlin at the end of the same month, thus making defeat virtually certain.

5. The last weeks of the war and the first days of peace

How German women experienced the last weeks of the war and the first days of peace depended on a variety of factors, not least where they lived geographically. In popular memory (and also as a matter of historical fact) those women who found themselves in areas conquered by the Red Army suffered far more than anybody else.[88] News of the atrocities committed by drunken Soviet soldiers against helpless civilians had begun to emerge as early as October 1944, when the Wehrmacht briefly reoccupied the town of Nemmersdorf in East Prussia and discovered the bodies of 62 women and girls who had been raped and mutilated.[89] After a brief hiatus the Soviets renewed their offensive towards Berlin in January 1945. From this point onwards multiple mass rape became the most visible and most vile means of terrorising the conquered German populations of East Prussia, Pomerania and Silesia, with the estimated number of victims ranging from tens of thousands to 2 million.[90] According to a secret memorandum on the behaviour of the Red Army in captured German territory, drawn up by Wehrmacht intelligence officers on 22 February 1945, most rapes took place 'under the influence of alcohol'. The victims were 'girls and women of all ages from 8 to 68' and they were usually forced to submit to their assailants 'at gunpoint'. Reports even came in of women being attacked by 'up to 24 officers and Red Army regulars at a time'.[91] These impressions can also be confirmed from Soviet sources. Thus the Russian playwright Zakhar Agranenko, who served as a marine officer in East Prussia in 1944–45, recorded in his diary in January 1945: 'Red Army soldiers don't believe in "individual liaisons" with German women. Nine, ten, twelve men at a time – they rape them on a collective basis'.[92] And the Soviet journalist Natalya Gesse later wrote: 'The Russian soldiers were raping every German female from eight to eighty. It was an army of rapists.'[93]

Apart from rape and the fear of rape, there were other dangers to face. As the Soviets advanced, the home front and the fighting front increasingly melted into one, with no place to hide. Hundreds of thousands of German men – husbands, fathers and sons – were killed after October 1944 while fighting in the *Volksturm* (home army), and many more Germans of both sexes were shipped off to the Soviet Union to work as slave labourers in the Gulag, often not returning until many years after the war, if at all.[94] At least 1 million German civilians from the east also perished from hunger or froze to death during the long westward flight of refugees ahead of the advancing Soviet troops in the winter of 1944–45.[95] While the deportees were mostly able-bodied men, the refugees were mostly women, children and the elderly. Often they had to leave their homes on foot or in horse-drawn wagons, as all other forms of transport had been requisitioned for the final last-ditch stand against the Soviets. One teenage girl later recorded the gruesome scenes of death and devastation she witnessed during a trek from the eastern edge of East Prussia through to Kahlberg on the Baltic coast in late January and early February 1945:

> Mothers in a fit of madness threw their children into the sea. People hanged themselves; others fell upon dead horses, cutting bits of flesh and roasting them on open fires. Women gave birth in the wagons. Everyone thought only of himself – no one could help the sick or the wounded.[96]

Even those refugees who managed to make it into the relative safety of the area beyond the Oder–Neiße line still faced a life of extreme hardship and poverty. Many were forced to live in overcrowded refugee camps or in less populated rural areas where accommodation could still be found for them. This caused much resentment among locals, especially when outsiders were seen to be given preferential treatment in terms of housing and food allocations.[97] Meanwhile, the initial wave of refugees from the east in the winter of 1944–45 was followed by a much bigger wave of German expellees (*Vertriebene*) who were driven from their homes in Poland, Czechoslovakia, Hungary, Yugoslavia, Romania and the Soviet Union itself in the aftermath of the Potsdam agreements of July 1945. In all, nearly 6 million ethnic Germans had fled to the western zones of occupation by October 1946, and a further 3.6 million to the Soviet zone (the future GDR).[98] Most of them had lost all their possessions, and many of them came in large family groups in which there was no employable adult male.[99]

In the western and central parts of Germany conditions were also desperate at the end of the war, but not quite as grim as in the east. In many small towns and villages local dignitaries managed to negotiate a quick surrender to the advancing enemy in order to minimise bloodshed. This strategy was not without risk, however, and those who raised the white flag too early could find themselves being executed as traitors by the SS and other diehard Nazis in the last days of the war.[100] After the surrender, liberated prisoners of war and foreign workers occasionally went on the rampage, looting and stealing food, and terrorising the local population, especially women. Sometimes they were accompanied by groups of Allied soldiers who egged them on.[101] In most cases, however, these bouts of lawlessness were short-lived. Indeed, former forced workers, usually Poles or French POWs, often continued to work voluntarily on the farms they had been allocated to for several months after the war, partly because they had developed a friendship with their German employers and partly because food was more plentiful there than in their own home countries. There were also instances of POWs helping to negotiate surrenders. In Wendelsheim near Tübingen in south-western Germany, for instance, 'French prisoners of war immediately reported to their invading countrymen that "they had been well-treated here during their fifty-eight-month stay" and asked that the troops should leave the village unmolested, which they did.'[102] In other parts of rural Württemberg, too, it was frequently reported that villagers welcomed the arrival of American troops on the grounds that 'it isn't the Russians who are coming, but civilised people'.[103]

Women living in the ruined cities of northern and central Germany fared less well. With the collapse of the Nazi regime, supplies of food and fuel dried up almost completely, and urban populations were left at the mercy of the occupying forces. In Berlin, surrounded and conquered by the Soviets in late April 1945, women were also once again in great danger of sexual assault. With the fighting now virtually over and the Wehrmacht no longer a threat, however, rape was seen less as a means of exacting revenge or terrorising the population, and more as the 'sexual spoils of war'.[104] Groups of drunken soldiers thus went looking for their female victims at night, flashing torches into bunkers and attics and quite literally taking their pick. For many months, girls and younger women rarely appeared in public at all, especially during the 'hunting hours' after dark. Inge Deutschkron, for example, the Jewish woman who at 22 years of age had just emerged from over two years of hiding underground from the Nazis, had to stay for several days and nights on the roof of a neighbouring house with a group of other women, including one who had already been raped.

> At meal times we climbed down [from the roof] and ate, while Aunt Lisa or my mother kept guard and sounded the warning if any Soviet soldiers came near the house. Then we climbed back up the ladder, pulled it up behind us, closed up the hatch and placed a bucket of water on top, so that anybody opening the hatch would find [this bucket] falling on their heads.[105]

Occasionally German men were on hand to remonstrate with Soviet soldiers, but only very rarely. For instance, in Inge Deutschkron's account a local man stayed on the roof with her and the other women, but he was unable to do anything to protect them. In fact, he was temporarily arrested on suspicion of being a German soldier. He was virtually the only young man around on their street.[106] In other accounts teenage sons tried to put up a futile resistance in order to defend their mothers, only to be shot in the process. Husbands, if present at the scene of an attack, often felt completely powerless to intervene. Hanna Gerlitz, for instance, remembered how, after being raped by two Soviet officers, 'I had to console my husband and help restore his courage. He cried like a baby.'[107] Sometimes, too, husbands and fiancés reacted by disowning women who had been raped, preferring to blame the victims rather than face the reality that they had been unable to offer them protection. One woman could still recall many years later what her fiancé Gerd had said when he returned to Berlin a few weeks after the end of the war to find that she and the other women she was living with had all been attacked:

> 'You've turned into shameless bitches – every one of you in this house'. And he grimaced. 'I can't bear to listen to these stories. You've lost all your standards, the whole lot of you!' And what could I say? I crept into a corner and sulked. I couldn't cry. All this seemed so silly, so hopeless.[108]

According to some estimates, about one in three women (500,000 out of 1.5 million) living in Berlin at the end of the war were raped by Russian soldiers. The total number of rapes was even higher because many women were attacked more than once.[109] Not surprisingly, suicide, abortion and sexually transmitted infections were rampant in the first months after the war. Semi-legal abortions were performed by doctors in public hospitals, sometimes up until the last month of pregnancy, and a black market thrived in illegal abortions as well.[110] Other women took to prostituting themselves in order to get enough to eat or in the hope of gaining a 'protector' against other would-be rapists.[111] One unrepentant Russian tank commander later claimed: 'They all lifted their skirts for us and lay on the bed.' He also boasted that 'two million of our children were born' in Germany, undoubtedly a gross exaggeration.[112]

Soldiers representing the western Allies also raped German women, although this happened less frequently and less systematically than in the Soviet zone. More common, indeed, was the 'grey area' of sexual favours in return for material rewards – usually chocolate and cigarettes, which British and American servicemen possessed in abundant supplies.[113] What most struck western observers about the Germany of 1945, however, was the huge surplus of women over men. The first post-war census in October 1946, for instance, revealed that there were 126 females for every 100 males. In Berlin this figure was even higher, with 146 females to 100 males.[114] Germany was now truly a 'country of women', and indeed it was to take at least one, if not two, generations before the demographic imbalance caused by the two world wars began to disappear.[115]

Notes

1 Kasberger, *Heldinnen waren wir keine*, pp. 180ff.
2 Stephenson, '"Emancipation" and its Problems', pp. 358–9.
3 See Annemarie Tröger, 'German Women's Memories of World War II', in: Margaret Randolph Higonnet *et al.* (eds), *Behind the Lines. Gender and the Two World Wars* (New Haven and London, 1987), pp. 285–99.
4 Gerhard Wilke, 'Village Life in Nazi Germany', in: Bessel (ed.), *Life in the Third Reich*, p. 23. Cf. Mark Roseman, 'World War II and Social Change in Germany', in: Arthur Marwick (ed.), *Total War and Social Change* (London, 1988), pp. 58–78, esp. pp. 70–1.
5 Figures in Schneider (ed.), *Frauen unterm Hakenkreuz*, p. 166. By the end of the war nearly 4 million German soldiers had been killed and some 11,700,000 were POWs. Cf. Frevert, *Women in German History*, pp. 257–8.
6 Stephenson, '"Emancipation" and its Problems', esp. pp. 351–61.
7 Kitchen, *Nazi Germany at War*, p. 143. Cf. the evidence in Noakes (ed.), *Nazism, 1919–1945*, Vol. 4, p. 333.
8 'Aus einem Geheimbericht des SD ... über eine spontane Volksempörung', 8 July 1943. Reproduced in: Schneider (ed.), *Frauen unterm Hakenkreuz*, pp. 158–9.
9 Cited in Frevert, *Women in German History*, p. 257.
10 Roseman, 'World War II and Social Change', p. 64. See also the monthly execution figures reproduced in Evans, *Rituals of Retribution*, p. 917.
11 Tröger, 'German Women's Memories', p. 296.
12 Cf. Herbert, *Hitler's Foreign Workers*, esp. pp. 359ff.
13 Stephenson, *Women in Nazi Germany*, p. 95.
14 Stephenson, *The Nazi Organisation of Women*, p. 189.
15 Marie 'Missie' Vassiltchikov, *Berlin Diaries, 1940–1945* (London, 1985), p. 12 (diary entry for 28 April 1940).

16 Ibid., p. 13 (diary entry for 7 May 1940).

17 Kershaw, *The Nazi Dictatorship*, p. 89.

18 Elizabeth Heineman, 'The Hour of the Woman. Memories of Germany's "Crisis Years" and West German National Identity', in: *American Historical Review* 101 (1996), pp. 354–95, esp. p. 387.

19 Roseman, 'World War II and Social Change', p. 62.

20 Cited in Marion Deicke, 'Und sie rauchten doch! Deutsche Moden, 1933–1945', in: *Zeit–Magazin*, 6 May 1983, pp. 30–40.

21 Noakes (ed.), *Nazism, 1919–1945*, Vol. 4, p. 526.

22 See e.g. the evidence in Stephenson, *Women in Nazi Germany*, p. 173.

23 Ibid., p. 105.

24 Kaplan, *Between Dignity and Despair*, p. 151.

25 Kitchen, *Nazi Germany at War*, p. 81.

26 Heineman, *What Difference Does a Husband Make?*, p. 46.

27 Stephenson, *Women in Nazi Germany*, p. 31.

28 Cited in Birthe Kundrus, '"Die Unmoral deutscher Soldatenfrauen". Diskurs, Alltagsverhalten und Ahndungspraxis, 1939–1945', in: Heinsohn *et al.* (eds), *Zwischen Karriere und Verfolgung*, p. 106.

29 Moeller, *Protecting Motherhood*, pp. 29–31.

30 Heineman, *What Difference Does a Husband Make?*, p. 48.

31 Ibid., p. 51.

32 Ibid., p. 47.

33 'Wer darf die Bezeichnung "Frau" führen?', in: *Völkischer Beobachter*, no. 236, 23 August 1940. Copy in BA Berlin, RLB-Pressearchiv, no. 7979, Bl. 126.

34 Heineman, *What Difference Does a Husband Make?*, p. 49.

35 On the *Lebensborn* programme see Catrine Clay and Michael Leapman, *Master Race. The* Lebensborn *Experiment in Nazi Germany* (London, 1995).

36 Ibid., p. 71.

37 Grossmann, *Reforming Sex*, pp. 151–2.

38 Ibid., p. 152.

39 Hepp, 'Vorhof zur Hölle', p. 250.

40 Kundrus, '"Die Unmoral deutscher Soldatenfrauen"', p. 96.

41 Hepp, 'Vorhof zur Hölle', esp. pp. 250–1.

42 Cf. Annette F. Timm, 'The Ambivalent Outsider. Prostitution, Promiscuity and VD Control in Nazi Berlin', in: Gellately and Stoltzfus (eds), *Social Outsiders*, pp. 192–211.

43 See also Heineman, *What Difference Does a Husband Make?*, esp. pp. 100–5.

44 Ibid., p. 55.

45 Kundrus, '"Die Unmoral deutscher Soldatenfrauen"', p. 107.

46 Heineman, *What Difference Does a Husband Make?*, p. 56.

47 Kitchen, *Nazi Germany at War*, pp. 156–7.

48 Noakes (ed.), *Nazism, 1919–1945*, Vol. 4, p. 385.

49 On the policing of sexual relations between Germans and Polish workers see Gellately, *The Gestapo and German Society*, esp. pp. 232–44. Also Kundrus, '"Die Unmoral deutscher Soldatenfrauen"', pp. 102–4.

50 Stephenson, '"Emancipation" and its Problems', pp. 356–8; Stephenson, 'Triangle: Foreign Workers, German Civilians and the Nazi Regime. War and Society in Württemberg, 1939–1945', in: *German Studies Review* 15 (1992), pp. 356–8.

51 Cf. Annemarie Tröger, 'Between Rape and Prostitution. Survival Strategies and Possibilities of Liberation of Berlin Women in 1945–48', in: Judith Friedlander, Alice Kessler-Harris and Carol Smith-Rosenberg (eds), *Women in Culture and Politics. A Century of Change* (Bloomington, 1986), pp. 97–117.

52 Moeller, *Protecting Motherhood*, p. 25.

53 Heineman, *What Difference Does a Husband Make?*, p. 57.
54 Gellately, *The Gestapo and German Society*, esp. pp. 143–4. See also Gellately, *Backing Hitler*, pp. 136–7.
55 Gellately, *Backing Hitler*, p. 164.
56 Schneider (ed.), *Frauen unterm Hakenkreuz*, p. 178.
57 Gellately, *Backing Hitler*, p. 86. Cf. Marxen, *Das Volk und sein Gerichtshof*, pp. 87–9.
58 Evans, *Rituals of Retribution*, p. 689.
59 On the treatment of petty criminals see Nikolaus Wachsmann, 'From Indefinite Confinement to Extermination. "Habitual Criminals" in the Third Reich', in: Gellately and Stoltzfus (eds), *Social Outsiders*, pp. 165–91. On prostitutes see Timm, 'The Ambivalent Outsider', *passim.*
60 Deutschkron, *Ich trug den gelben Stern*, pp. 154–5.
61 For examples see Joshi, 'Wives as Denouncers', *passim.*
62 Gellately, *The Gestapo and German Society*, p. 149.
63 Dördelmann, '"Aus einer gewissen Empörung"', p. 200.
64 Joshi, 'Wives as Denouncers', p. 420.
65 Cf. Dördelmann, '"Aus einer gewissen Empörung"', pp. 201–3. For recent studies of female denunciations see also Helga Schubert, *Judasfrauen. Zehn Fallgeschichten weiblicher Denunziation im Dritten Reich* (Frankfurt/Main, 1990); and Rita Wolters, *Verrat für die Volksgemeinschaft. Denunziantinnen im Dritten Reich* (Pfaffenweiler, 1996).
66 Johnson, *Nazi Terror*, pp. 368–9; Marxen, *Das Volk und sein Gerichtshof*, p. 74; Gisela Diewald-Kirkmann, *Politische Denunziation im NS-Regime oder die kleine Macht der 'Volksgenossen'* (Bonn, 1995), pp. 131–6.
67 'Zusammenarbeit zwischen NS-Frauenschaft und Reichsluftschutzbund', in: *Nationalsozialistische Partei-Korrespondenz*, no. 108, 10 May 1935. Copy in: BA Berlin, RLB-Pressearchiv, no. 7977, Bl. 20. See also Kitchen, *Nazi Germany at War*, p. 88.
68 Stephenson, *Women in Nazi Germany*, p. 100.
69 Ibid., p. 101. See also Stephenson, '"Emancipation" and its Problems', pp. 351–2.
70 Moeller, *Protecting Motherhood*, p. 19. See also Schoenbaum, *Hitler's Social Revolution*, p. 288.
71 On the Allied bombing campaign see Earl R. Beck, *Under the Bombs. The German Home Front, 1942–45* (Kentucky, 1986); Eleanor Hancock, *National Socialist Leadership and Total War* (New York, 1991); and Kitchen, *Nazi Germany at War*, esp. pp. 87–98.
72 Noakes (ed.), *Nazism, 1919–1945*, Vol. 4, p. 569.
73 Heineman, 'Hour of the Woman', p. 362.
74 Kitchen, *Nazi Germany at War*, p. 94.
75 Moeller, *Protecting Motherhood*, p. 20.
76 Figures in Stephenson, *Women in Nazi Germany*, p. 97, citing Ursula Büttner, '*Gomorrha'. Hamburg im Bombenkrieg. Die Wirkung der Luftangriffe auf Bevölkerung und Wirtschaft* (Hamburg, 1993), pp. 25–6.
77 Stephenson, 'Triangle', esp. pp. 343–52.
78 Gellately, *The Gestapo and German Society*, pp. 247–8.
79 Heineman, *What Difference Does a Husband Make?*, p. 57.
80 Ibid., p. 98.
81 See e.g. the article 'Raubstaat England', in: *NS-Frauenwarte*, 8 (1939/1940), pp. 336–7.
82 Kitchen, *Nazi Germany at War*, pp. 282–3.
83 Moeller, *Protecting Motherhood*, p. 24; Heineman, *What Difference Does a Husband Make?*, p. 81.

84 Sebastian Haffner, *Defying Hitler. A Memoir* (London, 2002), pp. 15–16.
85 Stephenson, '"Resistance" to "No Surrender"', p. 364.
86 Ursula von Kardorff, *Berliner Aufzeichnungen. Aus den Jahren 1942–1945*, 2nd edn (Munich, 1962), pp. 137–8 (diary entry for 12 April 1944).
87 Kitchen, *Nazi Germany at War*, p. 90.
88 See Heineman, 'Hour of the Woman', *passim*. Also Robert G. Moeller, 'War Stories. The Search for a Usable Past in the Federal Republic of Germany', in: *American Historical Review* 101 (1996), pp. 1008–48.
89 K. Erik Franzen, *Die Vertriebenen. Hitlers letzte Opfer* (Munich, 2002), pp. 40–1.
90 Heineman, *What Difference Does a Husband make?*, p. 81. On the rape of German women by Soviet soldiers see also Erika M. Hoerning, 'Frauen als Kriegsbeute', in: Lutz Niethammer and Alexander von Plato (eds), *'Wir kriegen jetzt andere Zeiten'. Auf der Suche nach der Erfahrung des Volkes im nachfaschistischen Ländern* (Bonn, 1985), pp. 327–46; Tröger, 'Between Rape and Prostitution', *passim*; Atina Grossmann, 'A Question of Silence. The Rape of German Women by Occupation Soldiers', in: Robert G. Moeller (ed.), *West Germany Under Construction. Politics, Society and Culture in the Adenauer Era* (Ann Arbor, Michigan, 1997), pp. 33–52; and Regina Mühlhauser, 'Vergewaltigung in Deutschland 1945. Nationaler Opferdiskurs und individuelles Erinnern betroffener Frauen', in: Klaus Neumann (ed.), *Nachkrieg in Deutschland* (Hamburg, 2001), pp. 384–408.
91 Alfred-Maurice de Zayas, *A Terrible Revenge. The Ethnic Cleansing of the East European Germans, 1944–1950* (New York, 1994), p. 44.
92 Beevor, *Berlin. The Downfall*, p. 28.
93 Cited in Anthony Beevor, 'Inside Story: They Raped Every German Female From Eight to 80', in: the *Guardian*, G2, 1 May 2002, p. 6.
94 Moeller, 'War Stories', p. 1026. Cf. de Zayas, *A Terrible Revenge*, pp. 116–24.
95 Noakes (ed.), *Nazism, 1919–1945*, Vol. 4, p. 664.
96 Ibid., p. 665.
97 See Frevert, *Women in German History*, p. 256, and Jill Stephenson, 'Nazism, Modern War and Rural Society in Württemberg, 1939–45', in: *Journal of Contemporary History* 32 (1997), pp. 339–56, esp. p. 355. Also Rainer Schulze, 'Growing Discontent. Relations Between Native and Refugee Populations in a Rural District in Western Germany after the Second World War', in: Moeller (ed.), *West Germany under Construction*, pp. 53–72.
98 Figures in Franzen, *Die Vertriebenen*, p. 324.
99 According to a report drawn up by the US military administration in April 1946, no more than 20 per cent of those expellees arriving in the American sector belonged to 'family units with employable male heads'. Cited in Heineman, *What Difference Does a Husband Make?*, p. 278, n. 13.
100 Stephenson, '"Resistance" to "No Surrender"', esp. pp. 355–65.
101 Stephenson, 'Triangle', p. 353.
102 Ibid., p. 354.
103 Stephenson, '"Resistance" to "No Surrender"', pp. 355–6.
104 Beevor, *Berlin. The Downfall*, p. 326. Cf. Hoerning, 'Frauen als Kriegsbeute', *passim*.
105 Deutschkron, *Ich trug den gelben Stern*, p. 179.
106 Ibid., p. 180.
107 Beevor, *Berlin. The Downfall*, p. 411.
108 Tröger, 'Between Rape and Prostitution', p. 112.
109 Grossmann, 'A Question of Silence', p. 35
110 Ibid., p. 45.
111 Tröger, 'Between Rape and Prostitution', pp. 103–4 and 113.

112 Beevor, 'Inside Story', p. 6.
113 Frevert, *Women in German History*, p. 258.
114 Moeller, *Protecting Motherhood*, p. 27.
115 Ibid., p. 2.

Conclusion

At the Potsdam conference in July 1945 the three main winning powers in the Second World War declared that the main objective of their joint military occupation of the former German Reich was the complete eradication of National Socialism – so that it could never again appear in Germany or threaten the peace of Europe. At the same time, in the decade or so after the Second World War, the renegotiation of gender roles played an important part in the German people's own efforts to come to terms with the social, economic, political and demographic legacy of the Nazi regime.[1] This was particularly important as the nation itself was soon split into two parts, the smaller communist east and the larger capitalist west, each with its own version of history and its own vision of the future. Politics and ideology thus became fused into one as the divisions of the Cold War hardened into open confrontation and the threat of a possible third world war.

In the immediate months following the German surrender, however, the daily struggle to find adequate food and shelter subsumed everything else, including politics. Indeed, it has become something of a cliché to argue that 'the end of the war [on the battlefield] meant no end to the war at home'[2] and that women were forced to 'fight for survival against hunger and all types of want', even after men had been defeated.[3] An important sociological study of Berlin families conducted by Hilde Thurnwald in 1946–47, for instance, paid hardly any attention to men, because, as the author argued, 'at present in these families women have moved into the central position as providers'.[4] The political language of collapse and gradual rebirth between 1945 and 1955 also had an explicitly gendered aspect to it. In East as well as West Germany, family, marriage and a 'healthy natural motherliness' were placed at the heart of programmes for social and economic recovery.[5] In 1985, the president of the West German Federal Republic, Richard von Weizsäcker, returned explicitly to this theme of the 'hour of the woman' when he said in a speech marking the fortieth anniversary of the end of the war:

> If the devastation and destruction, the barbarism and the inhumanity, did not inwardly shatter the people involved, if, slowly but surely, they

came to themselves after the war, then they owed it first and foremost to their womenfolk.[6]

However, historians should be very wary of accepting such statements at face value. While at least 3 million German soldiers were killed in the war, an estimated 2.3 million remained in Soviet POW camps in 1947; and it would be a further eight years before the final prisoners were released.[7] The post-war years were equally a 'struggle to survive' for these imprisoned soldiers, and many, perhaps up to 1 million, died while still in captivity.[8] Furthermore, the focus in women's narratives on food shortages and suffering tended to take them away from ideas about shared responsibility for Nazism and instead helped to construct an image of ordinary German civilians as 'victims'.[9] In the first three years after the war, for instance, there was a great deal of resentment towards the Allied occupation forces in general, who seemed determined to dismantle the best parts of German industry, and also a peculiar degree of hostility towards the British, who were accused of mismanaging, or worse still, attempting to ruin the German economy.[10] There were even protest marches and strikes against food shortages in 1946 and 1947, led largely by women and affecting the British zone in particular.[11]

Gradually, however, and especially after the currency reform in the western zones in June 1948, the idea of reconstruction became mingled with the rhetoric of the Cold War and the sense in which West Germany had to be built as a bulwark against the alleged destruction of family values and national identity in communist East Germany.[12] In retrospect it was even possible to build a myth around the 'Women of the Rubble' (*Trümmerfrauen*) as the heroines of Germany's 'zero hour' (*Stunde Null*), while forgetting that many of the women who actually cleared rubble from bomb sites in 1945–46 were former members of Nazi organisations, or the relatives and dependants of former Nazis, who were forced to perform this onerous work as a just retribution for past crimes.[13]

All of this raises important questions about what exactly the legacy of National Socialism was for German women. Indeed, as Elizabeth Heineman has shown, in most women's recollections the real time of hardship came not during the Third Reich but rather in the period 1945–48.[14] Constant fear of rape, lack of food and fuel, worries about accommodation, outbreaks of flu and other potentially lethal diseases, and the overriding absence of men were mingled here with the memory of having to work for wages that were practically worthless, and thus having to negotiate the black market in order to feed oneself and one's children.[15] Even after the prohibition on women's work in construction was lifted by the Allied Control Council Law No. 32 of July 1946, thus allowing 'ordinary' women to gain extra points on their ration cards by seeking employment in rubble clearance and on building sites, this was not considered to be a proper career but a stop-gap measure.[16] Most 'rubble women' were relieved when the immediate period of post-war reconstruction was over and the currency reform enabled them to return to the home (as it allowed their husbands to return home from post-war captivity).

After 1949 war widows in West Germany often pitied their counterparts in the communist east, who were denied decent pensions paid out in the new, re-valued Deutsche Mark, and were thus forced to continue in waged work outside the home.[17] Indeed, both Nazi propaganda and the experience of the war led to a hardening of anti-communist feeling in post-war West Germany, a trend that was actively encouraged by the American occupation authorities.[18] While US politicians and generals were calling for an effective end to the de-Nazification process and a concentration on the military threat from the USSR, however, many 'ordinary' West German women and men were becoming more open in their condemnation of those women who had developed relationships with American servicemen (the so-called 'Yankee sweethearts'). This was seen as insulting to the memory of the nearly 4 million dead German soldiers of the Second World War and even as a new 'stab in the back'. Gradually, reference to the real rape of women by Soviet and Allied soldiers became mingled in the official rhetoric of all political parties with the idea that the German people as a whole had been seduced, raped and abused in the period 1943–48, first by Hitler's 'no surrender' policy and then by the calamity of defeat and occupation at the hands of foreign armies.[19]

By contrast, the years of the Third Reich down to 1943 could be looked upon as a period of rising hopes for 'Aryan' women, with marriage loans, maternity benefits, limited professional openings for educated women, and so forth. Many younger women indeed appreciated the opportunity to become involved in the public life of the Third Reich, for instance through enlistment in the Nazi youth movement and labour service schemes or through shared enjoyment of what Alf Lüdtke describes as the 'occasional "highs" (*Rausch*) triggered by the ... heroic postures and military successes of the Nazi regime between 1936 and 1942'.[20] Others, however, disliked the coercive and militaristic side of National Socialist rule, preferring to opt out of such activities while continuing to share in the benefits of economic growth and recovery from the depression.

This dilemma can also be seen in the organisation of university life, for instance. While some recent studies have pointed to the emancipatory potential of the sharp growth in the number of female students after 1939, Jill Stephenson rightly argues that many women students enrolled on university courses simply to avoid being drafted into war work.[21] In fact, most of the additional students were recruited from the 'home economics' stream of girls' senior schools and were allowed into university only as an emergency wartime measure, a fact most of them were probably aware of. Possibly these students also had a good time while at university, and were certainly seen as being privileged, at least down to 1944–45, but they were hardly in a position to compete with men for the best academic grades.

Indeed, concerns were already being raised in 1942 that 'a large section of the female student body would never complete their course', largely because 'from the start [they had] never intended to do so'.[22]

'Emancipation', then, at least in the liberal feminist sense of equality of opportunity, was hardly on the Nazis' agenda in the 1930s and 1940s. The new divorce regulations in the Marriage Act of 1938 also generally favoured men over women, especially when they allowed adulterous husbands in some circumstances to go off and have second families without providing for the maintenance of the first.[23] On the whole, though, the regime was popular because it tended to treat 'Aryan' women, so long as they were politically reliable, with kid gloves, thus pandering in the main to traditional bourgeois tastes and sensibilities. Apart from those suspected of leading 'immoral lives', for instance, or those branded 'asocial', few soldiers' wives and war widows were forced to fend for themselves without state support, helping to foster the illusion that the '[moral] decline occurred with the collapse of, rather than during, Nazi rule'.[24]

Average family size also grew slightly during the 1930s and early 1940s, another indicator, perhaps, of social contentment. True, wealthy women who could afford expensive private consultations no longer had easy access to medically assisted abortions, in sharp contrast to the Weimar period, when Germany had the 'most lenient [abortion laws] in Western Europe'.[25] Nonetheless, with rising living standards and improvements in pre- and post-natal care, the issue of sex reform did not carry the same urgency for working-class women as it had in the 1920s, even if few wanted to have endless numbers of children. The introduction of the death penalty for illegal abortionists in 1943 was of course a blatant expression of the power of the patriarchal state to repress women. As Atina Grossmann says, it was also one further example of the 'coercive pronatalism' inherent in the Nazi discourse on 'Aryan' motherhood.[26]

The death penalty was indeed rigorously enforced, especially against Polish women in occupied Poland who were found to have assisted 'German' women to have unauthorised terminations.[27] However, in 1945, in the dying days of the regime, exceptions were made for German rape victims, who were allowed to abort foetuses up until the eighth month of pregnancy. Indeed, the Reich Ministry of Interior not only approved abortions in these cases but actively encouraged them on racial grounds, going so far as to order the setting up 'in large cities [of] special wards for the care of such women'.[28] This policy was continued by doctors in public hospitals after the end of the Third Reich, perhaps now more for humanitarian than racist reasons (and also to help save marriages). Eventually, though, the priorities of both the West and East German regimes dictated that abortion be recriminalised, as it was in both zones by 1950. This was very much in line with attempts to make the family the first line of defence in the attempted reconstruction of the nation.[29]

There were of course important differences between east and west after

1945. In East Germany there was perhaps a more radical break with the past. Thus, in the 1950s great emphasis was placed by the ruling Socialist Unity Party (SED) on the granting of both equal wages and an equal role to women within the production process. In theory at least, the regime intended to recruit more female workers, single and married, into industry and agriculture in order to meet its high production targets, although in practice at local level many managers of state-owned factories and farms continued to defend male privilege in the workplace while dismissing married women as 'double-earners'.[30]

In the 1960s, more concerted efforts were made to address the problems of poverty and discrimination faced by working-class women who worked full-time for a living, particularly single mothers and women with many children who had been widowed or divorced or abandoned by their husbands. Debates about gender inequalities in the workplace paved the way for the renewed legalisation in 1972 on abortion during the first 12 weeks of pregnancy, coupled with measures to give working women a real choice over whether or not to carry their pregnancies to term, for instance by expanding cost-free childcare facilities and schemes for maternity leave. At the same time, though, party workers continued to insist that the GDR needed more children if it was to meet the ideological objective of building socialism on German soil. Women were thus expected to play an equal part in production while also continuing to bear the larger share of work in the home and in the sphere of reproduction.[31] The growing militarisation of East German society in the 1950s and 1960s, especially following the reintroduction of compulsory national service for men in 1962, may also have helped to reinforce older assumptions and prejudices about the 'natural' division of labour between the sexes. Certainly it made it more difficult for women to advance into the upper ranks of the party and state hierarchy.[32]

In West Germany, meanwhile, single women in the 1950s faced discrimination in the form of tax laws that systematically favoured marriage, while married women were not encouraged to join the workforce or to establish a career at all, at least in the early years of the Federal Republic, and instead were directed towards viewing motherhood and the reconstruction of family life as their primary and proper vocation.[33] Until the 1980s few women made it into high-profile political positions at either state or federal level, and those who did tended to be single, or if married then without children.[34]

Abortion remained outlawed until 1973, and even after this the issue of when and on what grounds to permit medical abortions remained a bitterly contested area of public policy. In 1975, for instance, the Federal Supreme Court overturned a government bill, sponsored by the SPD and FDP parliamentary factions, that allowed for abortion-on-demand in the first trimester. Instead, the CDU/CSU view that the state had an 'obligation to see pregnancy carried to full term' was upheld, so that abortion remained technically illegal. In 1990, after German reunification, opponents of free choice led a campaign to prevent the continuation of the GDR model of abortion-on-demand in the first trimester. After a period of some uncertainty, in which the status quo in both parts of Germany was allowed to continue for a period of two years, the Bundestag and the Federal Court again clashed over whether a woman's right to choose could ever be recognised by the German state. In the end, the issue was fudged: doctors considering carrying out a termination are obliged to meet certain timing and counselling stipulations and must also inform the patient that abortion is fundamentally illegal and that 'the unborn child has its own right to life'.[35] Nonetheless, provided these conditions are met, neither doctors nor their patients can be prosecuted for terminations carried out in the first three months of pregnancy. In other words, as one critic puts it, 'in Germany today abortion is a favor for the needy, not a right'.[36]

The fight for and against female sexual liberation and women's reproductive rights thus runs like a thread of continuity, linking the Germany of the 1900s and 1920s to the Germany of the 1960s and beyond. So too does the struggle for equal wages and for equality of opportunity in education and in the workplace. Where the Nazis were unique, however, was in their 'ideological fantasies'[37] about racial purity. This accounts for both the appropriation of women's reproductive functions by the state in the form of compulsory sterilisations and the huge rise in state-sanctioned murder and abortion during the war. While patriarchy can continue to function in a variety of political settings, these levels of violence, coercion and murder can be sustained only in a regime committed to war and genocide. The female and male victims of National Socialism suffered in ways that were often very similar, and certainly they were sterilised and murdered in roughly equal numbers, but the introduction of racist principles into the intimate sphere of sexuality and human reproduction enabled the Nazis to exploit and humiliate women in particular. At the same the Third Reich, by calling into question the liberal conception of the family as a private refuge and source of emotional support (for instance through encouraging in some circumstances the denunciation and/or abandonment of husbands by wives and of parents by children) ultimately threatened a traditional bastion of male power and privilege too.[38]

German women do not share a collective burden of guilt for the crimes of the Nazis, but on an individual level some women were implicated in the murderous policies of the regime. Those who took part directly in acts of genocide or other crimes against humanity had the same outlook and the same prejudices as their male colleagues, for instance intense hatred of Marxists, Jews and 'Gypsies', and a belief in the importance of overt displays of physical strength and power at the expense of traditional Christian morality. This basic observation confirms the view that the Nazis were neither entirely reactionary nor entirely modern in their view of women and family, but somehow sought a 'third way' that was both anti-conservative and anti-liberal. Women were given a special function as childbearers and reproducers of the race, and were partly coerced into this role, but the Nazis nonetheless embraced equality to the extent that they believed that 'Aryans' of both sexes should have the right to exploit everybody else. In this sense, the year 1945 really was Germany's 'zero hour', a total defeat for the National Socialist regime and its barbaric racial ideology. In the years after the Second World War, the fate of the German nation was largely determined by the emerging Cold War between east and west. All the same, there were some continuities with the 1930s in the restoration politics of post-war West Germany, when motherhood and the family were once again 'reasserted and reified' as a means of forgetting the past and looking ahead to the future.[39]

Notes

1 On the renegotiation of gender roles see e.g. Katherine Pence, 'Labours of Consumption. Consumers in Post-war East and West German Reconstruction', in: Abrams and Harvey (eds), *Gender Relations in German History*, pp. 211–38.
2 Moeller, *Protecting Motherhood*, p. 3.
3 Eva Kolinsky, *Women in Contemporary Germany. Life, Work and Politics*, 2nd edn (Oxford, 1993), p. 27.
4 Hilde Thurnwald, *Gegenwartsprobleme Berliner Familien. Eine soziologische Untersuchung an 498 Familien* (Berlin, 1948), p. 10. Cf. Moeller, *Protecting Motherhood*, p. 11.
5 Grossmann, *Reforming Sex*, p. 191.
6 Moeller, *Protecting Motherhood*, p. 12.
7 Kolinsky, *Women in Contemporary Germany*, p. 25.
8 Moeller, 'War Stories', p. 1011.
9 Ibid. Cf. Moeller, *Protecting Motherhood*, p. 14, and Alf Lüdtke, '"Coming to Terms with the Past". Illusions of Remembering, Ways of Forgetting Nazism in West Germany', in: *Journal of Modern History* 65 (1993), pp. 542–72, esp. pp. 547–9.
10 Josef Foschepoth, 'German Reactions to Defeat and Occupation', in: Moeller (ed.), *West Germany Under Construction*, pp. 73–89.
11 Ibid., p. 83. Cf. Frevert, *Women in German History*, p. 257; Kolinsky, *Women in Contemporary Germany*, p. 26.
12 Moeller, *Protecting Motherhood*, pp. 5–6.
13 Heineman, 'Hour of the Woman', p. 375.
14 Ibid., p. 387.
15 Grossmann, *Reforming Sex*, p. 191.
16 Kolinsky, *Women in Contemporary Germany*, p. 35.
17 Heineman, *What Difference Does a Husband Make?*, pp. 196–201.
18 Moeller, *Protecting Motherhood*, p. 5; Lüdtke, '"Coming to Terms with the Past"', p. 550.
19 Grossmann, 'A Question of Silence', p. 38; Heineman, 'Hour of the Woman', pp. 369–70; Mühlhauser, 'Vergewaltigung in Deutschland', p. 392.
20 Lüdtke, '"Coming to Terms with the Past"', p. 551.
21 Stephenson, '"Emancipation" and its Problems', p. 348.
22 Ibid., p. 351.
23 Czarnowski, '"Der Wert der Ehe"', p. 89. As we saw in Chapter 3, however, the Marriage Law also allowed 'Aryan' women to divorce Jewish husbands, and in

such cases the husbands usually faced deportation and death. Jewish women married to 'Aryan men' were better protected, especially if they had children.

24 Heineman, 'Hour of the Woman', p. 381.
25 Usborne, *The Politics of the Body*, p. 174.
26 Grossmann, *Reforming Sex*, p. 151.
27 Ibid., p. 152.
28 Ibid., p. 153.
29 Ibid., p. 198.
30 Heineman, *What Difference Does a Husband Make?*, p. 186.
31 Grossmann, *Reforming Sex*, p. 214. On this theme see also Donna Harsch, 'Squaring the Circle. The Dilemmas and Evolution of Women's Policy', in: Patrick Major and Jonathan Osmond (eds), *The Workers' and Peasants' State. Communism and Society in East Germany under Ulbricht, 1945–71* (Manchester, 2002), pp. 151–70.
32 Cf. Corey Ross, '"Protecting the Accomplishments of Socialism"? The (Re)Militarisation of Life in the German Democratic Republic', in: ibid., pp. 78–93.
33 Tröger, 'Between Rape and Prostitution', pp. 114–15. Cf. Robert G. Moeller, 'Reconstructing the Family in Reconstruction Germany. Women and Social Policy in the Federal Republic, 1949–1955', in: Moeller (ed.), *West Germany under Construction*, pp. 109–33.
34 See e.g. Waltraud Cornelissen, 'Politische Partizipation von Frauen in der alten Bundesrepublik und im vereinten Deutschland', in: Gisela Helwig and Hildegard Maria Nickel (eds), *Frauen in Deutschland, 1945–1992* (Berlin, 1993), pp. 321–49. Also Frank Bösch, *Die Adenauer-CDU. Gründung, Aufstieg und Krise einer Erfolgspartei, 1945–1969* (Stuttgart and Munich, 2001), pp. 303 and 512, n. 95.
35 For the above see Grossmann, *Reforming Sex*, pp. 213–16.
36 Ibid., p. 215.
37 Burleigh, *The Third Reich*, p. 812.
38 Lisa Pine, 'Women and the Family', in: Panikos Panayi (ed.), *Weimar and Nazi Germany. Continuities and Discontinuities* (London, 2001), pp. 212–13. Cf. Joshi, 'Women as Denouncers', *passim*. It is of course true, as we saw in Chapter 7, that the Gestapo also sought ways of discouraging denunciations that had domestic motives only.
39 Moeller, *Protecting Motherhood*, p. 228.

Bibliography

Archives and museums

Staatsarchiv Bremen (StA Bremen)
Bundesarchiv Berlin (BA Berlin)
Forschungsstelle für Zeitgeschichte, Hamburg (FZH)
Niedersächsisches Hauptstaatsarchiv, Hanover (NHStA Hanover)
Historisches Museum, Hanover

Newspapers and journals

Der Angriff
Berliner Börsen-Zeitung
Berliner Lokal-Anzeiger
Berliner Tageblatt
Deutsche Allgemeine Zeitung
NS-Frauenwarte
Nationalsozialistische Landpost
Nationalsozialistische Monatshefte
Nationalsozialistische Partei-Korrespondenz
Völkischer Beobachter

Collections of documents

Kuhn, Annette and Rothe, Valentine (eds), *Frauen im Deutschen Faschismus*, 2 vols (Düsseldorf, 1982)
Noakes, Jeremy and Pridham, Geoffrey (eds), *Nazism, 1919–1945. A Documentary Reader*, 4 vols (Exeter, 1983–98)

Richarz, Monika (ed.), *Jewish Life in Germany. Memoirs from Three Centuries* (Bloomington and Indianapolis, 1991)

Schneider, Wolfgang (ed.), *Frauen unterm Hakenkreuz* (Hamburg, 2001)

Schüddekopf, Charles (ed.), *Der alltägliche Faschismus. Frauen im dritten Reich* (Bonn, 1982)

Selected books, articles and essays

Abrams, Lynn and Harvey, Elizabeth (eds), *Gender Relations in German History. Power, Agency and Experience from the Sixteenth to the Twentieth Century* (London, 1996)

Bajohr, Stefan, 'Weiblicher Arbeitsdienst im "Dritten Reich". Ein Konflikt zwischen Ideologie und Ökonomie', in: *Vierteljahrshefte für Zeitgeschichte* 28 (1980), pp. 331–57

Baumel, Judith Tydor, *Double Jeopardy. Gender and the Holocaust* (London, 1998)

Beevor, Anthony, *Berlin. The Downfall 1945* (London, 2002)

Bessel, Richard (ed.), *Life in the Third Reich* (Oxford, 1987)

——*Germany after the First World War* (Oxford, 1993)

Boak, Helen L., 'Women in Weimar Germany. The *Frauenfrage* and the Female Vote', in: Richard Bessel and E. J. Feuchtwanger (eds), *Social Change and Political Development in Weimar Germany* (London, 1981), pp. 155–73

——'National Socialism and Working-Class Women Before 1933', in: Conan Fischer (ed.), *The Rise of National Socialism and the Working Classes in Weimar Germany* (Oxford, 1996), pp. 163–88

——'The State as an Employer of Women in the Weimar Republic', in: W.R. Lee and Eve Rosenhaft (eds), *State, Social Policy and Social Change in Germany, 1880–1994*, 2nd edn (Oxford, 1997), pp. 64–101

Bock, Gisela, 'Racism and Sexism in Nazi Germany. Motherhood, Compulsory Sterilization and the State', in: Bridenthal *et al.* (eds), *When Biology Became Destiny*, pp. 271–96

——*Zwangssterilisation im Nationalsozialismus. Studien zur Rassenpolitik und Frauenpolitik* (Opladen, 1986)

——'Equality and Difference in National Socialist Racism', in: J. Wallach Scott (ed.), *Feminism and History* (Oxford, 1996), pp. 267–90

——'Ordinary Women in Nazi Germany: Perpetrators, Victims, Followers and Bystanders', in: Ofer and Weitzman (eds), *Women in the Holocaust*, pp. 85–100

——*Frauen in der europäischen Geschichte. Vom Mittelalter bis zur Gegenwart* (Munich, 2000)

Brady, Robert A., *The Spirit and Structure of German Fascism* (London, 1937)

Bremme, Gabriele, *Die politische Rolle der Frau in Deutschland. Eine Untersuchung über den Einfluß der Frauen bei Wahlen und ihre Teilnahme in Partei und Parlament* (Göttingen, 1956)

Bridenthal, Renate, Grossmann, Atina and Kaplan, Marion (eds), *When Biology Became Destiny. Women in Weimar and Nazi Germany* (New York, 1984)

Buber-Neumann, Margarete, *Milena* (London, 1990)

——*Als Gefangene bei Stalin und Hitler*, reprint (Munich, 2002)

Burleigh, Michael, *Death and Deliverance. 'Euthanasia' in Germany, 1900–1945* (Cambridge, 1994)

——(ed.), *Confronting the Nazi Past. New Debates on Modern German History* (London, 1996)

——*The Third Reich. A New History* (London, 2000)

Burleigh, Michael and Wippermann, Wolfgang, *The Racial State. Germany, 1933–1945* (Cambridge, 1991)

Crew, David (ed.), *Nazism and German Society, 1933–1945* (London, 1994)

Czarnowski, Gabriele, *Das kontrollierte Paar. Ehe- und Sexualpolitik im Nationalsozialismus* (Weinheim, 1991)

——'Der Wert der Ehe für die Volksgemeinschaft. Frauen und Männer in der nationalsozialistischen Ehepolitik', in: Heinsohn *et al.* (eds), *Zwischen Karriere und Verfolgung*, pp. 78–95

Daniel, Ute, *The War From Within. German Working-Class Women in the First World War* (Oxford, 1997)

Deutschkron, Inge, *Ich trug den gelben Stern* (Munich, 1985)

Diehl, Guida, *Die deutsche Frau und der Nationalsozialismus* (Eisenach, 1933)

Dördelmann, Katrin, '"Aus einer gewissen Empörung habe ich nun Anzeige erstattet". Verhalten und Motive von Denunziantinnen', in: Heinsohn *et al.* (eds), *Zwischen Karriere und Verfolgung*, pp. 189–205.

Evans, Richard J., *The Feminist Movement in Germany, 1894–1933* (London, 1976)

——*Rituals of Retribution. Capital Punishment in Germany, 1600–1987* (London, 1996)

Farquharson, John E., *The Plough and the Swastika. The NSDAP and Agriculture in Germany, 1928–1945* (London, 1976)

Fénelon, Fania, *Das Mädchenorchester in Auschwitz* (Munich, 1981)

Frauengruppe Faschismusforschung (ed.), *Mutterkreuz und Arbeitsbuch. Zur Geschichte der Frauen in der Weimarer Republik und im Nationalsozialismus* (Frankfurt/Main, 1981)

Frevert, Ute, *Women in German History. From Bourgeois Emancipation to Sexual Liberation* (Oxford, 1989)

Gellately, Robert, *The Gestapo and German Society. Enforcing Racial Policy, 1933–1945* (Oxford, 1990)

——*Backing Hitler. Consent and Coercion in Nazi Germany* (Oxford, 2001)

Gellately, Robert and Stoltzfus, Nathan (eds), *Social Outsiders in Nazi Germany* (Princeton, NJ, 2001)

Goldhagen, Daniel, *Hitler's Willing Executioners. Ordinary Germans and the Holocaust* (London, 1996)

Gottlieb, Julie V., *Feminine Fascism. Women in Britain's Fascist Movement, 1923–1945* (London, 2000)

——'"Motherly Hate". Gendering Anti-Semitism in the British Union of Fascists', in: *Gender and History* 14 (2002), pp. 294–320

Grossmann, Atina, 'Feminist Debates about Women and National Socialism', in: *Gender and History* 3 (1991), pp. 350–8

——*Reforming Sex. The German Movement for Birth Control and Abortion Reform, 1920–1950* (Oxford, 1995)

——'A Question of Silence. The Rape of German Women by Occupation Soldiers', in: Moeller (ed.), *West Germany Under Construction*, pp. 33–52

——'Women and the Holocaust. Four Recent Titles', in: *Holocaust and Genocide Studies* 16 (Spring 2002), pp. 94–108

Grunberger, Richard, *A Social History of the Third Reich* (London, 1971)

Haffner, Sebastian, *Defying Hitler. A Memoir* (London, 2002)

Harvey, Elizabeth, 'The Failure of Feminism? Young Women and the Bourgeois Feminist Movement in Weimar Germany, 1918–1933', in: *Central European History* 28 (1995), pp. 1–28

——'"Die deutsche Frau im Osten". "Rasse", Geschlecht und öffentlicher Raum im besetzten Polen, 1940–1944', in: *Archiv für Sozialgeschichte* 38 (1998), pp. 191–214

——'Culture and Society in Weimar Germany', in: Mary Fulbrook (ed.), *Twentieth Century Germany. Politics, Culture and Society, 1918–1990* (London, 2001), pp. 58–76

——'"We Forgot All Jews and Poles". German Women and the "Ethnic Struggle" in Nazi-occupied Poland', in: *Contemporary European History* 10 (2001), pp. 447–61

Haste, Cate, *Nazi Women. Hitler's Seduction of a Nation* (London, 2001)

Heineman, Elizabeth, 'The Hour of the Woman: Memories of Germany's "Crisis Years" and West German National Identity', in: *American Historical Review* 101 (1996), pp. 354–95

——*What Difference Does a Husband Make? Women and Marital Status in Nazi and Postwar Germany* (London, 1999)

Heinsohn, Kirsten, Vogel, Barbara and Weckel, Ulrike (eds), *Zwischen Karriere und Verfolgung. Handlungsräume von Frauen im national-sozialistischen Deutschland* (Frankfurt/Main and New York, 1997)

Hepp, Michael, 'Vorhof zur Hölle. Mädchen im "Jugendschutzlager" Uckermark', in: Angelika Ebbinghaus (ed.), *Opfer und Täterinnen. Frauenbiographien des Nationalsozialismus* (Frankfurt/Main, 1996), pp. 239–70

Herbert, Ulrich, *Hitler's Foreign Workers. Enforced Foreign Labor in Germany under the Third Reich* (Cambridge, 1997)

Hitler, Adolf, *Mein Kampf*, edited and with an introduction by Donald Cameron Watt (London, 1969)

Johnson, Eric A., *Nazi Terror. The Gestapo, Jews and Ordinary Germans* (New York, 1999)

Joshi, Vandana, 'The "Private" became "Public". Wives as Denouncers in the Third Reich', in: *Journal of Contemporary History* 37 (2002), pp. 419–35

Kaplan, Marion A., *Between Dignity and Despair. Jewish Life in Nazi Germany* (Oxford, 1998)

——'Keeping Calm and Weathering the Storm. Jewish Women's Responses to Daily Life in Nazi Germany, 1933–1939', in: Ofer and Weitzman (eds), *Women in the Holocaust*, pp. 39–54

Kardorff, Ursula von, *Berliner Aufzeichnungen. Aus den Jahren 1942 bis 1945*, 2nd edn (Munich, 1962)

Kater, Michael H., 'Frauen in der NS-Bewegung', in: *Vierteljahrshefte für Zeitgeschichte* 31 (1983), pp. 202–41

——*The Nazi Party. A Social Profile of Members and Leaders, 1919–1945* (Cambridge, Mass., 1983)

——Generationskonflikt als Entwicklungsfaktor in der NS-Bewegung vor 1933', in: *Geschichte und Gesellschaft* 11 (1985), pp. 217–43

Kershaw, Ian, *Popular Opinion and Political Dissent in the Third Reich. Bavaria, 1933–1945* (Oxford, 1983)

——*Hitler, Vol. 1: Hubris, 1889–1936* (London, 1998)

——*Hitler, Vol. 2: Nemesis, 1936–1945* (London, 2000)

——*The Nazi Dictatorship. Problems and Perspectives of Interpretation*, 4th edn (London, 2000)

Kirkpatrick, Clifford, *Woman in Nazi Germany* (London, 1939)

Kitchen, Martin, *Nazi Germany at War* (London, 1995)

Klaus, Martin, *Mädchen im 3. Reich. Der Bund Deutscher Mädel* (Cologne, 1998)

Klee, Ernst, *'Euthanasie' im NS-Staat. Die Vernichtung 'lebensunwerten Lebens'* (Frankfurt/Main, 1983)

Klemperer, Victor *LTI (Lingua Tertii Imperii). Notizbuch eines Philologen* (Leipzig, 1975)

——*I Shall Bear Witness. The Diaries of Victor Klemperer, 1933–1941* (London, 1998)

——*To the Bitter End. The Diaries of Victor Klemperer, 1942–1945* (London, 1999)

Koehn, Ilse, *Mischling, Second Degree. My Childhood in Nazi Germany* (London, 1981)

Kolinsky, Eva, *Women in Contemporary Germany. Life, Work and Politics*, rev. edn (Oxford, 1993)

Koonz, Claudia, *Mothers in the Fatherland. Women, the Family and Nazi Politics* (London, 1987)

Kundrus, Birthe, '"Die Unmoral deutscher Soldatenfrauen". Diskurs, Alltagsverhalten und Ahndungspraxis, 1939–1945', in: Heinsohn *et al.* (eds), *Zwischen Karriere und Verfolgung*, pp. 96–110

Lacey, Kate, 'Driving the Message Home: Nazi Propaganda in the Private Sphere', in: Abrams and Harvey (eds), *Gender Relations in German History*, pp. 189–210

Lange, Silivia, *Protestantische Frauen auf dem Weg in den Nationalsozialismus. Guida Diehls Neulandbewegung, 1916–1935* (Stuttgart, 1998)

Leber, Annedore (ed.), *Conscience in Revolt. Sixty-Four Stories of Resistance in Germany, 1933–1945*, reprint (Oxford, 1994)

Lengyel, Olga, *Five Chimneys*, reprint (St Albans, 1972)

Lewy, Guenter, *The Catholic Church and Nazi Germany*, new edn (New York, 2000)

———*The Nazi Persecution of the Gypsies* (Oxford, 2000)

Maier, Dieter, *Arbeitseinsatz und Deportation. Die Mitwirkung der Arbeitsverwaltung bei der nationalsozialistischen Judenverfolgung in den Jahren 1938–1945* (Berlin, 1994)

Maiwald, Stefan and Mischler, Gerd, *Sexualität unter dem Hakenkreuz. Manipulation und Vernichtung der Intimsphäre im NS-Staat* (Hamburg, 1999)

Marxen, Klaus, *Das Volk und sein Gerichtshof. Eine Studie zum national-sozialistischen Volksgerichtshof* (Frankfurt/Main, 1994)

Mason, Tim, 'Women in Germany, 1925–1940. Family, Welfare and Work', in: *History Workshop Journal* (1976), Part I, pp. 74–113, and Part II, pp. 5–32

———*Nazism, Fascism and the Working Class. Essays by Tim Mason*, edited by Jane Caplan (Cambridge, 1995)

———*Social Policy in the Third Reich. The Working Class and the 'National Community'*, edited by Jane Caplan (Oxford, 1995)

McFarland-Icke, Bronwyn Rebekah, *Nurses in Nazi Germany. Moral Choice in History* (Princeton, N.J., 1999)

McIntyre, Jill (i.e. Jill Stephenson), 'Women and the Professions in Germany, 1930–1940', in: Anthony Nicholls and Erich Matthias (eds), *German Democracy and the Triumph of Hitler. Essays in Recent German History* (London, 1971), pp. 175–213

Meyer, Beate, *'Jüdische Mischlinge'. Rassenpolitik und Verfolgungserfahrungen, 1933–1945* (Hamburg, 1999)

Milton, Sybil, 'Women and the Holocaust. The Case of German and German-Jewish Women', in: Bridenthal *et al.* (eds), *When Biology Became Destiny*, pp. 297–333

Moeller, Robert G., *Protecting Motherhood. Women and the Family in the Politics of Postwar West Germany* (Berkeley, Calif., 1993)

———(ed.), *West Germany Under Construction. Politics, Society and Culture in the Adenauer Era* (Ann Arbor, Michigan, 1997)

Mosse, George L., *Nationalism and Sexuality. Respectable and Abnormal Sexuality in Modern Europe* (London, 1985)

Münkel, Daniela, *Nationalsozialistische Agrarpolitik und Bauernalltag* (Frankfurt/Main, 1996)

Neiberger, Ami, 'An Uncommon Bond of Friendship. Family and Survival in Auschwitz', in: Rohrlich (ed.), *Resisting the Holocaust*, pp. 133–50

Ofer, Dalia and Weitzman, Lenore J. (eds), *Women in the Holocaust* (New Haven and London, 1998)

Overy, Richard, *War and Economy in the Third Reich* (Oxford, 1994)

Owings, Alison, *Frauen. German Women Recall the Third Reich* (London, 1993)

Peukert, Detlev J. K., *Inside Nazi Germany. Conformity, Opposition and Racism in Everyday Life* (London, 1987)

———*The Weimar Republic. The Crisis of Classical Modernity* (London, 1991)

Pine, Lisa, 'Hashude. The Imprisonment of "Asocial" Families in the Third Reich', in: *German History* 13 (1995), pp. 182–97

———*Nazi Family Policy, 1933–1945* (London, 1995)

Przyrembel, Alexandra, 'Transfixed by an Image. Ilse Koch, the "Kommandeuse of Buchenwald"', in: *German History* 19 (2001), pp. 369–99

Reagin, Nancy R., *A German Women's Movement. Class and Gender in Hanover, 1880–1933* (Chapel Hill and London, 1995)

———'Comparing Apples and Oranges. Housewives and the Politics of Consumption in Interwar Germany', in: Susan Strasser, Charles McGovern and Matthias Judt (eds), *Getting and Spending. European and American Consumer Societies in the Twentieth Century* (Washington D.C., 1998)

———'*Marktordnung* and autarkic Housekeeping. Housewives and Private Consumption under the Four Year Plan, 1936–1939', in: *German History* 19 (2001), pp. 162–84

Reese, Dagmar, 'Bund Deutscher Mädel – Zur Geschichte der weiblichen deutschen Jugend im Dritten Reich', in: Frauengruppe Faschismusforschung (ed.), *Mutterkreuz und Arbeitsbuch*, pp. 163–87

———'*Straff, aber nicht stramm – herb aber nicht derb'. Zur Vergesellschaftung von Mädchen durch den Bund Deutscher Mädel im sozialkulturellen Vergleich zweier Milieus* (Weinheim and Basel, 1989)

Rohrlich, Ruby (ed.), *Resisting the Holocaust* (Oxford, 1998)

Roseman, Mark, 'World War II and Social Change in Germany', in: Arthur Marwick (ed.), *Total War and Social Change* (London, 1988), pp. 58–78

———*The Villa, the Lake, the Meeting. Wannsee and the Final Solution* (London, 2002)

Rosenhaft, Eve, 'Women in Modern Germany', in: Gordon Martel (ed.), *Modern Germany Reconsidered, 1870–1945* (London, 1992), pp. 140–58

Rothfels, Hans, *The German Opposition to Hitler. An Assessment* (London, 1961)

Rupp, Leila J., *Mobilizing Women for War. German and American Propaganda, 1939–1945* (Princeton, N.J., 1978)

Sachse, Carola, *Industrial Housewives. Women's Social Work in the Factories of Nazi Germany*, introduced and edited by Jane Caplan (London, 1987)

Saldern, Adelheid von, 'Victims or Perpetrators? Controversies about the Role of Women in the Nazi State', in: Crew (ed.), *Nazism and German Society*, pp. 141–65

Schad, Martha, *Frauen gegen Hitler. Schicksale im Nationalsozialismus* (Munich, 2001)

Schmidt, Maruta and Dietz, Gabi (eds), *Frauen unterm Hakenkreuz* (West Berlin, 1983)

Schoenbaum, David, *Hitler's Social Revolution. Class and Status in Nazi Germany, 1933–1939* (London, 1967)

Scholtz-Klink, Gertrud, *Verpflichtung und Aufgabe der Frau im national-sozialistischen Staat* (Berlin, 1936)

———*Die Frau im Dritten Reich. Eine Dokumentation* (Tübingen, 1978)

Schoppmann, Claudia, 'National Socialist Policies Towards Female Homosexuality', in: Abrams and Harvey (eds), *Gender Relations in German History*, pp. 177–87

Schwarz, Gudrun, *Eine Frau an seiner Seite. Ehefrauen in der 'SS-Sippengemeinschaft'* (Hamburg, 1997)

———'Frauen in der SS. Sippenverband und Frauenkorps', in: Heinsohn *et al.* (eds), *Zwischen Karriere und Verfolgung*, pp. 233–44

Sneeringer, Julia, *Winning Women's Votes. Propaganda and Politics in Weimar Germany* (Chapel Hill and London, 2002)

Stachura, Peter D. (ed.), *The Shaping of the Nazi State* (London, 1978)

Steinweis, 'Weimar Political Culture and the Rise of National Socialism: The *Kampfbund für deutsche Kultur*', in: *Central European History* 24 (1991), pp. 402–23

Stephenson, Jill, *Women in Nazi Society* (London, 1975)

———'Girls' Higher Education in Germany in the 1930s', in: *Journal of Contemporary History* 10 (1975), pp. 41–69

———'The Nazi Organisation of Women, 1933–1939', in: Peter D. Stachura (ed.), *The Shaping of the Nazi State*, pp. 186–209

———*The Nazi Organisation of Women* (London, 1981)

———'Women's Labor Service in Nazi Germany', in: *Central European History* 15 (1982), pp. 241–65

———'National Socialism and Women Before 1933', in: Peter D. Stachura (ed.), *The Nazi* Machtergreifung (London, 1983), pp. 33–48

———'"Emancipation" and its problems. War and Society in Württemberg, 1939–1945', in: *European History Quarterly* 17 (1987), pp. 345–65

———'"Resistance" to "No Surrender". Popular Disobedience in

Württemberg in 1945', in: Francis R. Nicosia and Lawrence D. Stokes (eds), *Germans Against Nazism. Nonconformity, Opposition and Resistance in the Third Reich. Essays in Honour of Peter Hoffmann* (Oxford, 1990), pp. 351–67

——'Triangle: Foreign Workers, German Civilians and the Nazi Regime. War and Society in Württemberg, 1939–1945', in: *German Studies Review* 15 (1992), pp. 339–59

——'Nazism, Modern War and Rural Society in Württemberg, 1939–45', in: *Journal of Contemporary History* 32 (1997), pp. 339–56

——*Women in Nazi Germany* (London, 2001)

Stibbe, Matthew, 'Women and the Nazi State', in: *History Today* (November 1993), pp. 35–40

——'Nationalism, Anti–Feminism and the German Right, 1914–1920. A Reappraisal', in: *German History* 20 (2002), pp. 185–210

Stoltzfus, Nathan, *Resistance of the Heart. The Rosenstrasse Protest and Intermarriage in Nazi Germany* (New York, 1996)

——'Protest and Silence. Resistance Histories in Post-War Germany. The Missing Case of Intermarried Germans', in: Rohrlich (ed.), *Resisting the Holocaust*, pp. 151–78

Stümke, Hans-Georg, 'The Persecution of Homosexuals in Nazi Germany', in: Burleigh (ed.), *Confronting the Nazi Past*, pp. 154–66

Szepansky, Gerda, *Frauen leisten Widerstand, 1933–1945* (Frankfurt/Main, 1983)

Thälmann, Rita, *Frausein im Dritten Reich* (Frankfurt/Main and Berlin, 1987)

Thönnessen, Werner, *The Emancipation of Women. The Rise and Decline of the Women's Movement in German Social Democracy, 1863–1933* (London, 1973)

Tillion, Germaine, *Frauenkonzentrationslager Ravensbrück*, German translation (Frankfurt/Main, 2001)

Tröger, Annemarie, 'The Creation of a Female Assembly-Line Proletariat', in: Bridenthal *et al.* (eds), *When Biology Became Destiny*, pp. 237–70

——'Between Rape and Prostitution. Survival Strategies and Possibilities of Liberation of Berlin Women in 1945–48', in: Judith Friedlander, Alice Kessler-Harris and Carol Smith-Rosenberg (eds), *Women in Culture and Politics. A Century of Change* (Bloomington, 1986), pp. 97–117

——'German Women's Memories of World War II', in: Margaret Higonnet *et al.* (eds), *Behind the Lines. Gender and the Two World Wars* (New Haven and London, 1987), pp. 285–99

Usborne, Cornelie, *The Politics of the Body in Weimar Germany. Women's Reproductive Rights and Duties* (London, 1992)

Vassiltchikov, Marie, *The Berlin Diaries of Marie 'Missie' Vassiltchikov, 1940–1945* (London, 1985)

Weindling, Paul, *Health, Race and German Politics Between National Unification and Nazism, 1870–1945* (Cambridge, 1989)

Weyrather, Irmgard, 'Numerus Clausus für Frauen – Studentinnen im Nationalsozialismus', in: Frauengruppe Faschismusforschung (ed.), *Mutterkreuz und Arbeitsbuch*, pp. 131–62

——*Muttertag und Mutterkreuz. Die Kult um die 'deutsche Mutter' im Nationalsozialismus* (Frankfurt/Main, 1993)

Wickert, Christl , 'Frauen zwischen Dissens und Widerstand', in: Wolfgang Benz and Walter H. Pehle (eds), *Lexikon des deutschen Widerstandes* (Frankfurt/Main, 1994), pp. 140–55

——(ed.), *Frauen gegen die Diktatur – Widerstand und Verfolgung im nationalsozialistischen Deutschland* (Berlin, 1995)

Wiggershaus, Renate, *Frauen unterm Nationalsozialismus* (Wuppertal, 1984)

Wilke, Gerhard, 'Village Life in Nazi Germany', in: Bessel (ed.), *Life in the Third Reich*, pp. 17–24

Winkler, Dörte, *Frauenarbeit im 'Dritten Reich'* (Hamburg, 1977)

——'Frauenarbeit versus Ideologie. Probleme der weiblichen Erwerbstätigkeit in Deutschland, 1930–1945', in: *Archiv für Sozialgeschichte* 17 (1977), pp. 99–126

Zimmermann, Michael, 'The National Socialist "Solution of the Gypsy Question". Central Decisions, Local Initiatives and their Interrelation', in: *Holocaust and Genocide Studies* 15 (Winter 2001), pp. 412–27

Index